Designing Quality of Service Solutions for the Enterprise

Eric D. Siegel

Wiley Computer Publishing

John Wiley & Sons, Inc.

NEW YORK · CHICHESTER · WEINHEIM · BRISBANE · SINGAPORE · TORONTO

Publisher: Robert Ipsen
Editor: Carol Long
Managing Editor: Brian Snapp
Text Design & Composition: Rob Mauhar

Designations used by companies to distinguish their products are often claimed as trademarks. In all instances where John Wiley & Sons, Inc., is aware of a claim, the product names appear in initial capital or ALL CAPITAL LETTERS. Readers, however, should contact the appropriate companies for more complete information regarding trademarks and registration.

This book is printed on acid-free paper.

This publication is designed to provide accurate and authoritative information in regard to the subject matter covered. It is sold with the understanding that the publisher is not engaged in professional services. If professional advice or other expert assistance is required, the services of a competent professional person should be sought.

Library of Congress Cataloging-in-Publication Data:

Siegel, Eric D.
    Designing quality of service solutions for the enterprise / Eric
D. Siegel.
        p.   cm.
    "Wiley computer publishing."
    Includes bibliographical references (p.   ).
    ISBN 0-471-33313-1 (pbk.)
    1. Computer networks--Management.   2. Business enterprises-
-Computer networks.   3. Computer network protocols.   I. Title.
TK5105.5.S53   1999
658'.0546--dc21   99-43062
                                                               CIP

Printed in the United States of America.

10 9 8 7 6 5 4 3 2 1

CONTENTS

iii

T he purpose of this book is to help the reader decide if there is a real need for Quality of Service (QoS) and QoS-related policy-based networking in his or her enterprise network, and, if there is, how that need can be satisfied using technologies available in the marketplace. The reader will learn how to translate user needs and application program characteristics into QoS requirements and then will be able to take those requirements into discussions with technology vendors to design a satisfactory network.

Plan of the Book

This book starts with an overview of the technical and market forces behind the current interest in Quality of Service, Class of Service, and policy-based technologies. That introductory chapter is then followed by the two main sections of the book.

First, the book shows the reader how to convert the user's needs, expressed in nontechnical and nonnetworking language, into the technical specifications that are useful to the person designing a QoS solution. How do enterprise-wide trends in overall network architectural design affect the need for QoS and the technical requirements? What are the technical requirements that the user applications and their underlying communications protocols will place on the network infrastructure? How can those technical requirements be evaluated to determine the cost of alternative QoS designs? Given the cost and complexity, is QoS needed at all? Each chapter includes a detailed list of summary questions to help the reader derive QoS requirements from user, application, and enterprise needs.

Second, we look at the various technologies available to build QoS into a network and the ways that they can be assembled to satisfy the users' needs. Without getting too deeply into the details of their implementation, the book summarizes the advantages and disadvantages of each possible solution. The goal is to provide enough information so that the reader can understand, and discuss with vendors and colleagues, the implications of choosing each particular technology. Chapter 7, "Solution Building Blocks," includes a matrix that matches QoS technologies to the requirements derived in the first section of the book.

The individual chapters cover the following material:

Chapter 1, "The Importance of Quality of Service." The original Internet had only the most rudimentary facilities for Quality of Service, and even those simplistic facilities were rarely implemented or used. Recently, there has been a burst of interest in the area. This chapter first gives a brief working definition of QoS, Class of Service, and policy-based networking, then discusses the factors behind the recent interest in them.

Chapter 2, "Enterprise-Wide and User Requirements." We look at the overall principles, requirements, and constraints of the enterprise as a whole, then we show how to evaluate end-user requests and begin to derive the technical requirements that those requests will place on the network.

Chapter 3, "Applications and Infrastructure Issues." This chapter moves from the user and overall requirements into a discussion of the requirements of the particular applications and their protocols. Each type of application, especially those involving real-time speech, video, or client/server processing, has its own inherent requirements for transmission service. Their protocols also may have specialized requirements. Some protocols fail if those requirements are not met; others may interfere with the smooth operation of the network as a whole. This chapter first examines the specialized QoS requirements of real-time speech and video, and of client/server processing, then it moves on to protocols. It looks at all the common characteristics of protocols to help evaluate the QoS needs of the protocols underlying user applications. The chapter finishes with a quick look at the considerations and constraints resulting from the need to work with existing legacy networks.

Chapter 4, "Network QoS Design Specifications." Chapter 4 details the individual network QoS specifications and shows how they can be derived from the applications and protocol requirements described in Chapters 2 and 3. It is in this chapter that the final technical specifications for the network are developed and documented.

Chapter 5, "Requirements Methodology." The complete requirements planning methodology is then reviewed in Chapter 5.

Chapter 6, "Basic QoS Technologies." This chapter is a tutorial about the basic technologies used to provide Quality of Service solutions. Technologies discussed include the application program's interface, implicit methods of signaling for QoS, admission and policy control mechanisms, the statistical behavior of networks, queuing, and traffic shaping.

Chapter 7, "Solution Building Blocks." Chapter 7, the longest chapter in the book, contains the information about QoS solutions available in the market and closes with a few examples of QoS implementations. Topics covered include the following:

- Overprovisioning
- Isolation
- LAN QoS
- Frame Relay
- Asynchronous Transfer Mode (ATM) and its associated technologies, LAN Emulation (LANE) and Multi-Protocol over ATM (MPOA),
- IP Type of Service (TOS) and filtering
- IP Integrated Services and the Resource Reservation Protocol (RSVP)
- IP Differentiated Services (Diff-Serv), with a note about MultiProtocol Label Switching (MPLS)
- Traffic shaping
- QoS policy management and measurement

Intended Audience

The book is primarily intended as an architectural guide for practicing network architects and designers, although it can also be used by readers who need an overview of the area and by instructors of industry-oriented courses. Its orientation is toward the architectural use of technologies, not into the research of principles behind those technologies or into the details of their internal designs or particular implementations. It does assume a basic knowledge of data communications and packet-switching technology.

Network architects should read the book straight through, as chapters build on one another. Cross-references are included in each chapter to allow them to be read in any order, however, as the author realizes that few network professionals have the time to read a book completely—they usually have an immediate crisis that needs resolution!

Designers of applications that use modern networks will find much useful information in the book. It gives a good overview of the performance that can be expected from the network and the design rules that should be followed to avoid disappointing results when the application emerges from the lab and is placed in production use. Network architects and designers may therefore want to use some of the material from the book to prepare a set of recommendations for the applications designers and users within their organization, possibly using materials from the associated Web site.

Marketing and sales staff will also find the book useful, as it can give a solid overview of the various advantages and disadvantages of the technologies in the marketplace.

Designers of QoS products and researchers in the area can use the book as a broad introduction to relevant topics and to set the context of their work. Detailed information on the particular technologies in the depth needed for leading-edge research or detailed implementation plans for specific QoS technologies is not included in the book, as that would interfere with its primary task. The reader needing that information is referred to *Quality of Service: Delivering QoS on the Internet and in Corporate Networks* by Paul Ferguson and Geoff Huston [Ferguson], to *Inside the Internet's Resource reSerVation Protocol* by David Durham and Raj Yavatkar [Durham] (a broader book than its title indicates), and to *High Speed Networks: TCP/IP and ATM Design Principles* by William Stallings [Stallings], as well as to the many other references in the bibliography.

Web Site

This book has a Web site at

www.wiley.com/compbooks/siegel/

The companion Web site helps to keep the book current and to assist readers as they build their QoS solutions or as they teach and learn about them. The site includes the following:

- Microsoft PowerPoint presentations of each chapter's material
- Updated information for each chapter
- Updated references for all chapters, with links to relevant sites
- A list of errata (If you find an error, please tell me by going to the Web site! I'll post it quickly, so all of us can learn about it.)

CHAPTER 1

The Importance of Quality of Service

"All animals are equal, but some animals are more equal than others."

— A n i m a l   F a r m ,   G e o r g e   O r w e l l

For many years, the Internet functioned quite well without Quality of Service (QoS); the rudimentary QoS facility embedded in the basic Internet Protocol (IP) was generally ignored by network designers and users. Within the past few years, however, there has been an explosion of interest in the area, and all major Internet service providers and vendors are providing products that have Quality of Service features. What, then, is Quality of Service, and what are the meanings of the associated technologies for Class of Service (CoS) and for policy-based networking? And why is there suddenly interest in an area that was generally ignored for 20 years?

To answer these questions, this chapter first gives a brief working definition of QoS, CoS, and policy-based networking, then discusses the factors behind the interest in them.

Introduction

The Internet was originally designed to offer one level of service to everyone: *best effort*. A user transmitted his or her data into the network, and the network tried to deliver it to the correct recipient as quickly as possible and with as few errors as possible. There were no guarantees of transit time or even delivery; some packets never arrived at their destination. Unlike a telephone system, there were usually no busy signals—

the network would almost always accept data, but it would cope with congestion by simply discarding that data at the first congestion point.

A rudimentary form of prioritization was available, but it was rarely used. As most network traffic was electronic mail (e-mail) or file transfer, with a limited amount of remote terminal emulation, such service was more than acceptable. There wasn't any World Wide Web with its associated browser technology; there was virtually no voice or video over the Internet; the only alternative was to use very expensive dial-up connections or leased lines.

Additionally, the original users of the Internet were all U. S. government researchers and contractors studying network design. Internet service was provided free of charge, and no one was making a profit on the Internet or worrying about customer satisfaction. There was a very wide difference among different computers (much wider than today's), and the challenges of transmitting data among those implementations was sufficient to absorb everyone's interest. As the technology was new and still experimental, the episodes of poor performance were considered part of the normal experience; users were happy that the network was working at all.

As the Internet technology matured, the number of users of the network began to exceed the number of researchers into the network's technology. In 1975 ownership of the network was transferred from the Department of Defense's Advanced Research Projects Agency (ARPA) to the Defense Communications Agency. Tolerance of network performance problems decreased. Users were no longer satisfied by or interested in the explanatory, research-oriented memos that appeared from the original Internet contractor, Bolt Beranek and Newman (BBN), after each episode of poor performance or network failure. They wanted quick service, low error rates, and high availability. They also wanted greater interconnectivity among the various experimental and operational networks.

To improve network interoperability and availability, a new set of network software was developed. Called TCP/IP (Transmission Control Protocol/Internet Protocol), it replaced the original NCP (Network Control Protocol) on "Flag Day," January 1, 1983, and the current Internet technology went into production. Other TCP/IP-based networks appeared and were absorbed into the growing Internet. The Internet was becoming the core communications infrastructure for more than just U.S. networking researchers; it had evolved to support the international community, the military, computer scientists, and the whole academic world. Commercial networks using Internet technology had also appeared. Nevertheless, virtually all Internet communications still provided only one level of service, that of best effort.

In 1991 the regulations against commercial use of the Internet backbone were lifted, and the commercial networks and the Internet merged. By the end of 1991, over 5000 networks were a part of the Internet. In 1993 the first graphical Web browser, Mosaic, was released, and the Internet launched into a new phase of even more explosive growth. Because Mosaic and other Web browsers were so much more user friendly and versatile than the earlier forms of electronic mail, file transfer, and terminal emulation, nontechnical users found the new Web, built on the Internet backbone, to be a crucial part of their daily lives.

Commerce began on the Web, and, with electronic commerce (e-commerce) came more pressure for regulated unfairness (Quality of Service) in Internet performance. Users were paying directly for Internet use, and some were willing to pay extra for better performance to support new applications, such as real-time voice and video, that might save money over alternative telephone company connections. Even if the particular application didn't require unusually good performance for its operation, companies on the Internet wanted guarantees of good performance to ensure that their customers would be pleased with their experience of the company's Web presence. The ubiquitous best-effort service level was no longer enough.

Internet service and equipment vendors quickly responded to the demands for Quality of Service with a barrage of new offerings and a pile of confusing marketing literature. Each new attempt at technology from the Internet standards committees was quickly warped into a product announcement, and life became quite complex for network designers and users. It was to help decrease that confusion and ease the designer's job that this book was conceived.

Definitions

Quality of Service (QoS) and Differentiated Class of Service (CoS) are methods for providing enhanced services to network traffic. Policy-based networking is a recent, grander scheme for administering such services along with other services such as security.

Quality of Service (QoS)

Quality of Service (QoS) is a somewhat vague term referring to the technologies that classify network traffic and then ensure that some of that traffic receives special handling. The special handling may include attempts to provide improved error rates, lower network transit time (latency), and decreased latency variation (jitter). It may also include promises of high availability, which is a combination of mean (average) time between failures (MTBF) and mean time to repair (MTTR).

NOTE

The formula for availability is:

Availability = MTBF / (MTBF + MTTR)

In a chain of elements that must all function properly for the system as a whole to function, the availability of the system is the product of the individual availabilities. Total availability decreases as the number of elements increases.

Quality of Service facilities in some technologies, such as Asynchronous Transfer Mode (ATM), can be quite detailed, providing the user with explicit guarantees of average delay, delay variation (jitter), and data loss. But, as we will see in later chapters, QoS does not necessarily guarantee particular performance. Performance guarantees can be quite difficult and expensive to provide in packet-switched networks, and most applications and users can be satisfied with less stringent promises, such as prioritization only, without delay guarantees. Most modern applications automatically recover from lost data packets or can function in the presence of loss, and most users have learned to accept minor instances of increased network delay.

There is a second part to the definition of QoS: the description of how traffic is to be classified. Some QoS implementations provide per-flow classification, in which each individual flow is categorized and handled separately. This can be expensive if there are a lot of flows to be managed concurrently.

NOTE

A *flow* is defined as a sequence of data packets sharing the same combination of source and destination address, along with any other distinguishing characteristics that may be necessary to differentiate it from other flows sharing the same address pair. A flow in a packet-switched network is very similar to the concept of a circuit in a circuit-switched network or a virtual circuit in a frame relay, X.25, or ATM network. In some cases, the identifying information for a flow is referred to as the *five-tuple* (the combination of the source and destination addresses, IP port numbers, and protocol type).

Differentiated Class of Service (CoS)

Differentiated Class of Service (CoS) is a simpler alternative to QoS that was developed because of the expense of classifying traffic into flows and of maintaining and using per-flow information. Whereas QoS classifies packet streams into individual traffic flows, each of which may have a unique set of quality characteristics (error rate, latency, etc.), CoS is much coarser. It doesn't try to distinguish among individual flows; instead, it uses simpler methods to classify packets into one of a few categories. All packets within a particular category are then handled in the same way, with the same quality parameters, as set by the network managers. Unique per-flow quality information is not stored in the network devices.

Clearly CoS is a simpler technology than QoS, and this leads to some confusion in the marketplace. Vendors sometimes advertise QoS capabilities when, by the definitions just explained, their product offers only CoS capabilities. As there is no standard, generally accepted definition of QoS and CoS, the buyer must inquire closely to determine the precise capabilities provided.

NOTE This book uses "QoS" as an abbreviation for "QoS or CoS."

Policy-Based Networking

Both QoS and CoS require management control to prevent all of the users in the network from upgrading themselves to the highest service level. *Policy-based networking* is the latest, most sophisticated method for implementing that control. Policy-based networking allows much greater control over network performance than previous methods, as it provides facilities for end-to-end control and also allows dynamic changes to the rules as network utilization changes or as business needs dictate.

The primary idea behind policy-based networking is a generalization of the concept of access control lists, which have been used on mainframe computers for years. Once an individual user has been identified to the network along with the resource (network and application) that he or she is requesting, the network management system can decide whether to grant access and the quality of the access to be made available. The rules for access and for management of network resources are stored as *policies* and are managed by a *policy server*. The various network components (routers, switches, dial-in access devices, even the network interface cards on personal computers) can then ask the policy server for a decision when the user asks for network resources. The policy server, in turn, can send queries to other policy servers or to other enterprise databases before sending a reply.

Why Now?

During the first 20 years of the Internet's existence, Quality of Service was rarely considered. But recently the need for QoS began to grow.

- Commercial vendors began offering products and services that used Internet technology and could therefore be deployed either on the Internet itself or on private versions of the Internet (*intranets*).

- The new products and services, built to attract customers by using fancy graphics, multimedia, and a large amount of interaction, sometimes made large demands on Internet and intranet services in terms of quality factors such as bandwidth, latency, jitter, and error rate. While this might have been acceptable for experimental use on the early Internet, it was a problem when commercial sales of these products and services created tens of thousands of concurrent users. Even in the absence of unusual quality demands, the sheer number of users placed a severe load on the Internet and intranet backbones, resulting in congestion.

- Commercial users of the Internet were paying for access and were concerned with customer satisfaction and with communications costs. Poor Internet service meant dissatisfied or lost customers. It didn't just mean temporary delays when using file transfer to obtain research materials or when using remote terminal emulation to play the popular game of Hunt the Wumpus.

- Given the congestion on the Internet backbone, with the resulting quality problems, some users were willing to pay extra for better performance to support new applications. Typical of these was Internet voice, which might cost less than the alternative telephone company connections, but which required high-quality backbone service to make it work acceptably. Company management could be persuaded to pay a little extra for voice over the Internet, but, at the same time, they might not pay extra to deliver e-mail in two seconds instead of in two minutes. Internet Service Providers (ISPs) therefore began to investigate ways of providing traffic differentiation.

- Many users were beginning to combine previously existing networks into intranet enterprise backbones using Internet technology, but they discovered that the traffic from those previously separate networks did not always flow smoothly when sharing the same backbone. Some method of managing traffic flows was needed to ensure that enterprise users wouldn't revolt and reestablish the original separate networks.

There is therefore a combination of technical factors and market factors behind the current interest in QoS.

Technical Factors

Technical factors leading to QoS, which are discussed in more detail in the first half of this book, include application, protocol, and architectural requirements.

- Application requirements include the demands of new technologies such as real-time voice and video. These applications, which prefer end-to-end one-way delays less than 150 ms., are beginning to appear on intranets. Other applications, such as client/server, can make severe demands on the network if they are poorly designed—which, unfortunately, they often are. A badly built client/server application may perform dozens of data exchanges across the network to handle a single user transaction. Such applications work well on unloaded local area networks (LANs) in the development facility, but they cause major problems when moved into production on heavily loaded corporate LANs and on wide area networks (WANs).

- Transport and user protocol requirements include both the minimal needs of particular protocols to avoid their own failure and the need to regulate protocol behavior to prevent some protocols from harming overall network performance. As an example of protocol failure, many transactions that use legacy IBM protocols, such as those from IBM's Systems Network Architecture (SNA), may time out if network delays are greater than a few seconds, forcing the user to reconnect. As an example of network harm, some protocols, if unrestrained by the network's QoS facilities, can absorb all available network bandwidth and starve other, better-behaved, protocols. Without tight network control of latency and jitter, it's also possible that massive traffic flows with large data packets, such as those involved in file transfer, could disrupt real-time traffic flows, causing unwanted pauses in the flow and possible packet loss.

- Architectural requirements are the natural results of hierarchical traffic aggregation and of interconnecting network segments that have different speeds. Bottlenecks occur at transitions between high-bandwidth network sections and low-bandwidth sections. It is difficult to design aggregation points because new applications and usage patterns can quickly shift the traffic pattern to put stress in unanticipated areas, and overprovisioning—throwing bandwidth at the problem—isn't economically practical in many cases and is sometimes overwhelmed by unanticipated traffic. The increasing shift away from local data flows (e.g., from desktop PC to local printer) and toward enterprise-wide data flows (e.g., from desktop PC to intranet server or the Internet) exacerbates this problem.

As is discussed in Chapter 7's "Overprovisioning" section, pure bandwidth alone usually cannot solve all of these requirements, especially if there are bottlenecks in the network. Even if there's temporarily enough bandwidth, network management personnel are hard pressed to keep ahead of the bandwidth demands of the users and their new applications. Any temporary surge in bandwidth demand—a common occurrence in modern networks—results in uncontrolled losses of data from random users; there's no way to ensure that critical applications and users will continue to get network service. Worse, an unanticipated permanent rise in bandwidth needs can cause major disruptions of those critical applications and users during the weeks or months while the network is being upgraded to handle the new aggregate demands. QoS is becoming important to network architects because it promises to help them handle these requirements.

Market Factors

There are also market factors behind the interest in QoS. Responding to the delays and problems appearing on many networks, network providers and equipment vendors have rushed to embrace QoS as a way to differentiate their products and increase their profits. At the same time, certain vendors have used their lack of complex QoS as a marketing advantage. And user organizations, which have to pay the bill for all of this, are trying to regulate usage and decrease their total cost of ownership. Particular examples include these:

- Many Internet Service Providers (ISPs) are offering guarantees of availability and maximum latency (subject to certain restrictions) to differentiate their product in a crowded marketplace.

- Vendors of network routers and switches have also discovered that QoS capabilities are a market differentiator. Vendors boast of the particular QoS standards that are supported and the number of different quality classes that the device can manage. Other vendors, possibly those without the ability to support such facilities, emphasize the native speed and bandwidth of their devices and claim that the additional complexity of multiple queues and QoS management (the "QoS tax") is unnecessary and unproven.

- Network managers are trying to provide more fairness in their billing for the enterprise network backbone. The per-user charge, or "seat charge," used by many organizations is being replaced by more sophisticated service-level agreements and by the new policy-based networking. These techniques demand that the network managers be able to monitor and regulate the flow of user traffic into the network, restricting users to their agreed traffic characteristics. They also require that the network manager be able to provide the promised service levels and be able to prove that those service levels were achieved. Without these new techniques, and the technologies to support them, user organizations may withdraw from enterprise backbones and build their own dedicated networks to avoid backbone contention and perceived unfairness in paying for the network.

- Finally, network users are aware that some applications are more valuable to the business than others, and that some applications are worth the additional money that the network provider may charge for superior-quality network service.

Summary

Pressures for Quality of Service (QoS) grew because some users were willing to pay extra for better performance to increase their productivity or to support new applications, such as voice and video. The merging of different networks into multiservice backbones also increased the need for traffic flow differentiation to control network backbone performance and to allocate costs fairly. In response, suppliers and vendors of Internet connectivity and technology began to bring QoS to the marketplace.

Quality of Service, the original method for traffic differentiation, distinguishes among individual user-to-user connections and then handles each one separately to provide its requested quality, as measured by end-to-end delay (latency), latency variation (jitter), availability, and more. Differentiated Class of Service (CoS) is coarser; it groups connections into a few classes and handles all the connections in a class in the same way. And policy-based networking is the latest technology being used to manage the assignment of QoS or CoS to connections. It takes into consideration the user identity, the application being used, the overall state of the network backbone, and other factors, then directs the various network components appropriately.

CHAPTER 2

Enterprise-Wide and User Requirements

To determine the technical requirements for QoS, we'll start by examining the user needs and the needs of their organizations. It's those needs that drive network design, and it's the assumptions behind those needs that can cause problems if we haven't considered them properly. By looking at them clearly, we'll be able to avoid some of the more common implementation problems caused by unrealistic assumptions, incorrect assumptions, and misunderstandings about the costs and capabilities of technology and the willingness of users to pay for these technologies or to manage them.

In many cases, we'll eventually find that there isn't any need for complex QoS technologies. Simple Class of Service technology, or no QoS at all, may be what is needed. The enterprise must weigh the complexity and cost of QoS solutions against the enterprise's needs, picking and choosing among the QoS solutions to find a set that satisfies the most important needs at the least cost. To do that, however, we must be prepared to investigate the major network applications in some depth—and that is what this chapter and Chapter 3 are about. We can't evaluate the cost/benefit tradeoffs without understanding the cost. But, first, we'll start with a couple of examples.

Examples

QoS can be very useful, but it's not free—it requires an investment in time, money, and design to make it operate well, and it may not be worth the investment in all cases. Two classic examples, network consolidation and the need for new applications, illustrate these points.

Network Consolidation

Over the years, most enterprises have accumulated a number of separate networks, each designed to support its own set of applications. Consolidation of these separate networks into one corporate backbone network is a common use of QoS and often promises to save money while increasing flexibility. The hope is that QoS technologies can be used to ensure that each application will be able to function at least as well as if it were still on its original network. But, as we'll see, the combination of previously separate applications into one network can cause unanticipated problems. Applications may interfere with each other, may try to steal bandwidth, and may impose requirements that, although reasonable on a smaller network, are unreasonable or too expensive on a larger one. Careful integration between applications and their underlying transports may fall apart because of the less specialized facilities offered by a consolidated network. It may therefore be found that keeping one or more applications off the corporate backbone is more cost-effective, and more practical, than investing in the QoS facilities that are needed to ensure that these applications can function properly in a shared environment.

Our first example uses the technology of voice over data networks, which is called packet voice. The promise of lower costs through integration of data and voice networks has led many organizations to try this technology. Dozens of small startup companies, each with its own marketing department, have sprung up over the past few years to push packet voice, and the major data and voice/telephone companies have also entered the field. It's difficult for an executive to pick up an airline magazine without reading about how a competitor has cut the telephone budget practically to zero by using packet voice, so it's not surprising when a network manager gets the telephone call suggesting that packet voice is the way to go.

Our example begins when, as a result of suggestions from corporate management, a network manager and some of his or her staff try out the packet voice applications being demonstrated at some of the booths on the floor of a major computer and networking show. They're quite impressed. Voice quality is excellent, the system works with standard telephone handsets or with computer headsets, and the vendor promises that it can easily interoperate with the public telephone system. Voice quality across the show floor is great, and it's also excellent on a call over the vendor's internal network to the product manager back in California.

The problems start when the equipment is installed back home and the executive staff tries it for a long-distance call. Voice quality can be good, but it has a tendency to fade in and out as the system tries to compensate for lost or delayed data packets. At times, the conversation breaks up entirely. And the worst part is that there's a perceptible time delay in the conversation. It isn't quite as bad as over a satellite link, but it's still noticeable. Of course, it irritates the hard-charging top managers more than others, but it's that group of managers who can make life miserable for the network administrators.

Another source of pain for network management is that voice is much more sensitive to network delay than most traffic, so performance problems that weren't noticed before are now very noticeable. Minor traffic delays or packet losses that had absolutely no effect in the case of electronic mail or file transfers, and that had only minor effects in the case of transaction processing, can cause obvious problems in voice transmission. To add to the issues facing network managers, the question of enhancing the enterprise backbone to improve packet voice performance appears. People start to wonder who is going to pay for the new equipment and facilities. Should it be all of the users or just the voice users whose dissatisfaction caused the pressure for upgrades?

The problems over the internal network would be easier to live with if they weren't so random. It's impossible to predict when voice fading, or conversation dropout, or long transmission delays will occur. The only general rule is that everything becomes worse when there's a work crunch. The end of the month is an example: The voice traffic must compete with order entry, last-minute file transfers, and other network traffic.

Voice over the Internet is an experiment that is also tried and that fails almost instantly. The time delay and the dropouts are unbearable and unpredictable. Hopes of sending some corporate voice traffic over Internet links are quickly buried. There's clearly no chance of using such links to talk to customers or suppliers without making special arrangements with all of the ISPs involved.

Yet the promise of packet voice is still there. The hope of lower costs was the reason that corporate executives first became interested, and that hope still exists. And packet voice offers a lot besides lower costs. Because it uses the same infrastructure as data, it can more easily be integrated into unified messaging, where voice and electronic mail are combined into a single mailbox. There's also hope of a unified system of message filtering and alerting. Having data messages and calls follow an employee around the company or the world becomes more practical with an integrated system. The chance to talk to potential customers through their Web browser interfaces is also a tantalizing opportunity.

For these reasons, solutions must be found to the problems of packet voice, and QoS is an obvious candidate. QoS may be able to give packet voice the special handling it needs to perform properly over shared backbone trunks, thereby allowing packet voice to live up to its potential. With QoS in the picture, consolidation of voice and data over the same backbone network may be more acceptable.

New Applications

Another common use of QoS is to improve the operation of existing networks. Most networks don't have a proper architecture; instead, they've grown over the years as new applications were developed and as the corporation changed. New corporate functions, reorganized systems, relocated work groups, telecommuting—all these have their effects on the underlying network and can cause overall performance to be unsatisfactory, even if networks aren't being consolidated. When new application design methodologies such as client/server and Web-based implementation are added to the need for new applications, the effect on an existing network is such that many applications can begin to fail.

As an example, let's assume that the Human Resources (HR) department decides to reduce its headcount by implementing a new system for employees to enter their own address, insurance, and retirement fund changes to the HR database. The programmers use a client/server methodology and develop a user-friendly, intuitive interface for the company's employees. After all, most people will make changes only once a year. The program developers rightly believe that a cryptic, terse interface with little online help will simply send employees back to their telephone and to the old way of calling HR staffers for help. So a number of staff-years of effort are put into development of the client interface, and a good design emerges—at least, it's good from the point of view of the employees and the HR department's customers. It's easy to use; it doesn't really require any training; and most employees are willing to give it a try and are favorably impressed.

The programmers are pleased, and they implement the new client/server system in their development lab, which is equipped with all the latest networking technology. After all, the programmers, being technologists, would hardly sit still for a lab based on old VT-100 terminals and current-loop interfaces. They understand the advantages of, and demand, the latest in 100Base-T switched Ethernet connectivity between their workstations and the server computers. Their management, figuring that buying a few 100Base-T Ethernet switches and 100Base-T network interface cards (NICs) is an inexpensive way to buy improved morale, quickly supplies the necessary hardware.

Development of the new system goes forward. There are the standard sets of design questions and worries, but the network isn't really considered. It's part of the plumbing, and it works almost all of the time. A few tangles emerge in the client/server design, and they are solved, after a certain amount of discussion, by increasing the interaction between the client and the server. That's convenient, and it avoids a lot of redesign.

The help screens are stored in the client, as it's believed that they will be unchanging and may as well be part of the client program. Some other reference materials are also part of the client program, again motivated by the belief that they won't change. Unfortunately, both of these assumptions are shown to be incorrect when the alpha release appears. It's installed in the development lab, and HR representatives and a few non-HR employees are invited in to try it.

The HR representatives, who hadn't mentioned the fact that insurance and retirement fund regulations change constantly (they hadn't been asked by the programmers), make some casual comments about that one day while using the alpha release. The help screens' programmer, sitting nearby, overhears the comments and is startled. The programmer, after all, had never made any changes to his retirement fund. He's hoping to leave for a startup in a couple of years anyway and make a few million dollars, so he doesn't make any contributions at all. He didn't realize that there are often large changes to the mix of funds and to the complex federal requirements. Now he has a problem! The help screens will need revisions for each change. But the problem is resolved quickly, in time for the beta release, by ensuring that the client will always check its revision number against the server and will download a new copy of the entire client, including the help screens, if the revision number is out of date.

The beta release is installed, as was the alpha release, in the development lab and in the HR department. (A new LAN is installed for HR, much to their delight, courtesy of the project.) Things work well; no one's really looking for problems anyway—it'll kill the schedule—and so the foundation is laid for a major disaster.

When the application is finally rolled out, it doesn't take long before the complaints arrive. The high number of data exchanges between the client and the server ensures that what's perceived as a single transaction by the user is actually 10 back-and-forth interchanges between client and server. Any delay in the network is multiplied by 10, and users begin complaining about how each mouse click on their new, friendly graphical interface takes far too much time. When client and server were separated by only a couple of Ethernet segments and a fast 100BaseT Ethernet switch, it was a matter of a couple of milliseconds for each interchange. The central server in HR is many miles away from the typical corporate user, however, and it takes maybe 100 milliseconds or more for each interchange when that transmitted block of data has to go over wide area links and congested routers. User transactions that were completed in the blink of an eye in the lab are now taking a couple of seconds or more.

But that's not the worst of it. How often does someone use the system? Once a year? And how often does the help screen and other client-stored data change? A couple of times a year? The result is that each employee update of the database commonly starts with a download of a multimegabyte client application. That quick fix to the problem of changing help screens has caused worldwide traffic congestion that is threatening to choke the network. There are always a few dozen employees in the world at any given time who are trying to update their employee records, and that's enough to jam the corporate backbone.

The situation is now critical. The order-entry and other transaction traffic on which the corporation depends is being delayed by the new HR system. A couple of sales representatives updating their insurance records at the end of the year are enough to ensure that for 15 minutes no one on the sales floor can complete a customer order entry. Corporate management gets involved, and everyone's stress level ratchets up a few more notches, just in time for the holidays.

At this point, under pressure to do something quickly, network management proposes the following:

- Immediate withdrawal of the new HR application from production. (But what about the next application that comes along? And what happens to the money that HR has sunk into its new application?)
- Immediate increase in enterprise-wide bandwidth. (But who's going to pay for this? Will it be enough to handle the client downloads? And how long will it take to implement?)
- Use of QoS technology to confine the HR application to a restricted amount of bandwidth, protecting the critical enterprise transactions from interference. (But is the technology available? How costly is it, and how long will it take to implement? Is it manageable?)

The quick answer is to withdraw and redesign the HR application, giving immediate network relief while consideration is given to long-term solutions. Employees go back to calling HR with their changes or filling out paper forms, and the programmers scramble to decrease the use of multiple client/server interactions and major downloads. Corporate managers begin investigating the establishment of a testing lab to certify applications for deployment on the network.

For the long term, the HR department proposes a dedicated network or dial-in, which the corporate network managers automatically oppose as leading to fragmentation of the corporate backbone. The network managers can see where HR's idea leads: Every application will have its own network, just as it was in the old days. Expenses will rise, and corporate networking flexibility will drop. Each specialized network will have its own characteristics, its own equipment and operating procedures, maybe even its own carriers and circuits. Management will be a nightmare. The alternative of increasing bandwidth everywhere is hardly any better. The money isn't available to provide massive bandwidth increases, and any bandwidth increase could easily be absorbed by just a few more concurrent downloads of the entire HR client software package.

QoS technology to allocate bandwidth looks as if it might be able to save the day. With QoS, network management can provide bandwidth in proportion to payments and Service Level Agreements from user groups, such as HR. Groups that don't properly design their applications will have only themselves to blame when they find it expensive to buy additional bandwidth or network service from the corporate managers. The only questions are what type of QoS to install and whether it will live up to its advertising.

The HR department argues that adding dial-out modems or modem pools to existing networks isn't that difficult and will cost far less than a major redesign of the software, a major increase in the capacity of the corporate networks, or new QoS technologies—which might not even work. Using modems is low tech; the expense is predictable; and it isn't HR's problem that such a design may not be the best for the corporation as a whole.

Both network management and HR need to work together, with the network architects and the applications programmers, to develop a long-term, structured plan.

Hard and Soft Requirements

The two examples of situations driving the need for QoS were fun to write, and, I hope, gave some insight into the problems facing network management that lead to the consideration of QoS technologies. Although we can't look at all the possible uses of a network that could cause management to consider QoS, it is possible to describe a structured methodology to handle the planning for QoS regardless of the uses. The basis for that methodology is built in these early chapters, and the methodology itself is summarized in Chapter 5, "Requirements Methodology."

In this first step, we derive those QoS requirements that we can obtain simply by working with network users, before we begin to dig into the insides of the applications and their designs. We can do this because certain applications, such as person-to-person voice communications, have some network requirements that do not depend on the particular application or network technology used. The users can tell us what they're doing on the network now and what they'd like to do if the technology is there and the cost is reasonable. They can also explain what their assumptions are about performance and cost. And they may be able to tell us the advantages that new network uses will bring to the enterprise—which will help justify the expense of new QoS and network equipment and services. Some of these requirements, often called hard requirements, probably won't change as discussions with applications designers and network architects go forward, and we should be able to quantify them and thereby begin our list of network QoS requirements.

An example of a hard requirement may be the end-to-end latency requirement of a person-to-person voice circuit. As we'll discuss in the "Real-Time Delay" section of this chapter, the round-trip delay should be less than 300 milliseconds in most interactive voice applications. This is an example of a hard maximum requirement for many user situations. No amount of fiddling with application-level technologies can stretch this requirement to allow greater delays, and certain applications can make the situation more difficult for the network because the application itself can absorb considerable amounts of the latency budget. For a large subset of voice users, QoS solutions that cannot provide round-trip delays of less than 300 milliseconds are simply not worth considering regardless of the application trade-offs that can be made.

Another example of a hard requirement that we can find at this stage is the amount of error-free bandwidth needed to complete transfer of compressed batch data files. If the enterprise needs to transfer a certain number of gigabytes of data between certain hours, and if further compression is impractical, then the network simply must be able to provide that bandwidth. And the error rate must be low enough to ensure that the data files are transmitted error free in the required time period, after an allowance for retransmission of erroneous data blocks. QoS solutions that cannot provide the required bandwidth and error rate are unacceptable.

Many of the user requirements that are developed at this stage are softer, however. They're more dependent on the particular applications used or on trade-offs between cost and quality. Soft requirements may change, or we might encounter some difficulty in defining them precisely. The goal when working with users at this point is to begin to list the possible trade-offs for the soft requirements, as the list will help structure the discussion when we meet later with the applications designers who can help to focus the decisions and reach some conclusions about the QoS requirements.

An example of a soft requirement is driven by the possible cost-sensitivity of packet voice communications, such as voice over IP. Some users may be willing to trade voice quality and user-perceived end-to-end latency for cost reduction. Their requirement for end-to-end latency as seen by the user may vary depending on the cost of providing low-latency connections and compression equipment. It's therefore a soft requirement to be taken to the next phase of the requirements process for discussions with applications and network technologists. Such users should list the possible voice quality versus cost trade-offs that they are willing to consider.

Another example is driven by the need for students in a Distance Learning classroom to communicate with their instructor. The instructors and course developers, who are the users of the Distance Learning classrooms, may start with a requirement for full-motion, two-way videoconferencing between students and instructors. After all, that permits the greatest amount of interaction. Unlike hard requirements, however, this requirement could be modified and still permit Distance Learning to function. The users might be influenced by cost considerations to move away from full-motion, two-way videoconferencing and toward the use of an audio teleconference for student responses, possibly with a computer whiteboard capability. The hard requirement for latency remains, but the requirement for the bandwidth to support video is a soft one. The users should consider the cost that they're willing to bear to provide increasing levels of student communications.

Hard and soft QoS requirements appear in almost all situations and for almost all types of requirements. The typical soft QoS requirements that are found at this stage are the result of user wish-lists of features; they're in the same areas as the hard QoS application requirements, but they have additional considerations associated with them. The easiest way of distinguishing soft from hard QoS requirements is simply to ask users what they'd like to have if transmission were free and instantaneous, then work toward the opposite situation, that of expensive and slow, to see what happens to the requirements. This line of questioning should be used in talking with users about all the requirements discussed in this chapter.

Enterprise Requirements

The enterprise as a whole has requirements and constraints within which any network architecture and design must work. It's important to locate and document these early, as late discovery of such requirements and constraints can cause major implementation difficulties. This is especially important if consultants will be used in the network design, as they may not be aware of deep-seated assumptions held by everyone in the enterprise. They'll have to be told about the ways that the enterprise does things, the ways that the enterprise spends money and allocates resources, the priorities that the enterprise as a whole gives to building for the future as opposed to building just for today, and many more issues.

The summary list at the end of the chapter, "Enterprise-Wide Requirements and Constraints," can be used as a guide to uncovering and documenting these enterprise-wide issues. It is certainly not exhaustive, but it should give a good starting point for discussions with senior management. There are two groups of issues: first, Enterprise Principles and second, QoS Control, Guarantees, and Accounting.

Enterprise Principles

Principles are simple statements about an enterprise's beliefs; they are derived from the enterprise's goals, from its restraints in the world, and from its internal values. It is these principles that tie the overall network design, and the QoS design, to the enterprise's culture and long-range goals. Without consideration of the enterprise's principles, even the most technically sophisticated network design will fail during implementation. Users won't want to use the new network; enterprise controls may be unable to work with it; funding may dry up.

Principles cannot be developed by the networking team in a vacuum; they must be tied to corporate goals and the corporate culture. The networking team will have to work with an organization's management to discover and document the principles that influence the network, if they aren't already written. Some representative principles are the following:

- "The network must be optimized for flexibility, not just low cost."
- "We're in a low-margin business; the network must be as inexpensive as possible."
- "We will not implement bleeding-edge technologies or services; instead, we will wait until they are proven through large-scale implementation in the commercial marketplace."
- "We gain our market advantage from using bleeding-edge technologies. We are willing to invest in them if there's a reasonable expectation that they'll work and if their working will give us a distinct edge in the market."
- "We are committed to supplying the same caliber of networking and infrastructure services worldwide, to all of our offices and personnel. While this may cost more in some situations, it's worth it because of the cost reductions in application design and the feeling of unity it brings to our worldwide workforce."

- "We have a partnership with AT&T; they are our strategic telecommunications supplier. Wherever possible, we will use AT&T services."

- "We allow our external partners to have almost complete access to our internal systems; we're committed to treating them as members of the organization."

- "We're in a cut-throat business where partnerships change often; we form partner relationships but keep them arm's-length and controlled."

To begin discovering what an enterprise's principles are, let's start by looking at a possible set of enterprise principles, listed in the sidebar that follows. Note that it should always be possible to argue the position opposite to that of the principle. For example, if the enterprise's risk acceptance position is to be an early adopter of new technologies, the opposite position could also be a viable one—that of being a conservative implementer of well-proven technologies. If the opposite position can't be argued, then it's questionable whether the position should be stated. After all, there's no need to make a formal position out of statements that no one can disagree with and that are accepted by everyone in the industry. (For further explanations of principles, see the discussions at www.netreference.com, from which much of this section is derived.)

The first principle in the list is whether the enterprise uses technology as a competitive edge. Some enterprises use technologies in their competitive strategies, possibly by using technology-created efficiencies in product design and manufacturing as a way of decreasing the cost of the product. Or they could use the communications technologies themselves

---

Enterprise Principles

- Technology as competitive edge (efficiencies; market differentiation)
- Willingness to spend effort and money to get future flexibility
- Risk acceptance (early adopters)
- Uniform versus localized/optimal solutions
- Fairness in resource allocation versus simplicity
- Planning horizon
- Willingness to outsource and to allow competition with internal network service
- Vendor relationship (specified vendor list; reciprocal arrangements)

as a way of differentiating their products in the market. For example, they could use Web-based interfaces to stream video demonstrations to prospective buyers, or they could allow online ordering through Web interfaces or specialized remote kiosks located in shopping malls, with teleconferencing facilities in the kiosks to allow the customers to talk to sales staff if necessary. If the enterprise is focused on using technology as an edge, it may be willing to invest in QoS facilities if it can be shown that they generate that edge.

The willingness to spend money to gain flexibility is another important enterprise principle. Some enterprises don't spend money unless and until that expense can't be delayed any longer. Offices are cramped; some workers have their desks in hallways; old IBM 3270 terminals are still connected to IBM 3274 controllers with coaxial cables that bulge out of ceilings. Others go to the opposite extreme: They invest in any new technology that comes down the pike, in the hopes of buying an advantage in the market; they build or rent large buildings thinking that they'll grow into them. The usual situation is somewhere in between. Reasonable willingness to spend in advance of immediate need is especially important in QoS installations, as it's often useful to install QoS facilities enterprise-wide. Such large-scale installations give the enterprise the flexibility to adapt as workgroups move from one building to another, or as they are reorganized, or as their work applications are redesigned. With a flexible QoS backbone, crucial new applications that depend on high-performance communications can be implemented quickly, without waiting for extensive network redesign, acquisition, and implementation. Enterprise-wide QoS installations, however, can be costly and sometimes can be difficult to implement. Worse, sometimes the expensive flexibility is never used. It's therefore important to know the enterprise's view about spending money to gain possible future flexibility.

Allied to the enterprise's willingness to spend on technology is its willingness to spend on relatively untried technologies. Usually the technological edge is available only in cutting-edge products, which come complete with a whole set of surprises—some quite unpleasant. Quality of Service technologies are no exception to this rule; indeed, given the state of the QoS industry, they're a prime example of how the cutting-edge technologies may be problematic or surprising. Will the enterprise be willing to use QoS technologies that have been in the marketplace only for a year or less and that may come from small companies? Or will it insist on proven, older QoS technologies?

In many cases QoS is needed only by a small part of the enterprise, or different QoS characteristics are needed by different user groups. Allowing locally optimized QoS facilities may be more cost-effective and may sidestep some of the early-adopter, cutting-edge technology problems that might be encountered by large-scale, enterprise-wide installations. Later integration of these different islands of QoS technology may be more difficult than if they had been designed to meet a uniform specification. It's therefore useful to know if the enterprise allows a fragmented implementation of network technologies or whether it insists on uniform, enterprise-wide implementations.

Another issue is that of fairness. QoS technologies can provide very fine-grained resource allocation and billing tools, but they are complex and can be expensive. Some organizations are willing to pay the price for these tools and are willing to cope with the detailed bills that result. Other organizations choose simplicity over fairness, believing that the expense and management hours consumed by detailed resource allocation technologies aren't worth the additional fairness that results.

A further question focuses on the enterprise's planning horizon. Unfortunately, some QoS technologies and standards are so fluid that it's difficult to plan one year into the future, not to mention three or five years. An enterprise that insists on long-range planning may have some difficulties with the fluid state of QoS technologies, and the network designers may therefore have to work with only those vendors that can prove they have a solid, long-term plan. With such a plan from a credible vendor, the enterprise may be willing to commit to a QoS technology path even though those technologies are still evolving.

If the entire issue of QoS technologies appears too problematic, an alternative to QoS may be outsourcing a particular application to an alternative communications vendor. For example, the local telephone company could install leased lines, or the local ISP could provide specialized packet services for a new multicast application. Some enterprises forbid this type of bypass of the enterprise's network groups; other enterprises encourage it. The possible presence of such competition is important, as it alters the amount of money that the network group may receive and the set of possible connectivity alternatives. For example, the option of using external leased lines may cause the users to ask for leased-line equivalents from the enterprise networking group. Leased-line equivalents may not be the ideal technical solution for a particular application, but the network group may be forced to propose it to allow an apples-to-apples comparison with the outside vendor.

Finally, some enterprises have special relationships with certain vendors. These relationships may be of long standing, and they may be the result of reciprocal arrangements or long-term contracts. For example, an enterprise may have a multiyear contract with a local telephone company under which it is obligated to use that company's data service. Using another company's services because they have a desired type of QoS may not be an option. Similarly, there may be long-standing arrangements with a small list of equipment vendors. QoS solutions provided by vendors not on the list will be very difficult to obtain.

QoS Control, Guarantees, and Accounting

In addition to the organization's statement of principles, the operation of the budget and the budget cycle is a major influence on the architecture of real-world QoS networks. The team should be sure that it understands how budget decisions are made and what the planning life cycle and timeline are. Use of techniques such as Total Cost of Ownership (TCO) will greatly influence the ways in which QoS decisions are made and presented; they will also influence the outcome in some cases. After all, if a decision can't be justified by the rules of the organization, whatever you may think of those rules, it probably won't go forward. An organization that uses pure Return on Investment (ROI) calculations to justify investments may not be able to justify some types of QoS technology, as such investments are *enabling*—that is, they form the base from which some future, still unspecified, jump into a new market can be made, but they don't produce a monetary benefit immediately. Without the QoS technology investments, that jump might be impossible; but you might not be able to justify the QoS investment in an organization that has no mechanism for adding opportunity value or enabling technology value to its cost equations.

A number of QoS requirements may be specified by the enterprise at large, not left to the discretion of the individual user groups. These issues will also appear in a later section, "User Requirements," but it's important to see first if there are enterprise-wide specifications for them.

Most enterprises aren't willing to allow their users to set their own network QoS levels and priorities without management control. "If upgrades are free, all airline passengers will fly first class." But the technologies that allow users to request priorities and that allow the network to validate those priorities on a case-by-case basis are new and complex. Few applications exist that allow user control of QoS levels to be passed from the user through the application interface to the underlying communications services, and few systems exist for validating those requests against a centrally controlled authorization database. Many network managers would simply prefer to set all QoS characteristics themselves, without direct control by users through their user application. Even if sophisticated QoS policy control technologies were well proven, highly standardized, and inexpensive, there would still be a lot of design and policy work to be done by management before those controls could be used effectively. (That work can start even before the technologies are implemented.)

It's also important to consider whether the organization will use prioritization instead of absolute performance guarantees. Many QoS technologies cannot easily provide absolute guarantees, and many organizations don't need such guarantees. If users are willing to accept prioritization, how should the network management set relative priorities among applications? Who has the authority to set the priorities, and do they vary from time to time?

The network billing, cost-recovery, and budgeting mechanism is also a crucial item in the QoS planner's set of requirements and constraints. In many organizations, network charges are per seat—that is, the charge is based on the number of physical connections, not on the services provided over those connections. Such organizations have chosen simplicity over fairness. Moving to more complex billing, based on QoS, will involve quite a bit of work.

Once users are paying for QoS, they'll start asking for accurate accounting. It's therefore important to know the normal practice of the organization. Network usage accounting may be expected; if so, users may expect precise accounting for each data packet that flows. It's important to determine if the enterprise will accept statistical sampling or measurements by proxy workstations controlled by network management instead of precise accounting for every packet and connection. If billing is based on usage, managers will start asking for the controls they'll need to ensure that their telecommunications expenses are within budget. Such control requires real-time accounting across the network, to intercept unauthorized or excessive network usage as it occurs, possibly forcing that usage into a lower, less expensive QoS level.

With accounting for QoS usage and performance may come penalties for lack of performance. If the organization allows penalties, it's important to discover the form that they take. What is the possible effect on the network organization of failure to meet QoS promises, and what are the penalty structures that external competitors for network services may be asked to meet? The form and structure of QoS performance penalties may influence the types of QoS technologies that can be considered for the enterprise.

Another basic question is whether all users of the enterprise backbone are charged for services and for QoS-enabling facilities that are used only by a few. Even if QoS facilities aren't installed, the problem remains: Should all users of the enterprise backbone pay for the high usage by a few users or organizations? If that's the case, the enterprise will probably find that groups are optimizing their own budgets at the expense of the enterprise as a whole. They may inflict poorly designed applications on the network backbone, as the expense of fixing the applications to be more sparing of network resources costs them money but brings no immediate financial advantage. It's also important to uncover any alternative sources of funding for QoS facilities that may be enabling to the enterprise as a whole, even though it can't be strictly justified on the basis of current cost savings for existing applications and can't be billed to specific users.

Finally, the team should understand the way that new equipment and services are introduced into the organization, the method for paying for procurement and maintenance, and the way that existing equipment and services are retired. This influences the funding that will be available and the speed with which the organization will be willing to invest. How long is the depreciation cycle on old equipment? If it's retired, how is the remaining depreciation charged off, and which organizational department is stuck with the bill? Which organizations are responsible for new expenses, and for the training and migration costs that are the result of new technologies? Are user groups expected to provide their own training, or will the network group have to pay the bill? Is there really any money available for this? Clearly, the network group must investigate a large set of questions; the technical specifications alone aren't sufficient to build a successful network in the real world.

User Requirements

In this section we'll discuss the specific requirements of network users. Although we can't anticipate all of the applications that users may connect to the network, we can look at the typical requirements that QoS-sensitive applications have. This will suggest the issues that should be investigated about any user application that is asking for QoS. The requirements and considerations range from the Quality of Service requirements, such as latency and bandwidth, to administrative considerations, such as required proof that QoS is being delivered as promised. The user requirements are as follows:

- User locations
- Availability
- Specialized user-oriented quality measures
- QoS control, guarantees, and alternatives

After discussions with application and network technologists, these requirements, outlined in the summary list "User QoS Requirements" at the end of the chapter, will become a part of the Network QoS requirements described and listed in Chapter 4, "Network QoS Design Specifications," if it is decided that the enterprise is willing to make the investment to provide QoS for the application. In this chapter, our focus is on the initial user hard and soft requirements without considering the requirements made by the underlying applications and network technologies.

User Locations

The first piece of information needed by a network designer is usually a rough diagram of the location of the network's users, including both the individual application users and the application's servers. More detailed information for the final network QoS requirements is collected in Chapter 4, "Network QoS Design Specifications," but the preliminary information gathered here is needed to begin the discussions with applications and network technologists.

The diagram need not be absolutely accurate; it only needs to alert the application and network specialists about the geographic issues that may be involved in providing QoS capabilities to the users. That's why it's important to include any clustering of user (and application server) locations that might be able to use LAN or MAN (metropolitan area network) facilities. It's also important to include location information about mobile and remote users that may be using restricted-bandwidth or high-error-rate links. If servers are used, the server locations may not be known at this point, and the number of servers and the server hierarchy, if any, may also be unknown. That's not unusual; the location and organization of the servers will be developed later, as the costs and practicalities of possible network options are discussed with the application designers.

Remote and mobile users can place major demands on QoS facilities if they try to achieve the same performance levels as users on LANs at the enterprise hubs. In most cases, such attempts will fail anyway, so it's important that the expectations of the users be set appropriately during early discussions. Users should be asked if any segmentation of the user community is possible—to give lesser-quality service to remote and mobile users, for example. In many cases, a single user may have to learn to use two different interfaces: one while directly connected to a high-speed LAN, the other while dialing in, using the Internet, or using a mobile radio system. An example of this segmentation is in the use of Web-based sales information. The high-performance Web connections typically make generous use of graphics, whereas the low-performance Web connections are text based. In some cases it may make sense to use office visits to download graphics and application programs that are then used while on the road. It may even be possible to use a CD-ROM to enhance the data downloaded over a low-performance connection.

There are also some unusual geographic situations that may cause QoS problems and should therefore be documented for discussion at this early stage. These are situations involving underserved geographic areas, such as in sparsely populated areas with poor telecommunications services or in third-world countries that are only recently upgrading their telecommunications. In both of these situations, the existing telephone lines may be unable to provide service at speeds above 9600 bps, and their error rate and reliability may be very poor. Installing a new service may be almost impossible because all existing land lines are already in use.

The new telecommunication infrastructures being installed in these underserved locations are not a panacea. They are often based on specialized designs that use satellite or some form of radio. These designs provide quick connectivity and good voice service, but their data characteristics must be carefully investigated. It shouldn't be assumed that because speech quality is good, the link is usable for 56 kbps dial-up modems. Latency may be a major issue, especially with satellite-based links; and system bandwidth will almost certainly be restricted. Connections that travel from one side of the street to the other in the town may have to travel all the way to the urban center and back, as the new infrastructure may depend on equipment that's located there. As a result, point-to-point connections within a small town may be worse than connections from the town to the urban center; alternatives that bypass the local telecommunications carrier may need to be considered.

Availability

The first QoS issue is that of availability, and it's important to define the term carefully, with the full participation of the users. The technical definition of availability is the Mean Time Between Failures (MTBF) divided by the total time that the network could have been available (MTBF + Mean Time To Repair), but the issue for users is more complex than this simple definition. A more detailed definition is therefore necessary. The task of defining availability can be divided into three major areas: first, the definitions of connected and available, as seen by the user; second, the specification of the times of day and days of the month during which the system availability matters to the user; and third, the measurement techniques that will be used to evaluate the availability of the system.

It's important that the users and the network administration agree on the meaning of the term connected. The network administration may think that a user is connected when that user can reach a network router, but the user isn't normally interested in that definition. Instead, most users think that they're connected when they can reach all of their servers and applications. In the case of applications that are server-based, user groups would probably want to define network availability in terms of the percentage of users who can reach all of the application servers or a certain percentage of the servers. There might even be different tiers of availability, in which the network would have to guarantee the highest availability during the working day and a lower tier of availability during other times. If the application is not server-based, but is a diffused application in which users contact each other directly, the users might want to define network availability in terms of the percentage of users who could contact a certain percentage of other users.

Unfortunately, a definition that requires measuring the connectivity among all possible combinations of users and servers is probably too difficult or expensive to measure directly. Such a definition needs to include a description of an acceptable measurement sampling technique that can be used to generate measurements based on a sampled percentage of users. For example, some users would accept sampling software embedded in the client side of user applications, whereas others might prefer that sampling be done by workstations running special client software that are operated by the network administration.

The next step after defining *connected* is to define the meaning of *unavailable*. A network is clearly unavailable if it becomes impossible to establish new connections and to send data on existing connections, but it can also be effectively unavailable before such a complete breakdown in the network service occurs. There are many examples of network situations that can be unavailable to the user but would be defined as available by the network administration unless the term *unavailable* is carefully defined. For example, it may be possible to continue to use existing data paths but impossible to establish new ones, or it may be possible for the network signaling to build a path that can't be used because of massive congestion along the route. Or the error rate may be so high that virtually all packets are retransmitted again and again, with some never arriving in uncorrupted form. Applications may fail because they can't receive data before their time-out timers expire; users may abandon connections and applications when they find that their screens freeze, waiting for data that takes too long to arrive.

The meaning of unavailable should also include the length of time that the network must be unavailable before that failure is officially included in the statistics. This helps describe the acceptable and unacceptable patterns of availability. For example, one set of users might state that "the network is unavailable if more than 10 percent of the users cannot initiate a connection or successfully transfer a transaction's worth of data to any of the Primary Servers for a period of more than five minutes." Another requirement might be worded as, "the network will be available for at least 98 percent of the 10-minute intervals during the work day and will never fail to be available for more than six consecutive intervals."

Time dependencies are an important part of the availability requirements. Many organizations don't care about network performance during the weekends or the middle of the night. Others, however, may run 24×7 operations or may rely on their network for worldwide connectivity. In some cases, the day of the week, or of the month, or of the quarter may also matter for QoS. A particular application may not require high levels of QoS during most of the month but rise to the highest priority level on the last day of the month when all orders must be booked and the accounts closed.

Finally, it may be necessary to allow certain executives or others to grab a high QoS whenever they demand it. This latter case may require creative engineering. For example, teleconferencing for intragroup communications might normally use a service such as the Internet, which has unpredictable service levels. If a group teleconference is interrupted by poor QoS, the group members will simply grumble and then reschedule, with no great loss—or, at least, not a loss that anyone's manager is willing to pay extra to avoid. But if an executive wants to teleconference with major customers at a remote location, then the unpredictable Internet isn't good enough; special high-QoS telecommunications circuits must be made available during the teleconference.

Specialized User-Oriented Quality Measures

These are the most interesting measures in the chapter. Here, the network designer has to work with the users to figure out exactly what are the best measures of quality *as perceived by the users*. It's important to avoid substituting measurements of underlying factors in place of measuring the end-user experience itself. For example, file transfer elapsed time is the quality measure in which users of file-transfer applications are interested. Network delay is a factor in that elapsed time, and it can be measured, but it isn't the user's quality measure in this case. It's quite possible that network delay will be low at the same time that file transfer time is unbearably high because a high packet loss rate can cause a file-transfer application to throttle back on its transmissions. Measuring the root causes of user quality measures as an aid to defining and improving network performance is discussed in Chapter 4, "Network QoS Design Specifications"; it's important to note that this chapter focuses on the user quality measurements themselves.

Depending on the particular application, user quality measures can range from specialized measures such as the Mean Opinion Score (MOS) used to evaluate speech transmission, to standard measures such as throughput and elapsed time used for file transfer. The application designers should be asked to contribute here, and they'll later be asked to help translate these user-oriented measures into network QoS measures.

Although there are many different types of specialized quality measures for user applications, it is usually possible to start by looking for quality measures that fall into four major categories:

- Real-time delay
- Interactive response time
- File transfer
- Audio/video

These categories should cover most of the specialized areas that depend on Network QoS. Other measures are possible, and a brainstorming session with users and applications designers is necessary to be sure that important measures haven't been overlooked. In many cases, however, these four categories will be sufficient.

Real-Time Delay

Delay is simply the user-perceived delay in one direction, from the user to the server (or vice versa) in the case of a server-focused application, or from the user to another user in the case of a diffused application, which doesn't use servers. Real-time delay is usually important for interactive voice and video, as used in packet voice and in teleconferencing, and for other uses where network delay must be short and bounded, such as process control.

Delay is composed of many factors that are discussed in detail in Chapter 3, "Applications and Infrastructure Issues," and Chapter 4, "Network QoS Design Specifications"; this chapter is concerned only with the total delay as seen by the end users.

In some cases, there are generally accepted standards for delay, such as the International Telecommunications Union's ITU-T G.114 [ITU G.114], which recommends a maximum of 300 millisecond round-trip delay for voice. But even these standards are only a starting point for discussions with the users. In the case of voice, users may be willing to accept longer delays, of 400 milliseconds or more, if the delay will greatly decrease their cost. They may also want different delay requirements for different communities of users; for example, 300 millisecond round-trip for communications with customers and 600 milliseconds round-trip for internal communications. Studies have found that communications with round-trip delays above 600 milliseconds are rejected by approximately 40 percent of real telephone users. [Cox] The ITU's G.114 standard specifies 800 millisecond round-trip delay as the maximum for all but the most unusual cases. In some applications, delay is not a QoS requirement to be measured. File transfers, electronic mail, fax transmission, communications with voice mail mailboxes, streaming video, and streaming audio—none of these has stringent delay requirements. Instead, they have throughput and elapsed time requirements, as discussed in the next sections. Their throughput performance may depend on delay, but it's the throughput, not the delay, that is important to the end user. Simple measurements of the delay may be misleading because there are many reasons for poor throughput in addition to long transmission delays.

Surprisingly, Web pages usually don't have a QoS delay requirement; their quality, as perceived by users, is based on the total download time of the files that constitute the Web page. The file download times are best specified using the standard file transfer quality measures of throughput and elapsed time. The delay of individual packets is only roughly associated with Web download times because it doesn't take the inter-packet spacing into consideration. Low-delay transmission of individual packets doesn't guarantee excellent user-perceived Web download speed quality if those packets are widely spaced because of congestion in the network or if they require many retransmissions because of errors.

Interactive Response Time

Many applications depend on interaction between client and server. This interaction is typically called a transaction, and it involves the user's filling out one or more screens of data and then getting an acknowledgment from the server host. A large number of applications can be described by this transaction model; it includes information requests, order entries, interactive searches, bank transactions, on-demand status reports, and database inserts.

User satisfaction is often based on the speed and predictability of this interaction. When people are involved, they're willing to accept longer response times in exchange for less variability in that response time. They want the response time to be predictable. People also want the response time to be proportional to the perceived amount of work that's involved. Therefore, the users should be asked about their willingness to accept longer response times for certain transactions. Application designers should also consider methods to ensure that transaction response times have low time variation within each transaction type.

It's important to separate the user's view of the transaction from the application's view. The user may see an entire set of screen input and server responses as one transaction, whereas the application may see each client/server exchange of data as a separate transaction. This can be very confusing if a single screen of data requires two, three, or more exchanges of data between the client software and the server. The network delay is multiplied by the number of such data exchanges to calculate the effective user-perceived response time. Therefore, moving a successful application from a fast LAN to a slow WAN may uncover a major response time problem if this multiplier situation exists. If the network performance measure is based on the application's view of the transaction, network management may not understand the problem that the users face. They'll see that the exchange time has increased, but they won't realize the user impact because they'll be unaware of the multiplier effect.

Of course, the user's view of response time includes more than the total exchange times of the client/server interactions. Most of the interactive response time of an application is usually due to the delays within the server. Discussions with application designers in subsequent design steps will break down the overall user response time into network QoS factors and into other performance requirements that will be placed on the server and client systems. The network QoS factors are enumerated in Chapter 4, "Network QoS Design Specifications," as a combination of network latency, error characteristics, and bandwidth usage. At this time, however, all that's important is the end user's view.

File Transfer

File transfer performance measures apply to many seemingly different applications. Standard file transfer through the Internet's FTP (File Transfer Protocol) applications is included, but so are electronic mail, Web page downloads, a workstation's use of files stored on a local file server, and streaming audio and video. All of these use file transfer as an underlying mechanism, and, more importantly for this discussion, their user-perceived quality depends on the quality measures of file transfer performance.

For example, Web pages are simply short files that contain instructions for building the page along with references to other files containing images or more instructions. The total time to download the entire Web page file is important, not the network delay in moving individual packets within the file. Network congestion or lost packets can make the Web page server decrease its packet transmission rate (as discussed in Chapter 3, "Applications and Infrastructure Issues"), with the result that total time to download a Web page is increased while packet transmission delay may remain the same.

Streaming video and audio are also file transfers, not real-time applications. Their receiving software builds a large buffer to absorb network delay variations, and most streaming video and audio will ask for retransmissions of lost or erroneous packets. Real-time video and audio are quite different. They can't wait for the retransmission to be completed, so they'll accept a certain packet loss or error rate. The best performance measures of real-time video and audio are therefore a combination of real-time delay and the factors discussed in the next section. The best performance measures of streaming video and audio are a combination of the next section's factors with the file transfer measure of error-free bytes per minute.

File transfer implies error-free transmission of a set of data records. The time it takes to transmit a specific record is less important than the time it takes to achieve error-free transmission of the entire file. If the per-record transmission time is important, interactive response time is a better measure of user QoS than file transfer.

The performance of a file transfer can be measured in two equivalent ways. Error-free bytes per minute, sometimes called goodput, is the measure that makes the most sense for applications such as streaming video that need a reasonably steady data rate to avoid interruption. Their requirement is that each minute during the day (or during the availability period) must provide the required rate.

File transfer requirements stated in terms of elapsed time for a certain size file can be more useful than goodput in the case of large-scale batch file transfers, such as the transfer of major database updates. These requirements are usually stated with a deadline, such as a requirement that a 500-megabyte file be transferred between midnight and 2:00 A.M. Minute-by-minute variations in error-free transmission rate are acceptable, as long as the deadline is met.

Audio/Video

Audio and video quality measurement is a specialized area itself. The measurements for each situation should be decided in consultation with the users and the application designers, but a few examples will serve to illustrate the types of measurement that are possible.

Audio and Speech Requirements

For music and other nonvoice forms of audio, it's simplest to use the standard measurements of signal-to-noise ratio and distortion used in the audio recording industry. These measurements should be chosen as a result of discussions with users and with application developers; examples are the frequency response curve and the Total Harmonic Distortion.

Most network designers, however, find that their customers are primarily interested in transmitting speech, a specialized form of audio with less stringent networking requirements. Speech uses less network capacity than music for three reasons. First, the frequency range of speech is much narrower than that of music; second, perfect fidelity isn't needed for speech to be understandable; third, a lot of research has gone into the development of specialized compression algorithms specifically designed for speech.

Speech compression algorithms work by constructing a mathematical model of the human voice. While the result of these compression techniques can be very good voice quality, transmission of pure tones is usually poor. For example, some of these algorithms cannot transmit high-speed modem signals or the familiar telephone dialing tones accurately. Therefore, measuring the success of these algorithms by using standard audio recording measures is misleading. Instead, it's important to use measures that represent the human perception of speech's quality and intelligibility. Speech quality is a measure of how good the speech is in terms of being acceptable to telephone users (including being low-noise and lifelike), whereas intelligibility is a measure of how well words can be distinguished over the communications link.

The telephone companies have developed a number of measures for speech quality over the years. The most widely used is the Mean Opinion Score (MOS), which is a subjective method based on a technique called the Absolute Category Rating (ACR) described in the international standard

ITU-T Recommendation P.800, "Telephone Transmission Quality Methods for Objective and Subjective Assessment of Quality—Methods for Subjective Determination of Transmission Quality" (a revision of ITU-T Recommendation P.80) [ITU P.800]. Objective measures of speech quality also exist; for example, ITU-T Recommendation P.861, "Objective quality measurement of telephone-band (300 - 3400 Hz) speech codecs," [ITU P.861] which describes the Perceptual Speech Quality Measure (PSQM), but these are recent and aren't as commonly used as the MOS measure or other subjective measures.

The MOS measure is useful in evaluating the ability of systems to carry speech that will be acceptable to users. However, because it is based on using volunteers to listen to standardized speech samples under standardized ambient conditions and vote on their acceptability, it can be difficult to compare MOS values from different testing sessions or laboratories. MOS values range from 1 to 5, with scores in the range of 4 through 5 considered good quality for public telephone networks (toll quality speech) and scores between 3 and 4 considered usable for private communications. Scores between 2 and 3 are understandable, but they sound synthetic and are obviously distorted. Most speech compressors used in business systems fall within a very narrow MOS range, typically between 3.9 and 4.2. For example, the MOS value for the ITU-T G.711 standard for voice encoding at 64 kbps on the public telephone system is approximately 4.2, whereas the MOS value for speech encoding and compression at 8 kbps using the ITU-T G.729 standard is approximately 3.9. The standard MOS table is shown in Table 2.1.

A different set of subjective voice quality measures, ANSI S3.2-1989 (R 1995), "American National Standard for Measuring the Intelligibility of Speech Over Communication Systems," [ANSI S3.2] focuses on intelligibility, not on subjective quality as judged by listeners. It specifies trained listener

Table 2.1 Speech Mean Opinion Score (MOS)

MOS	ATTRIBUTES
5	Excellent
4	Good
3	Fair
2	Poor
1	Bad

panels that try to distinguish between similar-sounding words that are read from a standardized list by trained speakers in a controlled environment. There are also standards in the ITU-T P.800 family that describe similar methods for evaluating intelligibility. The ITU-T has issued a reference book on the topic, the *ITU-T Handbook on Telephonometry* [ITU].

Video Requirements

Video can be more complex to specify than audio or voice. First, there must be a specification of the video image to be carried, as performance is highly dependent on the size of the image and the amount of motion in the image. The image size, as shown in Table 2.2, could be given in terms of the Common Intermediate Format (CIF) and Quarter CIF (QCIF) teleconferencing standards, or in terms of PC or television standards.

For PC monitors, each of the primary additive colors (red, green, and blue) is specified separately, with a total of 8, 16, or 24 bits per pixel. But

Table 2.2 Video Image Sizes

STANDARD	HORIZONTAL PIXELS (PICTURE ELEMENTS)	VERTICAL PIXELS (LINES)
CIF	352	288
QCIF	176	144
PC - VGA	640	480
PC - SVGA	800	600
PC - XGA	1024	768
TV - Analog - US*	430	340
TV - Analog - Europe*	430	410
TV - BT.601 - US**	720	483
TV - BT.601 - Europe**	720	576
HDTV-Main	1280	720
HDTV-High	1920	1080

* Analog TV's pixel proportions are approximate; conversion from TV image characteristics to digital pixel counts is complex, and there are different variants of the standards in the different countries. These values are given here as a rough indicator of picture quality.

** ITU-R BT.601 is the standard for digital TV used in television production studios; it was formerly called CCIR 601.

The non-PC standards all give the number of luminance, or gray-scale, pixels; the number of color pixels for them is lower.

the television and teleconferencing standards are not that simple. They transmit the luminance (gray scale) and the color portions of the image separately, using two separate signals to represent the color portion of the image. They then save transmission bandwidth by using fewer pixels for the color than for the luminance portions of the image because the human eye is less sensitive to color than to gray scale. For example, CIF uses 352×288 luminance pixels, but only 176×144 color pixels. Each of the three signals (one luminance and two color) is usually 8 bits, but some applications use 10 bits for greater accuracy.

Specifying the amount of motion could be done simply by specifying the rate at which new still images, or frames, must be shown. As examples, motion pictures are shown at 24 frames per second (fps), U. S. television is shown at 30 fps, and European television is shown at 25 fps. At least 10 fps are needed to provide an illusion of motion. Most teleconferencing uses 7.5 or 15 fps; the rate may vary depending on the bandwidth available.

Vendors usually specify the rate that their video compressor can handle frames when there's not much motion. The amount of compression will probably decrease drastically if you're transmitting a video of a sports match, although there won't be much of a decrease if you're transmitting a videoconference. The users should work with the video application designers to specify the amount of motion that they expect, possibly by choosing standardized video scenes that are available as part of the video quality measurement standards discussed below.

Users also need to specify the distortion that's acceptable. Standard television measures of video distortion could be used, such as the Peak Signal to Noise Ratio (PSNR) [Farber] and various definitions of distortion as used by television engineers, but these measures are not always easily correlated with viewer ratings of picture quality. To handle the situation (similar to the one that resulted in the MOS measures for speech), subjective ratings have been used for years; examples are the ITU-T standards in the P.900 series. These depend on viewers who watch standard videos and rank their appearance, or on tests of teleconference participants trying to accomplish a standardized task. Recently, as discussed in Tektronix-1997b [Gringeri, Wolf], some new, objective measures have been developed for picture quality. One of the leading measures is the Picture Quality Rating (PQR) metric. This metric is based on the Just Noticeable Difference Metric (JNDmetrix) developed by the Sarnoff Corporation. By combining the PQR measure, which can be evaluated by test instruments, with standard video scenes representative of the user's application, different compression algorithms and products can be compared by a tool that effectively replicates the assessment that would be given by a panel of viewers. There's also an American National (ANSI) Standard, T1.801.03 (1996), entitled "American National Standard for Telecommunications—Digital Transport of One-Way Video Telephony Signals—Parameters for Objective Performance Assessment [ANSI T1.801.03]." It is part of a series of ANSI standards on digital video quality [T1.801].

QoS Control, Guarantees, and Alternatives

The enterprise as a whole will have the major say in this topic, as was discussed in the Enterprise Requirements section of this chapter. Nevertheless, each group of application users may have their own requirements within the guidelines set by the enterprise at large. It is those requirements that are examined here.

The first question is whether users expect to control their QoS through an interface that's user-accessible on the application. For example, a user might mark his file transfer as high priority and then expect that it would take precedence over other transfers and even over Web browsing. There might be an additional charge for the service, but he'd expect that charge because of the superior QoS level that he would be receiving. The technologies to implement and validate those user-controlled requests are very new, but some users may try to demand such a service from the network. If users need frequent changes in the level of QoS furnished to their application, use of an API may be simpler than requiring that all changes be made by network administrators.

If user control of QoS is required, the associated question about policy control must also be asked. The danger is that if users are allowed unfettered access to the QoS capabilities of the network, they may set all of their network requests to the highest available priority. This would destroy the network's QoS differentiation, and it could also result in unexpectedly large charges for their organization. Policy-based management can control this situation, but policy server technology is even newer than the technologies that allow user control of QoS through their program's Application Program Interface (API).

Implementation of QoS, especially technologies that allow user control of QoS, may be much simpler if the network administration is allowed to specify the network interface equipment (e.g., the network interface cards in the workstations and servers) and the specialized network software that handles QoS policy. This equipment and software can then monitor outgoing traffic and enforce QoS service levels in association with the enterprise-wide network QoS policy servers. Some user groups will not allow the network managers to have such authority, however, so QoS levels must be enforced through network-owned equipment such as Ethernet switches and network routers.

Whether QoS levels are assigned by users or by the central network management, there is usually a need to prove that those levels have, indeed, been supplied. One technique is to use direct end-to-end measurements through software routines embedded in the user's communications software, but this requires access to the user's communication software. Another, similar technique is to have accounting software watch user flows as they pass through the devices, such as Ethernet switches, at the edge of the network. If every user flow doesn't need to be accounted for, then there could be statistical sampling of a few flows or the use of proxy workstations controlled by the network administration. The proxy workstations emulate user applications and measure the provided network performance. Their main advantage is that they do not require that any software be installed at the users' sites—a great help if users are outside the enterprise and would object to the insertion of foreign software into their systems. (See the "QoS Policy Management and Measurement" section in Chapter 7 for further discussions.)

If QoS levels have not been supplied as agreed, there may be a need to pay a penalty to users. It's important to understand the proofs that are required for these penalties to be imposed and the form of the penalties themselves. Some organizations may simply ask that their bill be reduced; others may demand an additional penalty for particularly severe problems.

Finally, network management should be told of any alternatives that exist to the use of the enterprise's networks. Some larger groups in the enterprise may have the authority to outsource their communications needs, and they'll then try to compare the outsourcer's proposals to those of their own enterprise's networking group. The form of those external proposals must be known if the internal group is to make an apples-to-apples comparison to their own proposal. In some cases, the price advantage of one of the groups competing for the business may be so compelling that its solution, even though technically not ideal, may require matching proposed solutions from all other competing groups. For example, an outside supplier's proposal for low-cost leased line circuits may not be the best solution for some applications, but a very low price may force the internal networking groups to offer the same type of service—at least for purposes of comparison.

Summary

We begin our analysis of QoS requirements by interviewing enterprise managers and staff to discover both the enterprise requirements and the user requirements. In both of these cases, some of the requirements are firmer than others, and it's important to work with the people involved to understand the trade-offs they're willing to make. Some requirements cannot be changed, regardless of cost or other difficulty; other requirements are surprisingly flexible. The network architect must know enough about network technologies and about user needs to propose solutions that the users may not have considered and to be able to estimate the cost and practicalities of those solutions.

Enterprise requirements include both the enterprise's principles, which are organizing factors that express the basic beliefs of the enterprise, and the control and accounting methods favored by the enterprise. Principles are important because they tie the network design to the enterprise's culture and long-range goals. There's no point asking to spend money on a future-oriented QoS system with all the possible features if the enterprise's philosophy is to spend money only when absolutely necessary, and only at the last possible moment. The control and accounting methods are important because they'll affect the way that the QoS system will roll out into production use. They'll also influence the type of accounting and measurement that the system will need and the way that the system will be paid for.

Analysis of user requirements also begins in this chapter; it includes geographic locations of the users, their availability requirements, and special user-oriented quality measures for applications such as file transfer and speech and video transmission. The next chapter will delve more deeply into these applications, to see how user requirements begin to create the requirements that the application will place on the underlying networks.

Enterprise-Wide Requirements and Constraints

Enterprise Principles:

1. Technology as competitive edge (efficiencies, market differentiation)
2. Willingness to spend effort and money to get future flexibility
3. Risk acceptance (early adopters)
4. Uniform versus localized/optimal solutions
5. Fairness in resource allocation versus simplicity
6. Planning horizon
7. Willingness to outsource and to allow competition with internal network service
8. Vendor relationship (specified vendor list; reciprocal arrangements)

QoS Control, Guarantees, and Accounting:

1. Willingness to allow QoS characteristics to be directly controlled by users; required validation and usage control by network policy servers
2. Method and authority for setting relative priorities (if used) among applications and users
3. Network services billing and cost-recovery mechanism (fixed per-seat rate, variable based on usage, SLA, etc.)
4. Budget planning and project life cycle procedures; use of TCO and ROI
5. Budgetary restrictions, depreciation schedules, chargeback schemes, sources of funding
6. Required proof that QoS is being provided (none, statistical sample, proxy measurements, direct end-to-end measurements, etc.)
7. Formal penalties for unacceptable performance

User QoS Requirements

Application Name:

User Group Identification:

Contacts:

Each application may have different groups of users with different QoS requirements; these should be specified separately.

User Locations:

Draw a rough diagram of the geography, including:

1. Geographic clustering that could use a LAN or MAN

2. Mobile and remote links (e.g., wireless, dial-up, via-Internet)

Availability:

1. Definition of Connected (end-to-end, to the network backbone, etc.)

2. Definition of Unavailable (can't transmit a transaction, etc.; duration of outage)

3. Time-of-day and other calendar-related sensitivities

4. Measurement techniques

Specialized User-Oriented Quality Measures:

Definition and standard for Quality as seen by users, including a discussion of the user's willingness to compromise and accept lower quality guarantees or simple prioritization in the areas of:

1. Real-Time Delay (one-way delay measurement)

2. Interactive Response Time (by transaction type); variability

3. File Transfer error-free bytes per minute or elapsed time

4. Quality measures for speech and video; e.g., MOS (Mean Opinion Score) for speech

5. Signal-to-noise ratio and distortion measures for audio and video

6. Definition of audio/video to be carried; e.g., frequency range and resolution for audio, image size (pixels), color depth (bits), frames per second, and type of image for video

QoS Control, Guarantees, and Alternatives:

1. QoS characteristics, if any, to be directly controlled through application API; of those, characteristics to be validated through network policy servers

2. Need for frequent changes in QoS furnished to application

3. Willingness of users to allow installation of network control software within user machines

continues

4. Required proof that QoS is being provided (none, statistical sample, proxy measurements, direct end-to-end measurements, etc.)

5. Penalties for unacceptable performance

6. External alternatives under consideration and the rationale (e.g., procurement of dedicated bandwidth from public carriers)

CHAPTER 3

Applications and Infrastructure Issues

Simply knowing the enterprise-wide requirements and the user requirements isn't sufficient to specify the network QoS requirements in sufficient detail to allow major architectural and cost/benefit decisions to be made. The structure of the applications, the protocols that they use, and the constraints of the existing legacy networks all interact with the network QoS requirements. Hard requirements have to be translated into network QoS requirements through the efforts of application designers working with network staff. Soft requirements may be changed or abandoned as the implications of various application designs and protocol choices are explored or as the constraints caused by the existing infrastructure are examined. This chapter examines three groups of issues that must be considered:

QoS-Sensitive Application Technologies focuses on the encoding and compression technologies for speech and video, as well as some QoS issues for client/server and message-based applications.

Protocol Issues describes the QoS-related issues that must be considered when evaluating protocols for use by applications.

Infrastructure Considerations and Constraints looks at the QoS issues surrounding the use of existing networking infrastructures. (The issues involving the enterprise's basic principles, its budget, and its planning procedures were discussed in Chapter 2, "Enterprise-Wide and User Requirements.")

Three summary lists at the end of the chapter outline the application technology, protocol, and infrastructure issues, as a guide for evaluating your particular examples.

QoS-Sensitive Application Technologies

Network designers don't need to care about most of the things that applications do internally. Most application processes simply don't concern the network; they concern only the application and its users, or the application and its database. But other application processes are intimately involved with the network, and some of those processes, such as those for video compression, are sensitive to network QoS. By discussing them with the application specialists, we can arrive at reasonable choices of both the application technologies and the network QoS facilities.

The basic task of this section is therefore to look at the QoS-sensitive technologies that are embedded in user applications, to determine their requirements. Those topics that we will examine here are as follows:

- Speech encoding and compression
- Video encoding and compression
- Application messaging and client/server interactions

The speech and video technologies are crucial components of the video-conferencing standards, as shown in Table 3.1, and those applications are major reasons for building QoS into backbone networks. It is those video and audio standards that are discussed in the speech and video topics.

The other major application reason for QoS is the need to give some data applications priority over others; that reason is discussed in the "Application Messaging and Client/Server Interactions" section, which follows the speech and video sections.

Speech Encoding and Compression

Low-cost speech transmission has been a major selling point of packet voice technology. All enterprises depend on voice communications within the organization and to connect to customers and affiliates. There's a great temptation to decrease this cost, if it can be done without causing major problems. But there are many other reasons for speech over

Table 3.1   Videoconferencing Standards

VIDEOCONFERENCING STANDARD	VIDEO STANDARDS	AUDIO STANDARDS	COMMENTS
H.310	MPEG-2	MPEG-2	For use directly over ATM with AAL-5
H.320	H.261, H.263	G.711, G.722, G.728	For dedicated links; e.g., ISDN, T1/E1, ATM circuit emulation with AAL-1 and CBR
H.323	H.261, H.263	G.723.1, G.711, G.722, G.728, G.729	For IP; uses RTP and RTCP
H.324	H.263	G.723.1	For PSTN, includes V.80

ATM technologies are discussed in Chapter 7, "Solution Building Blocks."

RTP and RTCP are the Real Time Protocol and the Real Time Control Protocol, used to carry and control real-time data; they contain timestamps and reports on network latency, jitter, and error rate.

V.80 is a modem standard used to increase transmission efficiency by decreasing the number of bits per byte on an asynchronous line from 10 to 8.

the network apart from the possible chance to reduce cost. For example, speech can be a part of an integrated system that includes messaging, where voice and electronic mail are combined into a single mailbox along with a unified system of message filtering and alerting. Both data and telephone calls can then easily follow an employee around the company or around the world. Integrated voice and data systems also promise the ability to talk to other employees or customers through Web browsers and other fusion devices. Carrying both voice and data over a shared communications facility therefore carries the promise not only of lower costs, but also of greater flexibility.

Each group of network users has its own reasons for wanting packet voice, and each group has its own implementation situations; these greatly affect the quality that the group will expect from the system. Therefore, many different standards have evolved to provide different levels of speech quality with different QoS requirements. We'll examine a couple of the standards here, but the analysis can be applied to any encoding and compression system.

Note that we aren't considering audio encoding and compression, which is used for music. The popular MP-3 (MPEG Layer 3) audio standard, derived from the video compression standards developed by MPEG (the Moving Picture Experts Group), is an example, as are other MPEG standards such as MPEG-AAC (MPEG Advanced Audio Coder) and the Dolby Laboratories audio coder AC-3. These technologies usually require relatively high bandwidths, such as 64 kbps or much higher, but they can offer excellent fidelity for music as well as speech. Their QoS requirements aren't usually as stringent as those for speech because they usually aren't transmitted under the strict latency requirements needed for interactive communications. In addition, some of these audio encoders, such as the RealAudio encoder, use sophisticated techniques for error correction that are excellent at concealing packet loss of 15 percent or more.

Encoding and Compression Technologies and Standards

The purest form of audio encoding is encoding alone, without compression. The analog sound pattern is repeatedly measured, and that measurement, encoded as a binary number, is transmitted. The receiver rebuilds a sound wave from the measurements, smoothes out the result, and delivers it to the listener. This is shown in Figure 3.1, where the incoming audio wave is converted into a series of 8-bit numbers. Each number represents a measurement, and there are 8000 measurements per second. Therefore, the resulting datastream requires 64 kbps to represent the sound. At the receiving end, each 8-bit measurement is converted into a voltage, and the produced waveform, which consists of voltage steps as shown, is then smoothed for delivery to the user. This method is called Pulse Code Modulation (PCM).

PCM is used in the International Telecommunications Union's (ITU's) ITU-T G.711 standard for a coder-decoder (codec). This is the standard codec that's used in telephone systems worldwide; it forms the base of most long-distance telephone communications. It has been proven in use for many years, and its voice quality is obviously acceptable to users. It is therefore a good benchmark for comparison. (See Table 3.2 for a list of ITU codecs.)

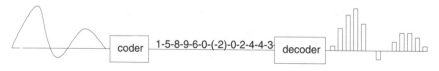

Figure 3.1   Encoding using Pulse Code Modulation (PCM).

Table 3.2   ITU Codecs

STANDARD	TECHNOLOGY	DATA RATE (KBPS)	ONE-WAY LATENCY	NOTES
G.711	PCM	64	< 1 ms.*	
G.722	ADPCM	64, 56, 48	2 ms.*	wideband, 50 Hz - 7 kHz
G.726, G.727	ADPCM	40, 32, 24, 16	< 1 ms.*	
G.728	LD-CELP	16	2 ms.*	computationally complex
G.729, G.729A	CS-ACELP	8	35 ms.	
G.723.1	MP-MLQ	6.3	100 ms.	
G.723.1	ACELP	5.3	100 ms.	

* The G.711, G.722, G.726, G.727, and G.728 codecs were designed for constant bit rate (CBR) links. When used on packet-switched networks, their latency increases because multiple measurements are put into each packet.

The ITU-T G.711 standard measures the incoming audio 8000 times per second, and it uses 8 bits to represent each measurement. The 8 bits are not linear, as more bits are used to encode lower amplitude signals than are used to encode higher amplitude signals. The specifications for that nonlinear encoding are named μ-law (for the United States and Japan) and A-law (for Europe); conversion is necessary on voice traffic that moves between the two standards. There isn't any built-in error detection or correction in G.711; it is the most vulnerable of all these standards to bit errors and can be unintelligible at a 1 percent random error rate. It prefers an error rate of 10^{-4}. This standard is normally used on constant bit rate (CBR) links, such as a digital telephone line; 160 measurements (20 milliseconds) are usually placed into a single packet on packet-switched networks, greatly increasing the latency.

Adaptive Differential PCM (ADPCM) is a variation of PCM that is also used in voice compression; it predicts the next measurement and then encodes the difference between the predicted and the actual measurement. This allows the measurement values to be smaller, which decreases the number of bits required. ADPCM is also less vulnerable to transmission errors than is PCM. ITU-T standards using ADPCM are G.722, G.726, and G.727. G.722 is designed for wideband voice. It handles 50 Hz through 7000 Hz and is therefore more pleasant and easier to listen to than codecs that are restricted to the normal telephone bandwidth of 300 Hz through 3400 Hz; it is often used for multiparty teleconferencing. G.726 and G.727 are telephone-bandwidth codecs. G.726 was designed for telephone links, and G.727 was designed for ISDN and Frame Relay. An interesting feature of G.727 is that transmission equipment is allowed to drop the least significant bits of the data to relieve network congestion. That gives better results than simply dropping entire measurements, but it depends on transmission equipment that understands the G.727 format. As was true for G.711, latency is greatly increased when packet-switched networks are used, because multiple measurements are placed into each packet.

The primary advantages of PCM and ADPCM are that they are simple to build and that they can add very little latency to the connection when used on CBR links. For example, a pair of G.711 codecs, one at each end of a conversation, adds less than 1 millisecond latency when used on a digital telephone line. Another virtue is that they can encode any frequency within their frequency range; more sophisticated encoders that are designed specifically for speech usually have trouble with pure tones. PCM can handle all standard telephone modem signals, and ADPCM running at 40 kbps or faster can encode 9600 bps modem signals successfully. There are also standard methods for converting ADPCM-coded signals into PCM, and vice versa, making interconnections to and within the telephone system straightforward.

To get more compression, engineers developed much more sophisticated methods than PCM or ADPCM. These methods build a model of human speech and then transmit the parameters of the model and the input signal for the model instead of transmitting the actual audio measurements. The result is very good speech quality at very low transmission rates, but most of these designs are specifically for human speech. They don't model anything else very well. For example, they usually can't transmit high-speed modem signals, and only some of them can transmit the standard telephone dialing tones. These types of speech coders, sometimes called vocoders, include the Low Delay Code-Excited Linear-Prediction (LD-CELP) codecs, the Conjugate-Structure Algebraic-Code-Excited Linear-Prediction (CS-ACELP) codecs, and the Multipulse Maximum-Likelihood-Quantization (MP-MLQ) codecs.

The main disadvantage of vocoders, in addition to the difficulties with nonspeech inputs, is that they are complex and must work hard to encode the incoming signal. They have to take a sample of the speech and analyze it to perform the compression, so latency through the encoder is usually much greater than through PCM-style methods. Instead of sampling continuously, they break incoming speech into time segments, called frames, and then work on each frame to encode it. They also compare the frame they're working on to a part of the next frame, a process called look-ahead. This increases their compression but further increases latency. The delay while the vocoder waits for its speech input sample to finish arriving can't be speeded up by increasing the vocoder's CPU speed; it's a feature of the algorithm and is called algorithmic delay. The time needed for processing a frame is usually the same as the frame size, and that processing time must be added to the algorithmic delay to get the total delay through the vocoder. Decoding delay at the receiving end varies, but it's reasonable to assume a delay approximately equal to the frame size.

The ITU-T's G.729 is our first example of a vocoder. It uses 10 millisecond speech frames, with a 5 millisecond look-ahead, for a total algorithmic delay of 15 milliseconds for encoding. To this must be added 10 milliseconds for the time needed to process a frame, for a total encoding delay of 25 milliseconds. As decoding delay is approximately 10 milliseconds, the total encode plus decode time in the vocoders alone is approximately 35 milliseconds. G.729A is compatible with G.729, but its encoding has slightly less quality and requires much less processing power. Output data packets for these vocoders are only 10 bytes long, and they have the ability to handle occasional packet loss by concealing that loss from the listener. Random errors that destroy too many packets cause problems, especially if there is more than 1 percent packet loss.

The G.723.1 standard is designed to provide excellent speech at very low rates. It is the recommended system for videotelephones, being a part of both the ITU-T's H.324 specification for videoconferencing over the public telephone system and H.323, for videoconferencing over IP. (Yes, G.723.1 is a strange-looking number. It's *not* a variant of G.723, which was absorbed into G.726 in 1990.) The main problem with G.723.1 is its delay. The frame size is 30 milliseconds, and there's a 7.5 millisecond look-ahead delay. The total algorithmic delay is therefore 37.5 milliseconds, and the processing delay is, as usual, equal to the frame size of 30 milliseconds. Therefore, encoding delay is 67.5 milliseconds. Decode delay is approximately equal to the frame size, for a total encode plus decode delay of approximately 100 milliseconds. Output data packets are 20 or 24 bytes long, depending on the encoding algorithm (ACELP for 20-byte packets and 5.3 kbps; MP-MLQ for 24-byte packets and 6.3 kbps). As is true for G.729, G.723.1 tries to conceal lost packets if they don't occur too frequently. Random errors that destroy more than 1 percent of packets cause obvious loss of quality, though speech is usually still understandable at a 10 percent random packet loss.

Finally, the G.728 standard is an unusual design that is very computationally complex, often requiring special hardware, but it has very low delay. It was designed for ISDN videotelephones and is not normally handled by standard telephone systems or by Internet-based systems. Because of its unusual design, it is surprisingly good at transmitting music as well as speech, giving quality that's equivalent to 32 kbps versions of G.726 and G.727. G.728 is also the best of all these codecs at handling random bit errors. It shows virtually no degradation at a bit error rate of 10^{-3}, and speech clarity is still good at a bit error rate of 10^{-2}. When used on packet-switched networks, the latency is increased because multiple measurements are put into each packet.

Judging the success of vocoder algorithms by using standard audio recording measures is misleading, because vocoders don't transmit pure tones well. Instead, it's important to use measures that represent the human perception of speech quality, such as the Mean Opinion Score (MOS) discussed in the "Audio/Video" section of Chapter 2, "Enterprise-Wide and User Requirements." All of the codecs in Table 3.2 cluster between 3.9 and 4.2 MOS, indicating that there's little difference among them. G.711 is at 4.2; G.723.1 is at 3.9. Very-low-speed vocoders (e.g., 2400 bps) tend to have MOS scores that are only slightly above 3.0.

The quality of the codec output deteriorates if there are lost measurements. For most systems, time gaps of approximately 0.1 second or longer are very difficult to fill with reasonable guesses about speech; the gap is almost always noticeable. For example, G.723.1 codecs, which normally have a MOS of approximately 3.9, drop to a MOS of approximately 3.4 if there are 3 percent lost packets. A MOS of 3.4 is still good, however, and G.723.1's speech clarity remains reasonable until random packet loss exceeds approximately 10 percent.

All of the data rates given in this subsection are for the encoded audio or speech alone, they don't include the additional overhead caused by the packet headers needed for transmission on packet-switched networks. Because of the very small size of speech data packets, packet headers have an unusually large impact on total data packet sizes. For example, a 6.4-kbps G.723.1 packet is 24 bytes, but to that must be added the packet headers associated with the transmission protocols if that packet is sent over a dial-up line. The usual complement of protocols (PPP, IP, UDP, and RTP) adds 48 bytes or more of (uncompressed) header, trailer, and escape characters. The startling result is that it can take 72 bytes to transmit the speech data packet, and more than 20 kbps could be needed to transmit that 6.4-kbps data rate on an asynchronous dial-up line! This need for packet overhead can be decreased by the use of compressed headers [RFC 2508], but it's still approximately 8 bytes of overhead. Some vendors may try to decrease the overhead by packing two or more speech data packets into each packet on the communications line, but then G.723.1 packets arrive in clumps instead of at evenly spaced 30 millisecond intervals. Additional buffering is needed at the receiver to handle these clumps, which increases latency.

There's even additional per-byte overhead if the data packets are transmitted on an asynchronous line. As discussed in Chapter 4, "Network QoS Design Specifications," asynchronous modems (e.g., V.34) transmit 10 bits per byte, not 8. The ITU-T V.80 feature of some asynchronous modems, however, allows 8-bit bytes, which increases transmission efficiency by 20 percent.

For more information on these topics, see [Cox, Kleijn, and Kostas].

QoS Requirements for Speech

The main network QoS issue for speech is latency, as speech is almost always a real-time, interactive application. (Connections to voice mailboxes and streaming audio will accept virtually any latency, of course.) The question of how much latency users will accept has been investigated in depth by the telephone companies, partially as a result of their experience with geosynchronous satellite communications links. The original hope, years ago, was that satellite communications could be used for long-distance and cross-oceanic communications. However, the round-trip delay of more than half a second caused major protests. Communications over a geosynchronous satellite doesn't fit what we've come to expect from a telephone call. Instead, it sounds as if it's going over a push-to-talk radio. Users rebelled, and the satellite links were relegated to bulk data traffic, which uses protocols that aren't affected by the latency. All transoceanic voice links now use submarine cables, and their latency is comfortably below 150 milliseconds one way.

With the coming of the Internet, the question of latency has reappeared. People may possibly accept lesser quality in return for lower cost or greater convenience, so there's great interest in determining the latencies and voice quality that users will accept. The ITU-T's standard for latency, G.114 [ITU G.114], suggests a maximum one-way latency of 150 milliseconds based on user studies, and it forms a baseline for comparison. Some users want less latency; other users can tolerate latencies on the order of the satellite delays—260 milliseconds one way. Studies have found that communications with one-way delays above 300 milliseconds are rejected by approximately 40 percent of real telephone users [Cox]. The ITU-T standard G.114 suggests that one-way delays of up to 400 milliseconds are acceptable for some applications and that delays over 400 milliseconds are acceptable in exceptional cases. That standard specifies 400 millisecond one-way delay as the maximum for all but the most unusual cases. But no one will mistake a circuit with a 250 millisecond or greater delay for one with telephone quality. A typical local telephone call through the public telephone network, which is the standard of comparison that's psychologically reinforced every day with every local call a person makes, has approximately 12 milliseconds of one-way latency.

To look closely at latency, the factor that usually causes the most difficulty with speech, we'll construct a latency budget for the speech encoding and compression application. The latency budget shows all of the delay factors in the chain between the talker and the listener. We'll examine the speech-specific factors here, while just summarizing the network-related latency factors that are discussed in more detail in Chapter 4, "Network QoS Design Specifications."

The network-related latency factors include the following:

Serialization delays, caused by the process of converting a byte or word in a computer's memory to or from a serial string of bits on the communications line

Electronic delays, the delay caused by communications electronics, such as by the modems in the path

Transmission delays, caused by the laws of physics (for example, a signal travels at two-thirds the speed of light when in a fiber-optic link)

Processing delays in the intermediate routers, switches, multiplexers, and other network equipment

Speech-specific latency factors include the following:

Dejitter delays, caused by the need to remove jitter from the received data stream. Jitter is the variation in delay caused by queues, buffering, packet rerouting, and other factors. Packets that arrive too late because of jitter are simply dropped by the codec. They become lost packets, degrading the output speech quality. The dejitter buffer delays all incoming packets, thereby allowing any late packets to arrive before the packets must be delivered to the decompression and decoding processor. The larger the dejitter buffer, the greater the chance that all packets will arrive. Most speech codecs are specified with an included dejitter buffer, but these buffers vary from one design to another. Unfortunately, large dejitter buffers increase the total delay through the system. Therefore, many speech systems now use an adaptive dejitter buffer, which varies its total delay depending on the jitter that it's seeing. As discussed in Chapter 4, "Network QoS Design Specifications," the dejitter buffer delay is commonly adjusted to be equal to the measured jitter when used for speech communications, but it may be set to two or more times the measured jitter when used for situations that don't tolerate errors well.

Processing and packet-handling delays in the speech transmitting and receiving devices. For PCs that are used for speech processing, this includes soundcard delays, operating system overhead, process dispatch scheduling time, applications program processing time, and transmission time through the protocol software. For specialized equipment, such as Internet telephones or gateways between telephone systems and the Internet, this includes hardware and software processing exclusive of the time used by the encoding and compression algorithms. This processing time can be large, on the order of many tens of milliseconds to considerably more than 100 milliseconds. A typical PC client or a gateway between a packet-switched network and the PSTN introduces a delay of approximately 150 milliseconds one-way. [Goodman]

Echo-handling delays caused by the electronics needed to cancel or suppress echoes. If the round-trip time exceeds approximately 25 milliseconds, it's important to remove the echoes on the line that are caused by the telephone system and by the microphone and speaker setup. The telephone system creates echoes because of the electronics involved in the two-wire to four-wire conversion that's done to connect the local telephone to the long-distance system. These telephone system echoes must be removed by the gateway between a telephone system and a packet voice system. Another type of echo, called an acoustic echo, is created when a free-standing microphone is used. An acoustic echo is caused by the microphone's picking up the received voice from the speaker and transmitting it back to its origin. These acoustic echoes can be avoided by using a telephone handset or other device (such as a high-end speakerphone) with built-in echo suppression. Fortunately, echo-handling devices for both types of echoes take less than 1 millisecond.

Codec delays, caused by the encoding and compression system, as discussed previously.

We're now ready to build the latency budget. For the sample budget in Table 3.3, we've chosen G.723.1 codecs for compatibility with the Internet teleconferencing standards. We expect the typical New York-to-San Francisco Internet delay to be approximately 100 milliseconds with a jitter of 30 milliseconds. We're using a dejitter buffer fixed at 1x the expected jitter, as these numbers are already going to look bad and we expect that

Table 3.3   Latency Budget Example for G.723.1

DELAY SOURCE	DELAY (MS.)	COMMENTS
Network		
Serialization	< 1	1.5 mb/s link, 64-byte packet
Electronic	0	No modems, and we're ignoring the delay for the leased line connection devices.
Transmission	100	We're combining Transmission Delay and Processing Delay into 100 ms. Internet Delay
Processing	–	
Speech Processing		
Dejitter	30	Using a 1x dejitter buffer, not the 2x needed to eliminate jitter.
Speech process	20	Time in the specialized speech processing software and hardware at both ends, exclusive of encoding (we're being very optimistic here).
Codec	100	ITU-T G.723.1 encode plus decode
TOTAL	250 ms.	*One way* delay.

only humans will be using the connection—not fax machines or modems. We're directly connected into the Internet at both ends with a 1.5 mbps link directly into an Internet backbone router; that eliminates the need for adding local telephone delays. And, as a final attempt to cut the delay number, we're using specialized hardware, not a PC.

Adding some real-life factors into this mix, such as a modem-based dial-up line at each end to connect to an ISP (an additional 40+ milliseconds per modem pair—*if* the modem's compression and error-correction are turned off) and the local telephone connection to the ISP (another 12 milliseconds of latency at each ISP), and we're already up to *355 milliseconds of latency one way*. Remember that our target is a maximum of 150 milliseconds of latency one way. We've not even added in the latency for the sound cards and the software overhead, if that's what's being used (easily another 150 milliseconds). We also haven't considered the latency through gateway connections to the public telephone system, if such conversion is required (another 150 milliseconds). The Internet latency could go to zero, and the one-way latency would still be unacceptable for many situations.

The problems with high-latency codecs should be apparent! The G.723.1 codec demands a high price in terms of latency for its compression abilities, and those abilities are restricted to speech only. However, G.723.1 is needed for compatibility with Internet-oriented video telephones; e.g., ITU-T's H.323 and H.324.

The long latencies associated with G.723.1 aren't a problem in videoconferencing, because of the even higher latencies associated with video compression. Video compression and decompression latencies, however, can vary as a result of the video's characteristics. Video frames may be dropped or repeated when there are compression or decompression delays. The resulting skew between the video and the audio output signal can be distracting to a videoconference participant if the audio is more than 20 milliseconds ahead of the video or more than 120 milliseconds behind it [Onvural].

The error rates and patterns on the network can greatly affect speech quality, especially if the error rates are over ten percent. Even error rates of one percent have an impact, as discussed above in the descriptions of the various codec standards. If error rates regularly exceed five or ten percent, speech quality can be usually be improved by using redundancy. Quality can also be improved on networks that can be configured to discard specially marked packets at congested nodes while sparing other packets. When using such networks, the codec can be designed to place less-important information in the packets that have a higher probability of discard.

Finally, if the packet voice system is to be connected into a normal telephone system, the additional issue of telephone signaling must be considered. It's not strictly a QoS issue, but remember that many of the codecs cannot transport telephone signaling tones.

Video Encoding and Compression

The technologies for video encoding and compression are different from those of speech encoding and compression, although the method for the calculation of interactive video's latency budget is the same. (Streaming video is basically a file transfer application; it doesn't have strict latency requirements.) A major difference is that straight, uncompressed coding of video is wildly impractical for transmission; it would result in data rates of approximately 10 mbps (low-resolution videoconferencing) to 210 mbps (studio-quality TV) or more. Therefore, all video signals transmitted on data networks are compressed.

The primary video encoding and compression standards in use today for high-quality video and videoconferencing are the MPEG (Moving Picture Experts Group) standards and the ITU-T videoconferencing standards H.261 and H.263. Proprietary methods, such as RealVideo, are used for low-bandwidth situations and for storing video as files on remote devices.

- The ITU-T standards are primarily designed for videoconferencing on low-speed links with lower resolution, typically 176×144 pixels at 5 or 10 frames per second, resulting in 20 kbps to 40 kbps. They are more efficient than MPEG at these low speeds.

- MPEG standards were designed for TV resolutions, for VCR-like operation (e.g., forward and reverse scanning), and for transmission speeds that are typically 1.5 mbps or higher, although the recent MPEG standards can work at much lower speeds.

- Various proprietary standards, such as Real Network's RealVideo and Sorenson Vision's Sorenson Video, are most commonly used for downloading streaming video at relatively low data rates over the Internet and for playing previously downloaded data files.

Companies such as Sorenson Vision have also enhanced the performance of the international standards while still allowing any standards-compliant decoder to handle the resulting bitstream (e.g., Sorenson EnVision).

The ITU-T standards' lower resolution and slightly poorer handling of motion in the frame are certainly acceptable for videoconferencing, which usually consists of rather static images of conference participants and of whiteboard drawings, not high-speed car chases and Hollywood-enhanced explosions. Note that even streaming video or major corporate broadcasts, which usually use MPEG, may be more convenient to transmit using the ITU-T standards if you expect that individuals may want to view the video using videoconferencing-style decoders.

Video Compression Techniques

Both MPEG and ITU-T video compression use the same basic compression theory. They can compress the video image both within the frame (spatially) and from frame to frame (temporally).

The first category of compression, called intra-coding, encodes a single video frame or portion of a frame without any information from adjacent video frames. These frames or frame pieces stand alone and are the base on which subsequent decompression and decoding are built.

If an entire frame is intra-coded, so that no piece of it has any dependency on any other frame, then that frame can be used as a resynchronization point in the video stream. Such frames, called key frames, are needed for locating video sequences during fast forward or reverse scanning, for editing, and for stopping propagation of errors from one frame to the next. An entire video presentation could be built of key frames alone, and many are.

When intra-coding is performed, adjacent identical and similar image blocks are compressed. Some of the information is lost in the compression through a process known as quantization. The amount of loss can be adjusted by varying the quantization, and compressors adjust the quantization as a way of controlling their output data rate. If the frame to be compressed has a lot of picture detail and the compressor's output buffers are nearly full, the compressor may coarsen the quantization to decrease picture quality and avoid overflowing the output buffers. The resulting picture is blocky, and sharp image outlines can be lost. In contrast, if the output buffers have plenty of room, the compressor may simply allow the quantization setting to remain, hoping that the next few video frames won't generate as much data when they are compressed.

Video compressors normally compress from frame to frame (*inter*-coding) as well as within a frame (*intra*-coding). The compression mechanism can notice that a particular piece of the image has moved, but not changed, from one video frame to the next. Instead of transmitting that piece of the image again, the encoder transmits instructions for the receiver to shift that portion of the image in the next video frame. The encoder looks at the action in the video, predicts the motion of groups of pixels (a *macroblock*), and then records the difference between that predicted motion and the actual motion seen in the video frame undergoing compression. This is called predictive inter-coding, as it's based on predicting the movement from a preceding frame. Frames built by predictive inter-coding typically require fewer than half of the bits that intra-coded frames require.

An advanced form of inter-coding is bidirectional inter-coding. This type of coding is an interpolation between adjacent frames. It's the most efficient type of coding in terms of bandwidth, typically requiring only one quarter of the bits of an intra-coded frame, and it has the additional advantage that its interpolations are more accurate because they are between two frames, not just a prediction from a preceding frame. For example, think of what happens in a video image if a door opens in a house, revealing the interior. Predictive inter-coded frames must encode everything revealed in the newly opened door, as the previous frame contains just an image of the closed door. But bidirectional inter-coded frames can interpolate by using the next frame, which includes an image of the completely open door. This is a great advantage in temporal data compression.

Unfortunately, bidirectional inter-coded frames require a lot of computation, and they force the encoder and decoder to store a number of frames in memory to handle the compression and decompression processes. The encoder must have both the preceding and following frames in memory before it can construct the intervening bidirectional inter-coded frames. It then transmits the bordering frames before the bidirectional inter-coded frames that are interpolated between them, which eases the job of the decoder. Needless to say, the resulting increase in encoding and decoding latency is considerable (typically 100 milliseconds), as is the increase in the necessary computational power. For these reasons, videoconferencing compression does not normally use this type of coding, and even some MPEG broadcasts omit them.

The recording engineer and the encoder set the mixture percentage of key frames and the more compressed inter-coded frames after considering the desired output transmission rate and the amount of change in the video image that's being encoded and compressed. Clearly, this is a lot easier for the engineer and the hardware if the encoding isn't being done in real-time. The encoding of movies for later streaming transmission may take a number of passes through the material, during which the mixture of frame types to be used in the final encoding and the number of bits allowed per frame is adjusted according to the scene. Various encoding plans can be tried, and the one resulting in the best combination of a low total number of bits with a high-quality picture can then be used. Real-time encoding is much more difficult; the video material must be encoded on the fly. A pipelining process is often used for high-quality video, in which incoming video is quickly examined to create an encoding plan, but this adds latency. The sophistication of this encoding process is a competitive area for compression technology vendors, as they can work to improve the resulting video quality while still remaining completely standards-compliant.

Nevertheless, for interactive video the rigorous latency demands result in suboptimal video compression. There's no time for fancy encoding plans, so bits are wasted or hurried changes must be made by the encoder in the quantization rate, resulting in blocky images, as the output buffers threaten to overflow. Efficient bidirectional inter-coding can't be used because it requires that an entire sequence of frames be stored before decompression can begin. The result is that video quality decreases as motion within the frame increases.

Finally, all video compression requires close synchronization between sender and receiver, therefore demanding large dejitter buffers if jitter is present. The decoder is juggling a lot of data, and it must produce a new video frame at the proper time to avoid major difficulties with the video display. If frames arrive late, the monitor will produce highly distracting flashes or the decoder may have to repeat a frame (causing synchronization loss, called skew, with the audio portion of the transmission); if frames arrive early, the input buffers to the decoder may overflow.

We'll now look at the ITU's videoconferencing standards and the MPEG standards in detail, followed by a brief look at proprietary systems.

Videoconferencing Standards

The ITU-T standard H.261 is the basic video standard for videoconferencing. It creates a video signal at a speed of p × 64 kbps, where p can be in the range 1 through 30. P is often set equal to 6, for a total speed of 384 kbps.

ITU-T H.261 was not designed for transmission of full TV video images; instead, it defines a smaller standard video image, the Common Intermediate Format (CIF), which contains 352 × 288 luminance (gray-scale) pixels and a quarter of that number (176 × 144) of chrominance, or color, pixels. It also defines smaller images: the Quarter CIF (QCIF) format with 176 × 144 luminance pixels, and (in H.263) the Sub-QCIF (SQCIF) frames, which are 128 × 96 luminance pixels. There are more luminance pixels than chrominance pixels because the human eye is more sensitive to gray scale than to color. Additional pixels result in a greater improvement in perceived image quality if they're used to increase gray-scale image detail instead of being used to improve color detail.

The ITU-T H.261 standard depends heavily on inter-coding image compression, as that is more efficient in bandwidth use than intra-coding—especially in typical videoconference situations that don't have a lot of change from frame to frame. Purely intra-coded frames, the key frames, are used as synchronization points because they don't depend on any other frames. After a key frame is sent, the encoder builds subsequent frames by sending only the predictive inter-coded changes, greatly decreasing the needed bandwidth. If a block of pixels in the frame (a macroblock) undergoes a major change from one input frame to the next, H.261 can intra-code that macroblock instead of trying to transmit the change vectors using inter-coding. The result is that most H.261 frames consist of predictive inter-coded macroblocks, with some intra-coded macroblocks included where there have been major changes.

If an error occurs in a macroblock, inter-coding will propagate that error into subsequent frames. To decrease the impact of those errors, the encoder ensures that there's never a string of more than 100 or so inter-coded macroblocks without an intra-coded macroblock to act as a clean restart point. Advanced encoders are also being discussed that will be able to accept feedback from the receiver's decoder and, based on that feedback, force the use of additional intra-coding to handle unusually error-prone circuits.

The ITU-T standards do not require the frequent generation of key frames. Therefore, ITU-T datastreams don't usually have a lot of resynchronization points for video editing or for offline playback functions such as fast forward or reverse scanning. The standard doesn't prohibit frequent key frame generation, but video transmission using the ITU-T standard is normally used for teleconferences that don't need those facilities and that don't want to spend the bandwidth needed to handle frequent key frames.

The ITU-T H.262 standard is identical to MPEG-2, which is discussed later and is not a pure videoconferencing standard.

ITU-T H.263 is an improved version of H.261, with support for speeds below 64 kbps and with some new image sizes: the Sub-QCIF format described previously, and 4CIF and 16CIF sizes that are 704×576 and 1408×1152 luminance pixels. H.263 also has new, optional encoding features that support, for example, bidirectional inter-coding between future and past frames. The bidirectional inter-coded macroblock information is transmitted with the next predictive inter-coded macroblock to increase efficiency. In effect, the predictive inter-coded macroblock of H.261 has been expanded to contain both its own information *and* the information needed to produce an earlier macroblock. Decoding the new PB-type macroblock allows the decoder to produce two frames simultaneously: a frame containing bidirectional inter-coding and a subsequent frame containing only predictive inter-coding. Because of this efficiency shortcut, there cannot be two bidirectional inter-coded frames in sequence.

The ITU-T compression standards fit the videoconferencing applications well, if enough bandwidth is available. When run at a 50:1 compression rate that produces approximately 50 kbps, H.263 QCIF at 10 fps is very acceptable for videoconferencing on a workstation screen. At higher compression rates, unenhanced H.263 QCIF at 10 fps produces a poor image if there's any motion at all. For example, a 140:1 compression rate producing QCIF at 10 fps and 20 kbps can be very poor. In such cases, proprietary enhancements to the H.263 standard can be useful. The ITU-T standards define the decoder, not the encoder, so it's possible to design enhanced encoders that adhere to the standard yet give markedly improved quality because of better encoding choices.

The ITU-T standards do not currently support scaling, which is the ability of a single datastream or group of datastreams to support multiple image qualities simultaneously. If different groups of receivers have different bandwidths available to them, then each group will need a completely separate ITU-T datastream either from the encoder or from transcoders that accept a high-quality datastream and produce a lower-quality datastream (at lower bandwidth) for further dissemination.

MPEG Standards

Unlike the ITU-T standards discussed previously, the MPEG standards, which are discussed at length in [Tektronix 1997a], were designed for the storage and playback of entertainment video, as well as for video transmission. The convenience of video playback (fast forward and reverse scanning) and the image quality were considered more important than the latency involved in the video coding and decoding process.

To enhance picture quality and provide enough synchronization points for editing and for forward and reverse scanning, MPEG datastreams have a large number of key frames, the frames that contain only intra-coded macroblocks. These key frames are called Intracoded Frames (I Frames). Frames that contain predictive inter-coded macroblocks are called Predictive Frames (P Frames), and frames containing bidirectional inter-coded macroblocks are called Bidirectional Frames (B Frames). PB macroblocks or frames, as are used in the ITU-T H.263 specification, aren't used by MPEG; MPEG datastreams can therefore have more than one B Frame in sequence. (See Figure 3.2.)

The MPEG specifications do not require any pattern of frame mixing, so the encoder can choose any mix desired to optimize quality, bandwidth utilization, or encoding efficiency. As do the videoconferencing standards, the MPEG specifications define the action of the decoder, not the encoder. Therefore, any frame mixture or encoding trick can be used, as long as the decoders can function properly. For example, a typical encoding pattern is IBBPBBPBBPBB; it repeats after every 12 frames. The sequence beginning with an I frame and ending with the frame before the next I frame is called a Group of Pictures (GOP). Because B Frames can't be decoded until the following I or P frame is received, the presence of B Frames increases latency. Frames must be held in buffers while the B Frames are encoded and then decoded. That's not a problem for playback of stored video, but it causes problems in real-time interactive video. At a rate of 25 fps, each buffered frame adds 40 milliseconds of delay.

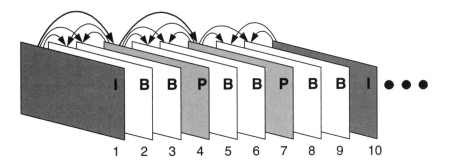

Figure 3.2 Video compression frame types.

All MPEG encoders vary their encoding rate because the sizes of the various types of frames vary and the mixture of frame types can vary. Encoders therefore contain large buffers (typically 100 milliseconds or more) to smooth out these variations and create a steady output stream. They may vary their encoding frame mixture and quantization to keep the output buffer filled, thereby maximizing image quality. For example, if the output buffer is almost empty, the encoder could increase quantization detail and also create a lot of I Frames; if the output buffer is almost full, the encoder could decrease quantization detail and also create a lot of the smaller P and B Frames. If the encoder is using pipelining to adjust its quantization, there can be an additional pipeline delay of 500 milliseconds or more while the encoder examines the incoming video and builds its encoding plan.

Because the MPEG packets contain different types of frames, as well as error recovery and clock-timing header information, some frames are more important to the decompressor/decoder than others. The packets with clocking information are the most important, followed by those with the I Frames on which other frames are built.

There are three MPEG video compression standards, MPEG-1, -2, and -4. MPEG-3, targeted at HDTV, was abandoned because HDTV compression was included in MPEG-2. MPEG-7 is a different standard, designed for describing and cataloging video, not for transmitting it.

MPEG-1

MPEG-1, the original MPEG, was designed for video storage and retrieval; it can encode and multiplex a single video stream with a stereo or mono audio track. It is designed for noninterlaced (non-TV) video and for VHS-like quality, and it can handle 352×288 pixels at noninterlaced

25 fps or 352 × 240 pixels at noninterlaced 30 fps. MPEG-1 is now used for CD-ROMs and for transmission at speeds up to 1.5 mbps.

MPEG-1 output streams can vary their bandwidth, but that is somewhat awkward and impractical. Such variations can occur only at specific points in the datastream and require coordination between the sender and receiver.

MPEG-2

MPEG-2 was developed for ATM, DVD, and set-top boxes; it is identical to ITU-T standard H.262. It adds multichannel audio capabilities, the ability to handle and multiplex different types of video signals, including HDTV and interlaced (TV) video, and improved compression. It also contains a special transport format (Transport Stream) for long-distance transmission, and it can generate variable-rate output datastreams. MPEG-2 decoders are backward compatible with MPEG-1. A typical transmission rate for VCR-quality video is a constant 1 mbps; a typical rate for TV-quality video is 5 mbps.

Because MPEG-2 must handle many different types of video, including HDTV with its many variations, there are different categories of MPEG-2. These categories are called profiles, and each profile is further subdivided into levels. The primary categories are Simple Profile/Main Level, which allows only standard definition TV with only I and P Frames, and the Main Profile, which contains many different levels corresponding to low-definition (352 × 288 pixel), standard-definition (720 × 576 pixel), and high-definition TV. An interesting profile is known as the 4:2:2 Profile; it is designed for compatibility with professional video editing equipment. Unlike the normal profiles, it includes the additional video data and synchronization information that is needed by that equipment.

The MPEG-2 datastream can be encoded to provide scalability by carrying a hierarchy of levels. One possible application allows standard-definition TVs to retrieve a standard definition TV signal, while high-definition TVs can combine the main MPEG-2 bitstream with an additional MPEG-2 enhancement layer bitstream to obtain the full HDTV signal.

MPEG-2 has two types of protocols to carry the output from the encoder: one for use within processing equipment and data storage systems, the Program Stream, and one for use on noisy long-distance links, the Transport Stream. It is the Transport Stream that's of interest to us. The Transport Stream is composed of fixed-length 188-byte packets, and those packets contain very accurate time stamps and special error-recovery information. The decoder uses those timestamps to synchronize the transmitted and received video signals, avoiding the problems that appear if a decoded frame arrives too early or too late at the video display, and it uses them to avoid skew between the audio and video.

The datastream from MPEG-2 can be generated at either a constant bit rate (CBR) or a variable bit rate (VBR). CBR is normally used for data transmission, whereas VBR is used for storage on DVD. The CBR method uses the same feedback methods used by MPEG-1 to adjust encoding rate as the output buffers fill or empty. The VBR method uses fewer bits, but it works best if the encoder can use multiple passes over the input video to create the most efficient encoding plan. An additional factor against using VBR for real-time transmission is that it is not available on most data transmission systems, particularly as the end-to-end delay must not vary despite massive changes in the bit rate—often 4:1 or more as an I Frame is followed by B Frames.

MPEG-2 works well with an ATM Cell Loss Ratio and an ATM Cell Error Ratio of approximately $1x10^{-8}$ [Ivancic] (which is approximately equivalent to a Bit Error Rate (BER) of $1x10^{-9}$ [Cuevas]), and it can automatically correct errors in its datastreams through the use of Forward Error Correction, which increases the size of the Transport Stream packets from 188 bytes to 204 bytes or more.

MPEG-4

MPEG-4 is a completely new system that was standardized in 1999; it is an architecture for true multimedia, with integrated video, audio, graphics, and text. It is designed to accommodate the ITU-T frame resolutions as well as TV resolutions, and it supports video at rates typically between 5 kbps and 4 mbps. The key difference from previous MPEG versions is that individual objects within the frame can be identified and manipulated. MPEG-4 also includes a new file format, mp4, which is designed for storing and exchanging complete MPEG-4 files between computer users.

Very low data rates are possible in MPEG-4, as are low total encode plus decode latencies. The MPEG-4 standard calls for a Low Delay Mode in which the maximum total encode plus decode latency is specified as 150 milliseconds at 24 kbps.

Because the individual objects within the frame are identified, much more sophisticated scaling mechanisms can be used that automatically create different datastreams depending on available bandwidth. Different users can then get appropriate bandwidth streams depending on their connectivity and on their display needs. A base layer gives the least common-denominator of information, and additional enhancement layers can be used to increase resolution at the cost of more bandwidth. This is an improvement over the hierarchies available in MPEG-2.

As is true for MPEG-2, MPEG-4 can recover from errors in its datastream. MPEG-4's specification calls for exceptionally good recovery abilities, with "usable video" at a random Bit Error Rate (BER) of 10^{-4} and a burst BER of 10^{-3} (maximum burst 10 milliseconds).

Proprietary Video Codecs

There are many proprietary video codecs, such as Sorenson Vision's Sorenson Video, Compression Technology's Cinepak, and Real Networks' RealVideo. Their decoders are widely distributed and usually free. These codecs are usually used for streaming video and for displaying video files that are locally stored, and their proprietary coding algorithms are not included in the international standards. Some of them are tuned for streaming video at very low data rates and high error rates, such as a 28.8 kb/s connection to the Internet. The vendors are also pushing vigorously into teleconferencing, especially on low-speed connections.

Although the best performance is usually with their purely proprietary codecs, most of these packages include the international standard algorithms as an option. Even when they use the international standards, quality is a primary area of competition. Most of the vendors take advantage of the fact that the international standards usually specify the decoding operation, not the encoding operation. Therefore, these packages can enhance the encoding operation, adding features or advanced encoding techniques to optimize the mixture of frame types and quantization, while remaining totally standards-compliant. This results in improved video display quality for all decoders, not just those built by the particular manufacturer.

QoS Requirements for Video

The QoS requirements that video will place on the network are discussed here, along with a summary of the advantages and disadvantages of the various video encoding and compression technologies.

MPEG-1 and MPEG-2 standards are intended primarily for movies and streaming video. They are generally impractical for videoconferencing, and their added features are unnecessary. Because they have a much larger number of key frames and much more intra-coded data than the typical ITU-T H.261 or H.263 encoding, they require more bandwidth. Their use of B Frames also greatly increases the latency, as multiple frames must be held in the system during the encoding and decoding cycles. They may use pipelining to create an encoding plan, adding up to 500 milliseconds of latency. And their fast-forward and reverse video scanning features and their editing features aren't needed during a videoconference.

The new MPEG-4 standard can be used in videoconferencing, however. It has a special Low-Delay Mode with a maximum delay through the encoder and decoder of 150 milliseconds. It can also handle low-speed links, which are typical of videoconferencing applications.

The videoconferencing ITU-T standards typically need only 200 milliseconds to 400 milliseconds total one-way latency through the encoder and decoder, which is acceptable. Their standard decoders don't provide the viewing flexibility provided by streamed or stored-video decoders, such as fast forward or reverse, because the videoconference situation doesn't need those capabilities. In some cases, however, movies and streaming video are sent using the ITU-T standards instead of the higher-quality MPEG because that allows decoding by videoconferencing equipment that may not be able to handle MPEG decoding.

For those designers planning on having an ATM backbone available, as discussed in Chapter 7, "Solution Building Blocks," it's important to note that the MPEG compression technologies are a closer fit to ATM Variable Bit Rate (VBR) with the ATM Adoption Layer type 5 (AAL-5) interface than they are to constant bit rate (CBR) links. For example, the ITU-T H.310 teleconferencing standard is explicitly designed for MPEG-2 video over ATM with AAL-5 and VBR. CBR links, however, are much easier to obtain, and most video streams cannot rely on ATM end-to-end. Most videoconferencing standards and most proprietary technologies are designed with CBR links in mind. They therefore use the CBR feature of ATM along with its AAL-1 interface. That's less efficient than using VBR with AAL-5, but it's more interoperable with non-ATM networks and end-user equipment.

Bandwidth requirements are greater for MPEG-1 and MPEG-2 than for the videoconferencing standards, primarily because MPEG tends to have a much higher percentage of key frames and intra-coded data. But MPEG-2 and MPEG-4 are designed to allow splitting of the datastream into base and enhanced picture streams (called layered coding, or enhancement layers), which allows different bandwidths to be derived from one encoding. Individual receivers can then decide on the picture quality they want. If layered coding isn't available, other possibilities are having the decoder drop B and P Frames to decrease the decoding processing power required or installing devices known as transcoders to recode at a lower rate and therefore decrease the bandwidth required. These transcoders can then be placed at the beginnings of low-bandwidth portions of the network to derive low-bandwidth, lower-quality datastreams as needed. If very low-bandwidth streaming video is needed, the proprietary codecs are better than those defined by international standards. Note that some of these low-bandwidth codecs are specifically designed for low data rates; increasing the bandwidth above a certain level may not greatly improve video quality.

MPEG-1, MPEG-2, and the ITU-T standards prefer an error rate that is better than an average BER of 10^{-9}. (MPEG-4, when it is implemented, will be much more forgiving of errors, as noted previously.) Video-conference participants are usually forgiving of the bright screen flashes and dropouts that occur when errors distort the received video; therefore, most users will accept the results of a higher average BER. Users are less forgiving of screen flashes and dropouts in movies, but nonmulticast streaming video can usually use retransmission to compensate for errors. Fortunately, all of the standards include the ability to recover from some errors, if the communications network can be persuaded to deliver erroneous packets instead of deleting them completely. The MPEG and the ITU-T standards, as well as proprietary codecs, can be used with Forward-Error-Correcting (FEC) codes, to detect and correct transmission errors without requiring the retransmission of frames that were incorrect when they were received the first time. Many of these codecs include such a feature as an option.

In any case, videoconferencing applications will usually have severe problems below 33 kbps, regardless of latency or error rate, because the larger video frames will block audio frames long enough to increase audio jitter and skew (the time differential between audio and video signals) to unacceptable levels. Work is being done in the IETF Integrated Services over Specific Link Layers (ISSLL) Working Group (http://ietf.org/html.charters/issll-charter.html) to handle this problem by forcing fragmentation of video and other large packets on slow links.

Application Messaging and Client/Server Interactions

Compared to the long discussions about speech and video encoding and compression, this discussion is mercifully short! The basic problem to be aware of is the sadly common tendency of application designers to couple their client and their server applications very tightly. Too many messages pass between client and server in the course of a single user-perceived transaction, and the result is a multiplier effect. If each user transaction requires, say, 10 back-and-forth interactions between the client application and the server application, then a 200 millisecond client/server interaction is multiplied into a 2 second delay. Any delay in the network infrastructure results in an increase in apparent transaction time by a factor of 10.

To avoid this situation, be sure that the applications designers have carefully considered the implications of some of their design decisions. Attempts to validate each separate field in an input screen through client/server interchanges are common causes of this difficulty. Needless to say, character-at-a-time interfaces, such as are used with UNIX GETCHAR() commands, are disastrous, as are X-window style GUI interfaces in which each mouse click may be a separate packet. Be sure that applications are tested early in their development cycle on a real WAN or on a special testing setup with a delay box inserted between client and server.

In the case of application messaging, the problems of client/server all apply. And here's one additional problem: a messaging system based on electronic mail (for example, some applications using MAPI, the Messaging Application Programming Interface) may have problems identifying its e-mail messages to the network in such a way that they don't get classed with real e-mail and are therefore delayed to allow other traffic to travel through the network more quickly.

Protocol Issues

Protocols are the sets of data formats and interchange rules that programs use while communicating, and each protocol has its own inherent requirements for transmission service. For example, some legacy protocols fail if the round-trip time delay exceeds a few seconds. Other protocols (e.g., TCP) are much more tolerant; they can handle up to a few minutes' delay. But TCP, and some other protocols, may try to absorb all of the available bandwidth, crowding out other users of the shared network backbone.

In some cases, a required protocol won't work well with the multiservice backbone network being designed. The equipment using that protocol may be expensive and inflexible, or the cost of redesigning an application to use more network-friendly protocols may be prohibitive. In those cases, it may be more practical to continue to use the legacy networks for that particular protocol. It's best to discover such situations before trying to force one of these protocols into the new backbone.

This section looks at the characteristics of protocols to help evaluate their QoS needs and the impact that they will have on the rest of the network. The focus here is on providing guidance for discussing protocol requirements with application designers and with QoS technology and service providers. It's important to know which questions to ask, and it's also important to know some of the standard techniques that could be used to handle various protocol difficulties. That will help application designers to select appropriate protocols for their applications, and it will help the network designers when they have to build the appropriate QoS capabilities into the network. The particular ways in which some of these protocols can also be used to *provide* QoS facilities are discussed later, in Chapter 7, "Solution Building Blocks."

When discussing protocol QoS requirements it's useful to keep in mind the basic protocol characteristics that have the greatest interaction with QoS facilities:

- Flow and congestion control
- Bandwidth
- Resilience

These characteristics are examined in detail in the following subsections, in which a description of the characteristics is followed by a discussion of their QoS considerations.

Flow and Congestion Control

Flow and congestion control allows a recipient of protocol traffic to adjust the rate at which that traffic arrives. With good flow control, the recipient and the network can adjust the incoming data rate to avoid the loss of data. If there's congestion at the receiver or at some point in the network, control can be exerted to avoid the loss of data or need for retransmissions caused by overflowing buffers.

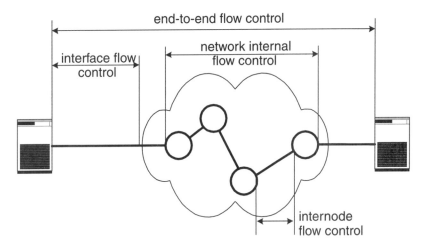

Figure 3.3 Flow and congestion control points.

Flow can be controlled in four places in the path between sender and receiver, as shown in Figure 3.3:

- End-to-end flow control, between the sender and receiver itself, without directly interacting with network components
- Network interface flow control, at the connections between the border network nodes and the network users
- Internode flow control, between individual intermediate network nodes
- Network internal flow control, between the first and last network border nodes, within the network, to avoid too much buffering inside the network

In this chapter, we're primarily concerned with the first two control points. We need to know the implications of application protocol choices, and those choices concern the network users' end-to-end flow control and the interfaces between the users and the network itself. The last two control points refer to methods that the network can use to control its flow and congestion internally, and that's covered later, in Chapter 6, "Basic QoS Technologies," and Chapter 7, "Solution Building Blocks."

The basic methods used to impose flow and congestion control on a datastream are these:

- Implicit Control

- Choke Packet
- Explicit Congestion Signaling
- Explicit Rate Signaling

These methods are discussed later in this chapter. But before that discussion, it's necessary to give a quick summary of the sliding-window protocols on which some of them depend.

Sliding-Window Protocols

Flow control is often combined with error control; a typical example is in the standard link-level protocols such as HDLC (High-level Data Link Control). In these protocols, the sender is allowed to transmit up to some maximum number of packets or bytes before receiving an acknowledgment. The protocol technique is called sliding window, and the number of packets or bytes that can be transmitted before the sender has to pause and wait for acknowledgments is called the window size. (Some protocols, such as HDLC, measure the window size in packets; others, such as TCP, measure the window size in bytes. The same considerations apply to both designs.) The original HDLC had three bits for packet numbering, allowing a maximum of seven packets outstanding before an acknowledgment had to be received. Some variations of HDLC allowed extension of the packet numbering field, allowing many more packets to be sent before an acknowledgment had to be received; some imposed additional restrictions (such as in X.25), restricting the number of packets outstanding to four or fewer. An option for TCP [RFC 1323] allows TCP's already large window size to be increased further.

The purpose of extensions of the packet numbering field was to allow efficient transmission on long-latency or high-speed links. If the link latency were long, as on a satellite link or a high-latency Internet connection, the sender could easily transmit seven packets and then be forced to stop and wait for an acknowledgment. That acknowledgment wouldn't be issued until at least one of the packets had arrived at the destination, and then it would be delayed by the latency on the return trip, as shown in Figure 3.4. By increasing the number of packets that could be outstanding, the sender could still be transmitting packets when the first acknowledgment made its way back from the receiver, as shown in Figure 3.5. That avoided inefficient pauses in the transmission stream.

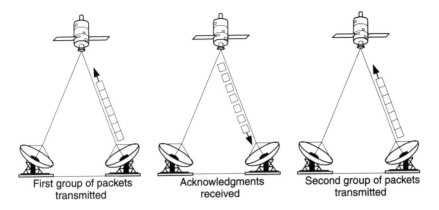

Figure 3.4 Small window size on a long-latency link.

Unfortunately, large transmission windows also mean that if there are problems somewhere in the transmission path, a massive number of packets will be sent into that problem area, adding to the difficulties. A sender that is allowed to transmit, say, 63 packets without receiving an acknowledgment will simply send those packets into the line before learning that the link is broken or hopelessly congested. The sender won't find out about the problem until a few seconds later, when the acknowledgments fail to arrive. The packets will then have to be retransmitted. For long-latency or high-bandwidth links, with large window sizes, megabytes of data may need to be retransmitted when that happens.

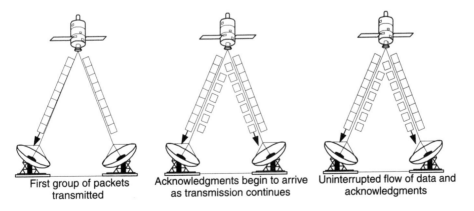

Figure 3.5 Extended window size on a long-latency link.

Two schemes are designed to avoid such massive retransmissions, and they can be used together. The first, selective retransmission, also called selective reject, is an error-recovery scheme that retransmits only the lost packet instead of retransmitting the lost packet and all of the packets that were transmitted after it. This mechanism is available in most window-based protocols as a special feature. It greatly decreases the retransmissions caused by short error bursts, but it requires more complex buffer management in the receiver.

For our discussions, the second scheme is more important. That is the use of the window as a flow control mechanism to avoid buffer overflow at the destination or at intermediate network nodes. The number of frames (or bytes) in the window is adjusted to match the available capacity of the receiver's buffers or the network capacity. Big bursts of data packets that overflow buffers are thereby avoided. If the network congestion increases, or if the recipient has trouble handling the incoming data, then the acknowledgments are delayed or the available window size, which is carried in the acknowledgment message, is decreased. That decreases the traffic flow into the problem buffers. This is a powerful technique, and it has been used in many different protocol families. For example:

- X.25 uses windowing to handle congestion problems at both the link level, to control all of a sender's flows simultaneously, and at the transport level, to control individual end-to-end flows.

- IBM's SNA uses a variation of windowing called pacing to control end-to-end flow and avoid buffer overflow problems.

- TCP uses a complex variant of windowing that is described next, in the "Implicit Control" section.

Implicit Control

Sliding-window protocols can be used to control flow implicitly, without the intervention of the network. The best example of this is the behavior of the Internet's Transmission Control Protocol, TCP.

TCP has a byte-oriented sliding-window protocol. Each byte in the data-stream is counted, and the TCP acknowledgments tell the sender the number of bytes that can still be transmitted without overflowing the receiving buffer at the final destination. Each TCP header contains a field that gives the sequence number of the first data byte in the packet, and each TCP acknowledgment contains a field that gives the sequence number of the next byte that the receiver is prepared to receive. There aren't any packet numbers because packets can be broken into smaller packets inside the network. Packet numbers would therefore be confusing and generally irrelevant; numbering the bytes themselves is easier. When a packet is subdivided, it's a simple matter to calculate the byte sequence numbers for the new packet headers. The acknowledgments are not affected because they acknowledge streams of bytes, not individual packets.

So far, the TCP flow control seems very straightforward. But some additional features add complexity because of the need to provide implicit flow control. The problem is that the Internet has grown to be much larger than originally anticipated. The designers of TCP assumed that the window size would be set to indicate the remaining buffer size in the receiver, to avoid overflowing the receiver's buffer. Congestion in the network itself was to be handled by special Source Quench packets and by the so-called self-clocking behavior of TCP's sliding window protocol. Neither of these mechanisms is sufficient for the modern Internet.

If there were sudden congestion in the network, the Source Quench choke packet was supposed to be used. As described in the next section, "Choke Packet," the congested router would send Source Quench packets back to the source to tell it to stop transmitting. Unfortunately, this technique didn't work on large networks, and it has been abandoned.

The other congestion control method, self-clocking behavior, is a side-effect of the normal operation of TCP's sliding-window protocol. The rate at which acknowledgments are received is a rough indication of the bandwidth of the most congested link in the packet's path. This is illustrated in Figures 3.6 and 3.7.

Figure 3.6 shows a simplified TCP acknowledgment behavior on an uncongested link. In this simple example, short acknowledgments are generated by the destination each time an incoming data packet is correctly received. The interarrival times of the acknowledgment packets are therefore equal to the interarrival times of the data packets.

When there is congestion on the path, the packets may start out on a high-speed, uncongested link from the sender, but then they hit a congested link and the effective data rate decreases. It now takes much longer to transmit each packet, and the buffers begin to fill inside the router that connects to the slow link. The packet interarrival time on the slow link

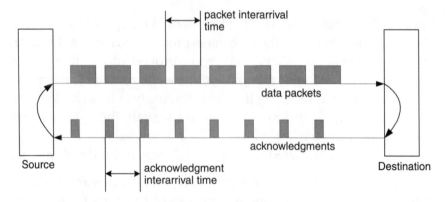

Figure 3.6 TCP acknowledgment flow on uncongested link.

is much greater than it was on the high-speed entry link. The exit link is high-speed, but that doesn't decrease the new, longer packet interarrival time. Instead, there are now long spaces between packets. The receiver still sends one acknowledgment per arriving data packet, so the new, longer spacing between arriving data packets is repeated in the acknowledgments. The result is that the sender eventually is throttled back to send packets only as fast as the slowest link can handle them because it can send a new packet only when an acknowledgment arrives for a previous packet. Figure 3.7 shows the result after the source has been throttled back by the decrease in the rate of arriving acknowledgments. Notice that the data packets on the slow link are longer because a slower

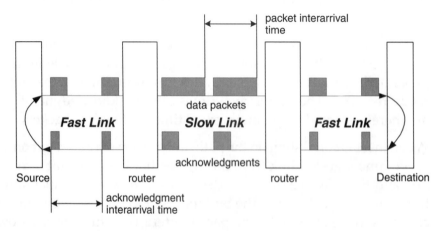

Figure 3.7 TCP acknowledgment flow on slow link.

link takes longer to transmit the bits than a faster link. The acknowledgment spacing is set by the packet interarrival time on the slowest link.

Unfortunately, self-clocking behavior, as shown in Figure 3.7, isn't sufficient on the modern Internet. The acknowledgments can be delayed for many reasons, only some of which are due to congestion on the sender's outbound link, and the feedback loop is too slow. At high data rates, massive amounts of data can be stuffed into the data path before the self-clocking scheme manages to throttle the transmissions. The original TCP designs would try to push the entire window's worth of data into the link as quickly as possible. If there was congestion, the buffers in the routers overflowed and retransmissions were therefore needed—which made the situation worse.

Because of these problems, many changes have been made to TCP implementations to help handle Internet congestion. None of these changes alters the TCP protocol standard; instead, they all take advantage of flexibility within the original standard. The result is a very sophisticated and complex method for inferring the capacity of a link without needing any signals from the routers. The protocol uses packet loss as one of the primary indicators that it is exceeding the link's capacity, and it automatically adjusts its transmission rate.

With the new TCP designs, packet transmission starts gradually on a new connection; this is called *slow start*. The sender probes the new connection to see how congested or slow it is. Only one or two packets are sent into the new connection, and each time an acknowledgment arrives from the receiver, the number of packets that the sender is willing to send before receiving an acknowledgment increases. For example, let's assume that the transmission window would allow 30,000 bytes and that 1500-byte packets are being used. An old-style TCP would try to send 20 packets immediately, the moment the connection opened. If there is congestion, then most of those packets would overflow router buffers and be lost, necessitating a retransmission. With slow start, TCP will send, say, only two 1500-byte packets initially. When the two acknowledgments arrive from the receiver, then it will send four more packets. (The maximum number transmitted has increased by one for each acknowledgment received.) When the four acknowledgments arrive, then it will try sending eight packets, and so forth. Eventually the number of packets that can be transmitted in a burst may increase to 20, the size needed to use the entire transmit window. The self-clocking behavior of TCP will also have the chance to act, spacing out the transmission of packets. This is a lot more gradual than simply stuffing all 20 packets into the link at the very start of the connection.

But what happens if there is congestion? TCP finds out by losing a packet—there's a buffer overflow somewhere. (TCP is using the loss of real user data to do its implicit congestion control!) When TCP determines, through some complex software logic, that a packet has been lost, it drastically cuts back the number of packets that can be transmitted in a burst. The TCP software now suspects that there's congestion, and sending a large block of packets into a congested network always causes problems. Because of that probable congestion, the TCP software is also much less aggressive about increasing the number of packets per burst than it was in slow start. When doing slow start, there was a good chance that there wasn't congestion, and TCP wants to increase the number of packets per burst as quickly as possible. But when TCP is reasonably sure that there's trouble in the network, it wants to increase much more cautiously. (For details of how this works, see [RFC 2001] and any of the major TCP/IP textbooks [Stevens, Stallings] for a description of slow start, dynamic window sizing on congestion, fast retransmit, fast recovery, and the other features of RFC 1122 and of the recent Berkeley TCP software named TCP Tahoe and TCP Reno; I've simplified greatly here.)

The end result of all this complexity is that TCP can infer the network bandwidth and adjust its transmission rate to match. The process isn't perfect, however. There's always the potential waste of network capacity as TCP goes through slow start or the various congestion recovery and avoidance algorithms, and real data packets must be retransmitted, adding to congestion and delay, whenever TCP transmits too quickly for the available bandwidth. If the bandwidth varies, TCP will always be either too conservative (wasting bandwidth as it slowly discovers the new, greater available bandwidth) or too aggressive (losing packets, which then must be retransmitted, as it transmits too frequently for the new, smaller bandwidth). TCP works best in channels where the bandwidth doesn't vary frequently and where packet loss is low; that allows the TCP packet rate to stabilize where it's controlled by the window size and TCP's self-clocking behavior.

As a final example of some of the problems inherent in implicit bandwidth control, we'll use the difficulty that TCP flows may have coexisting in a single transmission channel as they battle each other for bandwidth. In effect, they create varying bandwidth channels for each other, precisely the situation that TCP doesn't like. Some TCP implementations are more aggressive than others in increasing their packet transmission rate, and these will force the other TCP implementations that share the channel to give up their use of channel capacity as they lose packets and recover too slowly to match the aggressive implementation. Worse, if there are major buffer overflow problems in the routers, all of the flows will lose packets, and all of the flows will therefore cut their transmission rates and then rebuild those rates simultaneously. This results in waves of packets that periodically wash over the tops of the router buffers. It's a depressing scene for traffic engineers: First, massive amounts of traffic appear, causing widespread packet loss. Packet transmission rates are then forced to drop to the floor when TCP discovers those lost packets. The retransmitted packets trickle out of the senders gradually, with a lot of bandwidth potentially unused, as the TCP software in all the senders slowly increases the rate at which it's willing to transmit packets. These transmission rates then grow at approximately the same rate in all senders. Eventually the packet transmission rate is back to where it was before the buffer overflows, then it increases one more step—and then the buffer overflows again! There's widespread packet loss in all of the flows, then packet transmission rates drop to the floor, then—well, here we go again. This is called the *global synchronization problem*, and we'll see in Chapters 6, "Basic QoS Technologies," and Chapter 7, "Solution Building Blocks," how it can be handled by techniques such as Random Early Detection (RED).

Choke Packet

A very coarse method of congestion control is the use of a *choke packet*. Any node or receiver that's being overwhelmed by incoming traffic simply sends a choke packet to the sources of the traffic, forcing that traffic source to shut down immediately and remain shut until notified that it can restart. The original choke packet was simply the XOFF and XON characters used in early Teletype transmissions. A receiver with a full buffer transmitted the single character XOFF, which was usually represented as the combination of the Control and S keys on a keyboard. The transmitter stopped immediately and didn't restart until it received the XON character, which was usually represented by the combination of the Control and Q keys on a keyboard. Modern protocols such as the IEEE 802.3x protocol [IEEE 802.3x], used for congestion control on high-speed Ethernet LANs, are minor variations of this old XON/XOFF technique.

The Internet's basic protocol suite includes a special choke packet, the Source Quench, which was intended for use by overwhelmed routers, as mentioned in the preceding section.

Unfortunately, the choke packet is usually much too coarse a control mechanism. For example, the current Internet standard RFC 1812 recommends against the use of Source Quench because it was found to be an ineffective and unfair mechanism that nonetheless consumes network bandwidth while trying to do its job. Source Quench usually arrives too late at the source, after the receiver's or router's buffers have already overflowed, and it penalizes well-implemented senders while allowing others to continue transmitting.

Explicit Congestion Signaling

Many protocols include a method for signaling the sender explicitly when congestion occurs. The sender is then expected to alter his or her transmission rate. This is less abrupt than a choke packet, which simply demands that all transmission stop immediately, and it's much more efficient than implicit signaling, which reacts more slowly and wastes bandwidth.

An early example of explicit congestion signaling is in IBM's SNA, which included congestion indicators in its packet headers. If a packet traveled through a congested network node, that node could set the Change Window Indicator (CWI) flag in the packet's header. The recipient would notice that the CWI was set and therefore set a different flag, the Change Window Reply Indicator (CWRI), in the acknowledgment packet sent back to the flow's source. That source, seeing the CWRI, would know that congestion was occurring and would therefore decrease its window size. After the CWRI flags stop appearing, the source would start increasing its window size slowly.

More recently, Frame Relay is an example of a protocol that uses explicit congestion signaling. The Forward Explicit Congestion Notification (FECN) is used to inform the receiver that congestion is occurring, while the Backward Explicit Congestion Notification (BECN) is used to inform the sender. Most Frame Relay users ignore these signals, but some routers can be configured to adjust their internal queuing priorities and data rates when they receive them.

Another example of explicit congestion signaling appears in ATM. There are a whole set of flags and control options, but a simple example will show the general idea. ATM switches can use a special flag, the Explicit Forward Congestion Indicator (EFCI) in the ATM cell header, to inform the receiver that congestion is occurring. Depending on the situation and the type of ATM service category, the ATM system can then take action to decrease the transmission rate by signaling the transmitter. This is quite similar to the SNA schemes.

Finally, higher-level protocols used in voice and video transmissions, such as the Real Time Control Protocol (RTCP) used with the Real Time Protocol (RTP), include signaling features that can be used by the source to judge the amount of congestion and lost packets in the data path and to adjust the sending speed appropriately.

Explicit Rate Signaling

A few protocols, such as ATM's Available Bit Rate (ABR), include a very sophisticated mechanism for explicitly telling senders the rate at which they can transmit: Explicit Rate Signaling. This is different from telling them the available window, and it's different from simply allowing them to discover the maximum rate by receiving explicit congestion notifications or by losing transmitted data in an implicit signaling scheme. Protocols with explicit rate signaling avoid the inefficiencies created when the senders have to discover their available bandwidth through trial and error. Any ATM switch in the ABR route between sender and receiver can adjust the rate at any time by sending a special ATM ABR cell, the Resource Management (RM) cell. These RM cells can carry the EFCI and other explicit connection signaling flags (the Congestion Indicator, CI, and the No Increase, NI, flags), in which case ABR is using the simpler Explicit Congestion Signaling method. Alternatively, in second-generation ATM switches, the RM cells can carry those flags along with a set of explicit rate parameters such as the Explicit Cell Rate (ECR). The ECR sets the maximum transmission rate explicitly. Each ATM switch in the flow path has the right to decrease, but not increase, the ECR in flows that go through it. The switches use complex algorithms to ensure that they can handle the traffic at the ECRs that they've accepted in the flows that pass through them.

QoS Considerations

When evaluating protocols for use by applications, it's important to look for the characteristics that will have an impact on the QoS decisions.

Those characteristics are:

- A method, if any, for indicating that source should cut its transmission rate
- A method, if any, for responding to and working with explicit congestion signaling from the destination
- A method, if any, for responding to explicit congestion signaling from the network
- The ability to adjust to varying bandwidth and congestion within the network without undue packet losses; and the method that it uses to do this (does it cut transmission rate in response to packet loss?)

The first characteristic concerns backpressure from the network, the term used to refer to the ability of the network to get the sender to slow down the data transmission rate. This feature exists in almost all older protocols. For example, X.25 could cut either the layer 2 transmission window or the layer 3 transmission window, or both, to pressure the sender to decrease the transmission rate. At the physical layer, modems still use hardware (RTS/CTS) and software (XON/XOFF) signaling to exert backpressure. Some modern protocols, however, do not have this ability. A prime example is UDP, often used to carry voice and video. There's no way to backpressure the sender using just UDP; a higher-level protocol with a flow control signaling feature is needed. In many cases, the feature is absent or is ignored; the network must then simply drop packets if they're transmitted at too rapid a rate. Guarding against such out-of-profile transmissions (i.e., transmission rates that exceed the agreed-upon QoS characteristics profile for required bandwidth) is an important function of the entry nodes into, for example, Frame Relay and ATM networks. If those networks detect out-of-profile traffic, they mark that traffic with a Discard Eligible flag (Frame Relay) or a Cell Loss Priority flag (ATM) to have it discarded first, before in-profile traffic, if congestion is encountered.

The destination user may also want to signal that he can't accept traffic at the rate that it's being delivered from the network. If so, it's important to know if the protocol can handle the situation. Most protocols that provide this ability do it through manipulation of the window size; some have an explicit protocol signal, such as the Receive Not Ready (RNR) in HDLC or the Wait/Acknowledge (WACK) in the old IBM Binary Synchronous Communications protocols. Of course, the old physical-layer use of the

RTS/CTS electrical interface signals or the equally old use of XON/XOFF may appear in some situations. Modern high-speed Ethernet devices may use a variant of XON/XOFF, the 802.3x flow control signals, which can temporarily stop input to an Ethernet port.

The next item concerns the ability of the protocol software to work with explicit congestion signaling from the network. This usually takes the form of explicit congestion signaling, such as Frame Relay's BECN, or explicit rate signaling, such as ATM's Explicit Cell Rate parameter in Resource Management cells. The protocol software may need to be able to loop the congestion signal; that is, it may need to be able to receive a forward signal and convert it into a backward signal, so that the source of the traffic can be notified of the congestion. At this time, very few protocol software stacks can make use of any explicit signaling that they receive from the network.

The last item requires some thinking about the protocol and the network environment; it summarizes the ability of the protocol to perform implicit congestion control. This item is important because the network often can control bandwidth only indirectly. As mentioned previously, few protocol software stacks respond to explicit congestion signaling. Therefore, the network may try to restrict a flow's use of bandwidth through indirect means such as by deleting a data packet in the hope that the transmitter will detect the deletion and cut back its transmission rate. (This is a good assumption in the case of modern TCP software stacks; a poor assumption in the case of UDP.) Most older protocols were designed for dedicated links. They assume that any error loss is due to noise, and they immediately retransmit. Therefore, packet losses may cause an increase, not a decrease, in the data transmission rate from the source! Many other methods can be used to handle implicit congestion control; it is useful to read Chapter 6, "Basic QoS Technologies," and Chapter 7, "Solution Building Blocks," to learn about the techniques. In some cases, the network may even interfere directly with the window, if it's present, manipulating it and respacing the acknowledgments to smooth the traffic flow.

Bandwidth

This section is about the needs of the protocol for certain amounts of bandwidth and for certain characteristics of that available bandwidth. For example, many protocols, such as those designed for LANs, assume that bandwidth is almost free and usually uncongested; as a result, they tend to use broadcasts and multicasts liberally. That causes problems on networks where bandwidth is more expensive and constricted than on small, underutilized LANs. The bandwidth characteristics can be divided into three topics: the ability of the protocol to use high-speed or long-latency links, the protocol's assumptions about available broadcast or multicast facilities, and the protocol's requirements governing packet size and fragmentation.

High-Speed and Long-Latency Links

Most protocols, especially older protocols, were not designed to handle today's high-speed links. Even TCP, thought of as a modern protocol, can have problems at speeds greater than 100 mbps unless the Protect Against Wrapped Sequence numbers (PAWS) option of RFC 1323 is used, because TCP byte sequence numbers, used in acknowledgments, cannot normally be reused until two minutes have elapsed. (See [RFC 1323] for more information.)

The problem is even more severe with long-latency links, such as satellite links. In the original version of TCP, the data rate through a geosynchronous satellite is restricted to approximately 1 mbps because TCP will run out of byte sequence numbers. The original TCP maximum window size is 64 KB, and a 1 mbp/s link with a time delay of more than 500 milliseconds round trip can easily absorb more than 64 KB before the first acknowledgment makes its way back to the sender. (The TCP Window Scale option in RFC 1323 can handle this problem.) A very similar example is the HDLC protocol. In its standard form, HDLC has a maximum window size of seven. If each frame is 1500 bytes, seven frames are only 84,000 bits. At link speeds higher than 168,000 bps and a round-trip delay of more than 500 milliseconds, the entire 84,000 bits will be transmitted before the first acknowledgment is received by the sender, forcing a pause in transmission. HDLC therefore has an option to increase the number of possible outstanding frames to more than 60.

In addition to problems with the sequence numbers used for flow control and for error detection, there are problems with the retransmission of erroneous packets. At high data rates, megabytes of data can be transmitted before notification of an erroneous or missing packet makes its way back to the sender. Most window-based protocols must retransmit not only the erroneous or missing packet; they must retransmit all subsequent packets as well. This greatly simplifies buffer management at the receiver because it can simply discard all packets received after a missing packet. The packets will be retransmitted in sequence after the missing packet is itself retransmitted; there's therefore no need to hold a space for a retransmitted packet in the middle of a buffer filled with successfully received packets. Unfortunately, the simplification of the receiver's buffer management comes with a cost: At high transmission rates, large amounts of data may need to be retransmitted because just one packet was lost.

To solve the retransmission problem, selective acknowledgments are used. This has been an optional feature of protocols for a long time. Selective acknowledgments, also called selective rejects, allow the protocol to retransmit only the erroneous or missing packet; subsequent packets are not retransmitted if they arrived without errors. The receiver's packet reassembly and buffer management processes are much more complex, but a lot of bandwidth is saved when an error occurs. For example, the HDLC protocol has an optional Selective Reject to ask for the retransmission of a single packet without forcing the retransmission of all subsequent packets. Modern protocols also contain selective acknowledgment features, and TCP has been extended to include a selective acknowledgment (SACK) [RFC 2018].

Gateways can be used to help a protocol without built-in provisions for high-speed or long-latency links cross a link or a multiservice network with those characteristics. The gateway, shown in Figure 3.8, doesn't encapsulate the protocol. (Encapsulation is the process of encasing one protocol inside another one for transmission across a foreign network.) Instead, it terminates the protocol at both ends, using a more suitable protocol for the hop across the high-speed or long-latency link. In the example, HDLC with a window size of seven and no Selective Reject command is used on the terminating links, but the special satellite-mode HDLC, with Selective Reject and a window size of 63, is used on the

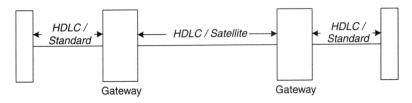

Figure 3.8 Protocol gateways.

satellite link. When a packet arrives at the gateway, it's acknowledged as if it had arrived at its final destination. It's then buffered, and the satellite-mode HDLC is used to carry it to the other gateway. That other gateway buffers it, then acts as if it were a user making a normal HDLC connection to the final destination.

This method of using protocol gateways is a common one for handling situations involving inefficient use of bandwidth. It's also used when protocols have timeout problems because of latency, as will be explained later. Neither of those situations can be helped by simple encapsulation.

Broadcast and Multicast

Most protocols originally designed for LANs assume that there's almost unlimited bandwidth and a built-in, hardware-based method for broadcast and multicasts. The protocols therefore use techniques that would never normally be used on wide area networks. Now that some of those protocols are migrating to WANs and to multiservice networks, problems occur.

Our first place to look for those problems is in the use of broadcasting as a substitute for an address-resolution directory service. All multiuser protocols need some method for associating user names (such as BuildingA .Printer5) with physical addresses (such as 23.68.92.59.23.10). In protocols designed for use with WANs, where broadcasts are expensive and difficult, there is a central directory list that is regularly copied to all users (such as the Hosts File on early TCP/IP systems), or there is an easily-found directory service at a standard location (such as the Domain Name System, DNS, in modern TCP/IP systems).

On LAN-based systems, however, the easiest way of handling address resolution is with broadcasts. One type of address resolution through broadcast is the broadcast query. A user looking for BuildingA.Printer5 simply transmits a query out to everyone on the LAN, and BuildingA.Printer5 then answers it, returning its physical address. All the other devices receive the query, read it, and then ignore it. An example of this technique is the IP protocol's Address Resolution Protocol (ARP) as used on Ethernet LANs. A user looking for, say, IP address 10.23.50.3 simply broadcasts the ARP query into the entire Ethernet, and the station with that IP address issues a reply giving its physical Ethernet address, such as 23.68.92.59.23.10. Another example is the original design for IBM's Token

Ring with Source-Route Bridging. It broadcasts the needed physical address to the entire network every time it's needed; there is no way of storing the information.

A different type of address resolution through broadcast is the periodic broadcast of name-address pairings, such as used by early versions of Novell NetWare. NetWare's Service Advertising Protocol (SAP) periodically broadcasts the network addresses of all printers and other servers to the entire network.

There are many variations of these name-handling broadcasts; the key is to look for them when protocols originally designed for broadcast-based media are moved to a multiservice network. If placed, unchanged, on a WAN with restricted or costly bandwidth, these constant directory broadcasts will flood the system.

Broadcasts are also used to ensure uniqueness. For example, the early protocols supporting NetBIOS ensured the uniqueness of names on the LAN by broadcasting new user names to find conflicts. Some protocol or applications systems use broadcasts as part of a licensing enforcement mechanism. They may broadcast their license serial numbers at frequent intervals to discover when the same single-user license is being used at many different locations. Any application or protocol that tries to guarantee the uniqueness of something, and that doesn't have a central registry database, may be using broadcasts or multicasts.

Protocols that use broadcasts and multicasts for naming or uniqueness can be adapted to WANs through the use of special directory servers; that's usually better than trying to provide the QoS needed to handle all the traffic they can generate. These servers maintain global directories and respond to the broadcast or multicast queries as if they were the requested user. Broadcasts and multicasts are filtered out of the WAN links at the router, and the directory servers coordinate with each other using point-to-point connections over a protocol such as TCP, as shown in Figure 3.9.

This method of using distributed, synchronized directory servers to handle broadcast-oriented protocols over a WAN is used extensively with IBM protocols. One example is the adaptation of NetBIOS-type protocols to WANs; another is the DLSw (Data Link Switching) method for handling SNA over a TCP/IP network, which uses distributed directory servers to associate SNA addresses with TCP/IP addresses.

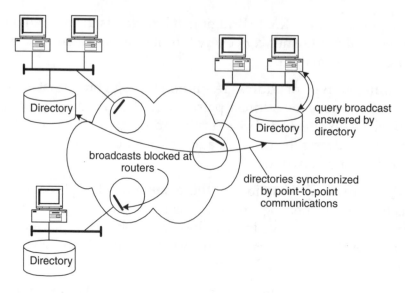

Figure 3.9 Using directories to remove broadcasts from a WAN.

Broadcasts and multicasts are also used for applications and protocols that must maintain consistent tables system-wide. Periodic broadcasts can be used to refresh all devices with the common information. This can be used by applications and also by the protocol itself. An example of the latter is the IEEE Spanning Tree protocol that is used to manage LAN bridges; it coordinates bridge configurations through the use of multicasts and a special packet.

Finally, of course, there are the pure broadcasting and multicasting applications, such as streaming audio and video. As discussed in Chapter 4, "Network QoS Design Specifications," these place far less load on media designed for these protocols than on media that are basically designed for point-to-point connections.

Low Cost, Constant Connectivity

This category includes the so-called watchdog or heartbeat protocols that retransmit at frequent intervals to check application health, the update and synchronization protocols that regularly coordinate geographically distributed tables, and the polling protocols that repeatedly connect to a remote device to check on its status. Their common thread is that they all assume that there's no problem with opening a connection to do a short data transfer at frequent, evenly spaced intervals. On LANs, that's true; on

WANs, there may be a price to be paid if long distances, on-demand links, or large numbers of devices are involved.

Many protocols need to detect a station that's gone offline without notifying others, and the use of intermittent watchdog or heartbeat packets is an obvious solution. The difficulty arises when the link to the station crosses a WAN. For example, Novell NetWare has an NCP Watchdog packet that it uses to detect disconnected stations and remove them from server tables. If the NetWare system contains a dial-on-demand WAN link, that link will be reconnected, by default, every five minutes simply to send the watchdog packet.

Synchronization protocols use frequent, regular multicasts to update tables; they may retransmit the entire table every few minutes, even if there are no changes, because of an assumption that the bandwidth is free and is always available.

Polling protocols connect to remote devices on a regular cycle to check for updates and changes, instead of registering their identity with those devices and waiting for them to send information when there's a change. Network management systems use these protocols to gather network device status data through the use of the Simple Network Management Protocol (SNMP), and Novell NetWare uses polling to allow printers to check the status of the print queue holding work for them on a remote system. Many legacy systems use polling to check remote terminals for incoming data; common examples are IBM systems.

If a protocol was designed for LANs or for multidrop WAN systems, it probably uses some of the techniques in this section. Fortunately, most of these systems have been modified so that they can use techniques that are friendlier to multiservice WANs, or there are so-called spoofing devices that remove the problem from the network.

A spoofing device emulates a watchdog, heartbeat, or polling protocol, as shown in Figure 3.10, to remove its traffic from the network. It absorbs polls or heartbeats on one side of the WAN link—it doesn't forward them over the WAN—and it generates polls or heartbeats on the other side of the link. It transmits data over the WAN link only if something changes. Unproductive polls or heartbeats are not transmitted.

Spoofing devices are commonly used to handle polling, and they communicate with each other using TCP/IP, X.25, or other standard protocols. They are available from specialty equipment manufacturers, such

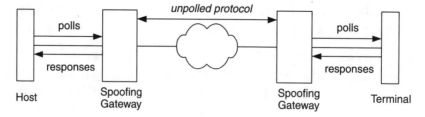

Figure 3.10 Spoofing.

as Black Box, which also supply a wide variety of gateways and other types of protocol and interface converters.

Packet Size, Fragmentation, and Multihop Behavior

All protocols have a maximum packet size, but those maximum sizes vary widely. In addition, many protocols don't allow packets to be sub-divided—fragmented—by the network before delivery. This is a problem if the protocol assumes that it can transmit, say, 8000-byte packets in their entirety without problems over a multiservice network. Encapsulation won't solve the problem of a packet that's too large for the network, as encapsulation only makes it larger. The packet may need to be fragmented at the entrance to the network and reassembled at the other end by special gateway devices, as shown in Figure 3.8.

The Internet protocols were designed to be fragmented by the network, as were some earlier legacy protocols, such as X.25. Protocols designed for multidrop lines or for special equipment in the days before the widespread use of IP were usually not designed for fragmentation.

In addition to packet length problems, some protocols designed for legacy networks expect small networks that have only a few hops. Unless these packets are encapsulated into another protocol, they'll probably have to handle more hops than they can deal with. For example, IBM's Token Ring protocol with Source-Route Bridging has a seven-hop maximum.

Resilience

The Internet protocols were designed to handle a wide range of networks and underlying media; they're able to work over a huge range of link latencies and error rates. Many legacy protocols assume low error rates and low latency on dedicated links with few or no intermediate routing hops.

The first problem with resilience is sensitivity to the time delays on modern multiservice networks. In some cases, the protocol timeout latencies cannot be increased; they're built into the protocol design itself. IBM's proprietary protocols had timeout problems when routed over IP-based networks until routers were reconfigured to give them priority over other traffic [Nolle]. The IBM protocol's packets would be delayed for a couple of seconds in a router's queues, and the IBM protocol, assuming that it was on a dedicated line, would disconnect the session because of the inferred line failure. It didn't understand that there was a buffer between one end of the line and the other.

Other resilience problems may appear with a few protocols. Check for protocols that are designed for low-error networks, especially if the multiservice network will need to traverse routes with high error rates, such as a route over cellular radio. Some protocols rely solely on timeouts to detect missing or erroneous packets, and they may stall for a couple of seconds each time a packet is damaged. They'll need to be encapsulated in some other protocol, possibly one with a forward-error-correcting code that can fix erroneous packets without waiting for a retransmission. They may need a gateway to convert them into a different, more resilient protocol for the trip across a link with a high error rate.

Finally, a few protocols may be designed for time-sensitive applications, such as real-time video, and may assume very low jitter in the network. Some of these were designed for use only on leased lines that had very stable transmission rates and no intermediate routers. (Commercial leased lines have extremely stable clock rates that can be used by terminals to synchronize attached equipment.) The devices attached by these protocols will be in severe trouble if they're always trying to compensate for the jitter that's characteristic of multiservice, multihop networks.

Infrastructure Considerations and Constraints

The technical considerations and constraints are the technical factors that must be considered when replacing or installing networking equipment.

Although they're not, strictly speaking, QoS considerations, the constraints imposed by existing network infrastructures and the organizational considerations imposed by the enterprise's principles and culture are important factors in QoS system design. There's no point in building a great QoS network on paper, just to find that there isn't any way to rewire buildings with that new fiber backbone, or that the corporation as a whole doesn't believe in spending to head off future problems that may not actually appear.

This section gives a brief summary of some of the issues involved with the technical considerations and constraints, as a way of helping network designers to avoid being surprised when they try to implement their plans. (The organizational considerations were discussed in Chapter 2, "Enterprise-Wide and User Requirements.") These issues include:

- The adaptability of existing network hardware and software to QoS
- The practicality of installing new data links inside and outside buildings
- The availability of necessary communications facilities from public carriers
- The cost-effectiveness, or practicality, of adapting legacy protocols and applications to new multiservice networks

Knowing the capabilities of the network's existing equipment is important when choosing QoS designs, as some existing equipment may already have QoS capabilities or be easily upgraded through simple software or hardware changes, while other equipment may need to be abandoned. It may also be found that the ideal QoS technology for a particular situation can't be installed because the needed connectivity or equipment is simply not available at the site. It may be that the expense of adapting existing applications and protocols to run on a new multiservice network is prohibitive. It's crucial to investigate those possibilities before making final plans.

In the great majority of cases, a new Quality of Service design must be added to an existing network. Unless the designer is allowed to throw everything out and start fresh, the first set of design constraints is always based on the capabilities of the existing network hardware and software. Most current routers are capable of some QoS function if they're given a software upgrade, and some other current network devices (LAN hubs and network interface cards, for example) are also able to handle some form of QoS. It goes without saying that the capabilities of existing equipment will greatly influence the choice of QoS solutions, and an inventory of existing equipment and its QoS capabilities is therefore needed before network design is started.

The possible need for new connectivity is also important. In some cases, additional connectivity cannot be added to a building because existing data communications links cannot be altered or enhanced. Many buildings cannot accommodate any more wiring, often because they were built before large-scale wiring ducts were a part of building structures. Wire has been stuffed into pipes, elevator shafts, and other places until obvious locations are filled, and it will now be extraordinarily expensive to add, or even to replace, the existing wire. Pulling fiber to replace wire introduces its own set of problems, as special fiber may be needed—at considerable expense—to snake through tight clearances and to withstand pulling forces and sharp bends. If, as often happens, there isn't any space left in existing ductwork, then fire codes may require that new ductwork be installed for any new wiring. Unfortunately, in some cases labor costs are very high because of local situations, and those labor costs make installation of any additional ductwork extremely expensive or even unthinkable. The plan to upgrade internode links may therefore need to be abandoned.

It may also be overly expensive or impossible to create new data links outside of the building. The telephone company may not have dark-fiber or unused cable facilities available, and it may be difficult or impossible to get the right-of-way necessary to connect buildings through underground cabling. Microwave or other types of links may be difficult to install because of licensing restrictions or simple physical obstacles. Satellite transmission using VSAT requires a view of the proper position in the sky, and VSAT introduces severe latency problems, especially if two VSAT users must communicate with each other. Such communication requires two complete hops (end stations in a VSAT network usually communicate only with the central base station, not directly with each other), for a total round-trip latency of over one second.

It's possible that planning to use a public carrier to avoid the problems of finding a way to install new data links may not be a solution. It's important to verify that the local communications companies are able to supply the service that you need where you need it in a timely manner. They may not have the required infrastructure, and the available staff may not be trained properly. In some parts of the world, it's easier to get a high-quality line to the United States than it is to get one from one town to another town 10 miles away.

Finally, it may be found after analysis that the legacy applications and protocols to be adapted to the new multiservice network are so unsuited to a modern networking environment that the cost of adapting them is prohibitive. Simply leaving them alone would be a better choice in that case! Again, it's best to discover that before spending time and effort on designing a network that will never be implemented.

Summary

Picking up where we left off in Chapter 2, "Enterprise-Wide and User Requirements," we now look at some QoS-sensitive applications in depth. These applications, which are speech and video compression applications and client/server applications, are those that usually drive the need for QoS facilities. They have a number of important technical characteristics that must be understood by the network architect who's trying to design a network that will support them.

Both speech and video technologies are very sensitive to jitter and to latency if they're to be used for real-time applications. Unfortunately, most compression technologies are, themselves, big consumers of latency. If there are only 150 milliseconds available to get speech from one person to another, and if the speech compression device itself uses 100 milliseconds, then there's not much slack left for the network, the modem delays, the dejitter processing, and more. As we show in the chapter, many of the optimistic dreams of voice over packet networks fall far short of reality—at least, with the technologies available today. We build a sample latency budget, and we look at the actual time delays involved in all of the upper-level technologies to get an idea of what the practicalities are. We can then see the possible trade-offs among different types of audio, speech, and video encoders—the low (1 millisecond) latency of G.711, used in the telephone system, contrasted with the high (100 milliseconds) latency of G.723.1, which is usually used with videoconferencing applications that have even worse video compression delays. We also look at the ITU and MPEG standards for video compression (ITU usually for videoconferencing, MPEG usually for streaming video). We finish with a quick reminder that in client/server applications it's important to keep track of the multiplier effect that occurs when there are a large number of back-and-forth interactions between client and server for each user-perceived transaction.

The chapter then proceeds to look in some detail at the protocols that underlie the applications. Many of these have their own QoS requirements if they're to operate efficiently and avoid interfering with other protocols or with the network itself. We look at the behavior of TCP and other protocols, and we develop the basic categories of problems that protocols can get into in multiservice networks—and the ways to handle those problems. We look at flow and congestion control, congestion signaling, rate control, bandwidth needs, latency considerations, broadcast effects on the network and the protocols, and other protocol details such as polling.

We then finish with a quick look at the constraints imposed by existing network infrastructures, to avoid building plans for QoS systems that will later prove too costly or impractical to implement.

Application Technology Issues

Application:

Contacts:

Audio/Speech Encoding and Compression:

These issues assume real-time audio or speech. Streaming audio or speech is a file transfer, which can be sent with an error-correcting protocol (e.g., TCP) and is not sensitive to latency.

1. Size of data packet and headers (there may be multiple speech frames within a packet)

2. Bandwidth requirements

3. Required error rate and error characteristics (random BER; burst BER with maximum length of burst)

4. Minimum latency through entire encode/compress/decompress/decode process (the Speech Processing portion of the latency budget) with zero dejitter buffer

5. Allowable error rate, lost frame rate *after* dejitter buffer (implies size of dejitter buffer when network jitter is known)

6. Native transport; that is, the transport for which the algorithm was designed (leased line or ATM CBR, ISDN, frame relay, packet, packet over dial-up link)

Video Encoding and Compression:

These questions assume real-time video. Streaming video is a file transfer, which can be sent with an error-correcting protocol (e.g., TCP). Streaming video can be encoded and compressed offline in a multipass, optimized process; it is not affected by latency or jitter.

1. Bandwidth characteristics: CBR or VBR (minimum/average/maximum burst b/s and maximum length of burst); possible use of layered encoding for enhanced video. Possible need for transcoders or multiple independent streams.

2. Bandwidth requirements, including possibility of base and enhanced video streams with different bandwidths.

3. Required error rate and error characteristics (random BER; burst BER with maximum length of burst).

4. Minimum latency through entire encode/compress/decompress/decode applications process with zero dejitter buffer (i.e., the latency budget excluding the network and the dejitter buffer).

5. Allowable error rate, lost frame rate *after* dejitter buffer (implies size of dejitter buffer when network jitter is known).

6. Availability of a native interface for ATM AAL-1 or AAL-5.

7. Availability of a native interface for RTP/RTCP. How does software respond to signals from RTCP that latency or error rate is deteriorating to some users?

8. Other methods for having the network signal the encoding/compression software to decrease bandwidth needs?

Application Messaging and Client/Server Interactions:

1. Preferred maximum latency between client and server

2. Methods that network can use to identify messages for preferential treatment, if necessary

Protocol Issues

Protocol:

Relevant Applications:

Contacts:

Flow and Congestion Control:
1. Method, if any, for indicating that source should cut its transmission rate
2. Method, if any, for responding to and working with explicit congestion signaling from the destination
3. Method, if any, for responding to explicit congestion signaling from the network
4. Ability to adjust to varying bandwidth and congestion within the network without undue packet losses; method that it uses to do this (Does it cut transmission rate in response to packet loss?)

Bandwidth:
1. Efficient use of high-speed or long-latency links (windowing; selective acknowledgment)
2. Broadcasts or multicasts
3. Assumption of low-cost, constant connectivity
4. Maximum packet size
5. Ability to handle packets that were fragmented by network
6. Maximum network hop count

Resilience:
1. Sensitivity to protocol timeouts, adjustability of timeout timers to handle long-latency networks
2. Sensitivity to particular error rates and patterns
3. Zero jitter requirements

Infrastructure Considerations and Constraints

Technical Considerations and Constraints:

1. Adaptability of existing network hardware and software to QoS
2. Practicality of installing new data links inside and outside buildings
3. Availability of necessary communications facilities from public carriers
4. Cost-effectiveness, or practicality, or adapting legacy protocols and applications to new multiservice network

CHAPTER 4

Network QoS Design Specifications

O nce it has been decided to provide QoS services, those services must be specified using parameters that are meaningful to network designers and to network equipment and service suppliers. They form the base for any discussion or consideration of alternative QoS technologies. Without them, it's virtually impossible to write a reasonable set of requirements or an RFP. Therefore, the higher-level requirements that were developed in Chapter 2, "Enterprise-Wide and User Requirements," and Chapter 3, "Applications and Infrastructure Issues," must eventually be converted into these network-level QoS parameters for use in the network design specifications.

This chapter introduces those network-level QoS parameters. Not all of these parameters will be used in a particular design, but they should all be considered. There is a separate subsection for each, grouped so that closely associated parameters are adjacent. Each parameter discussion starts with a definition and description, including the basic causes of the behavior regulated by the parameter. Then a discussion of what the parameter means in terms of its effect on applications and on the design of the network follows. Finally, some examples clarify the meaning of the parameter and discuss its design implications.

The parameters are as follows:

- Geography
- Traffic flow and multicast pattern

- Protocols
- Bandwidth usage pattern
- Bandwidth regulation
- Latency and jitter
- Error characteristics
- Availability
- QoS control and guarantees

The parameters are listed in specification format at the end of the chapter in the summary list entitled "Network QoS Specifications for Applications," which should be useful in documenting the Network QoS specifications for each application. That summary list, along with "Enterprise-Wide Requirements and Constraints" at the end of Chapter 2, and "Infrastructure Considerations and Constraints," at the end of Chapter 3, are the final inputs to the Network QoS design phase. They are discussed further in Chapter 5, "Requirements Methodology."

Geography

Complex and expensive QoS solutions may be necessary for some applications, but these solutions often don't need to be implemented on every node of the network. Instead, they can sometimes be restricted to the particular locations or regions where the users are connected. In many cases, not even the entire user region needs the QoS technology. For example, it may be that a particular application requiring a complex type of QoS is based in a server farm located in New York City, and the users are clustered in research labs in both the New York area and in Oxford. This is crucial information for the network designer, because he or she may be able to build a network that has special equipment at only a few locations: at the entrance to the server farm in New York, at the entrances to the research labs in New York and Oxford, and at key traffic relay points between them. There may not be any need to build an extensive, worldwide network of specialized QoS facilities if this is the only application needing that particular type of QoS.

The location of the network users and the pattern of traffic among them are therefore important pieces of the data needed before starting the QoS design work. We'll gather the traffic pattern information in such a way that later QoS requirements data can be associated with particular flows

Geography Specifications

Draw a diagram of the geography, showing:

1. **Geographic clustering that could use a LAN or MAN**
2. **Long-latency users (e.g., satellite)**
3. **Restricted-bandwidth users (e.g., using wireless LANs, Ricochet, dial-up, etc.)**
4. **High-error user (e.g., mobile)**

in the pattern; this will help us to describe the areas that the QoS solutions must control. To start, we'll need to create a sketch of the geography of the network and its users, one major application at a time.

A simple example is shown in Figure 4.1. User classes represent different groups of users from a data communications point of view: Class A, with needs for high-bandwidth, low-latency links; Class B, needing only

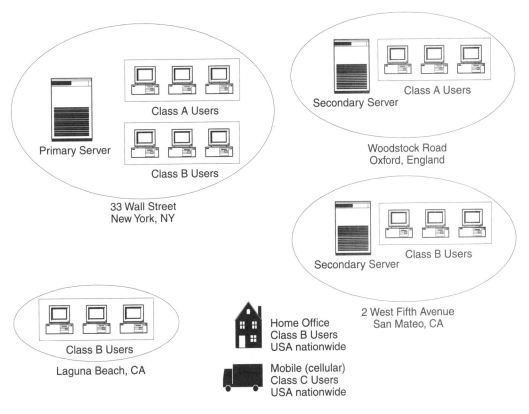

Figure 4.1 Application geography.

moderate bandwidth, in the 56-kbps range; and Class C, a restricted-bandwidth, high-error class used by service employees in their trucks to get brief, alphanumeric information. Data links aren't shown because this is a geographical diagram of the user locations only; more information, such as traffic flows, will be added later.

The major geographic issues important to the QoS designer are the location and size of user clusters, the problems associated with data communications to underserved areas of the world that may need special facilities (satellite, restricted-bandwidth links), and the cases of users who are using restricted-bandwidth or high-error links. These issues are discussed in the subsections that follow.

Clustering

Geography refers to the physical location of network users, whether those users are individuals with laptop PCs or large clustered server farms. We need to know the physical locations of the users, to establish the geographic reach of any necessary QoS facilities; we also need to know the clustering situation as it's seen by the network. We are interested in clustering because we need to know whether the users will be connected with LAN, MAN, or WAN technology, as these variations will influence the types of QoS solutions that we'll use. Clustering within a server, which isn't visible to the network, is not important to us.

Underserved Geographies

Another geographic consideration is that of location with respect to the availability of telecommunications facilities. Developed countries have an extensive communications infrastructure that can provide almost any type of communications link to any location in a reasonable time and at reasonable cost. Many locations in the world don't have such advantages, and that has a strong effect on the QoS capabilities that can be delivered to the user. The telephone infrastructure of many geographic regions is hard-pressed to provide even 9600 bps, and it is sometimes easier to get a high-speed data line between a major city and the United States than it is to get a high-speed line across the street.

In many cases, satellite or radio communication is necessary to reach users in these underserved locations. Even if the local telephone company agrees to provide a link to a remote location, that link will sometimes be provided through geosynchronous satellite, possibly by sharing a VSAT (Very Small Aperture Terminal) satellite link multiplexer in the local town. The problems of satellite and of radio, discussed in the next section, are simply substituted for the problems of using an old, error-prone, low-bandwidth telephone connection.

Satellite and Radio

Satellite communication is often used to reach users who are geographically isolated—on islands, on ships, or in sparsely populated locations, for example. Satellites are also a common solution for the problem of obtaining high-speed communications in underserved geographical areas. Unfortunately, satellites introduce unavoidable latency, which is upward of 260 milliseconds one way for satellites in geosynchronous orbit and 20 milliseconds one way for Low Earth Orbit (LEO) satellites [Ghani]. Situations requiring VSAT can result in surprisingly long latencies, as many VSAT connections require two hops through the satellite to connect together two subscribers who use the small VSAT dish antennas. (End stations in a VSAT network usually communicate only with the central base station, not directly with each other.) Some protocols can handle long latencies or can be adapted to it through the use of the special spoofing or quarantining equipment that is described in the "Protocol Issues" section of Chapter 3. User applications that require low latency may have major problems, and alternative arrangements for those applications may be necessary. For example, commercial-quality interactive voice over geosynchronous satellite is simply impossible, but it's easy over LEO satellite. Systems incorporating geosynchronous satellites should provide a mechanism for separating the datastreams into high-latency and low-latency streams, with the low-latency stream routed through some terrestrial system instead of through the satellite.

Radio communications includes satellite, microwave, commercial radio links, and cellular. The primary difficulty with radio is that its error rate is typically higher than that for normal land links and is affected by the weather. Microwaves, used by both terrestrial microwave and by satellite, are absorbed by water; therefore, microwave communication suffers during heavy rainstorms. Microwaves are also affected by sunspot activity, which is predictable far in advance, and by objects passing through the microwave beam. Cellular radio and commercial radio are adversely affected by metal structures that absorb and reflect radio signals; they also usually require licensing from government bodies that may restrict the high-power signals needed to overcome these situations. Although power and design can compensate for obstacles in the path between two unmoving radio users, the situation becomes far worse when one or both of those users are mobile. In such cases, discussed next, a low error rate at reasonable cost may be completely impractical. To obtain usable error rates, bandwidth may need to be severely restricted, often to only 9600 bps or less on older systems.

Remote and Mobile

More and more network users are now remote or mobile. Remote users are people with laptops who travel among enterprise locations and connect into the enterprise's network from many different offices, using the office wiring, or from outside the enterprise entirely, using the public telephone system or the Internet. The primary characteristic of remote users from the network's point of view is that they connect into the network from unpredictable points, often far away from their home office database. A classic example is the employee who works at home a few days per week, dialing into an ISP from home and therefore entering the enterprise's network a few thousand miles away, where the Internet connects to the enterprise. His traffic then needs to be backhauled through the enterprise network to his office, travelling thousands of miles (with the associated delays!) to finish only a couple of miles from where the journey started.

Remote users have some options to decrease their load on the network and to make network design easier. First, they can be set up to connect to the network at special locations that are equipped both to handle the QoS demands of their applications and to provide expedited service back to their home areas. This can make the job of the network easier than if remote users simply connect to any vacant port they can find anywhere in the enterprise—with the resulting problems of security, address conflicts, troubleshooting complexity, and the need to put QoS facilities on all of the possible ports that they might use. Second, when they connect through ISPs or similar services, those services can be set up to identify the user and then direct the connection to the best entrance into the enterprise, selecting from a set of gateways in different locations. As more and more enterprises use sophisticated ISP functions, such as Virtual Private Networks and security servers, this method of avoiding long backhauls will become more common.

Mobile users connect through untethered systems, such as cellular radio. They may be service providers with specialized terminals, salespeople with cellular antennas attached to laptops that they use for order entry and research, or corporate executives using cellular to send and receive electronic mail. Their primary characteristics from the network's point of view are the mobile connection's usually-restricted bandwidth, high error rates, and difficulty in handling QoS requirements. Many of the mobile users are also remote users; the travelling executive is an example. Others are not remote—their mobile connection enters the enterprise network locally, and they don't wander out of their area.

Applications that must work with mobile users often provide a special interface with decreased QoS requirements, as the cost of providing the bandwidth and error rate needed for graphics-intensive applications is usually prohibitive, when it can be provided at all. Specialized Web languages are available for such use, with greatly decreased transmission requirements; these Web languages can be used when mobile Web browsing is necessary for an enterprise's intranet application. In many cases, especially that of transaction entry, simple text can be substituted for graphics. The content needed for the transaction will still be there, and the data rate will be lower.

Designers of applications for mobile users should also give strong consideration to building a user client that can handle frequent communications interruptions. Mobile users are subject to frequent data loss and to frequent disconnects; the application will be more durable if it can perform some processing within the client without constant communications back to the central servers. An application that can validate and assemble a batch of transactions for transmission as a single file is much more durable, and usually much faster, than an application that can't complete a simple transaction without a couple of back-and-forth references to the central server database at the enterprise's headquarters. Any interruption in communications forces the user to restart the latter application, whereas the former version, which needs only to transfer a file, can keep trying to send the file for hours, sending a piece at a time, without irritating the user or involving him or her in all of the retransmission attempts. The additional effort on the part of the application designers to build specialized interfaces for mobile users is usually effort that's well spent. Trying to make a mobile system act as if it has all of the services and bandwidth of a fixed-location communications system can be quite expensive or completely impractical. The application designers will then find that they haven't escaped the problem at all; the users will complain, and the designers will have to build that specialized interface anyway.

Traffic Flow and Multicast Pattern

The next issue is that of the flow pattern. Design of a network to provide needed QoS to an application that has a simple server-focused, branching-tree traffic pattern is quite different from the design of a network that must provide QoS on demand to hundreds of individual users who are setting up a dense web of independent interconnections. And both of these situations are different from that of multicasting and broadcasting, which has its own set of issues.

Use of the flow specifications is illustrated in Figure 4.2, which continues the example started in Figure 4.1 by adding a few of the traffic flows. Note that the locations and bandwidth of the actual data links may be considerably different when the design is finally completed; this is a flow diagram only.

We'll first discuss the server-focused versus diffuse data patterns and their implications, followed by a discussion of multicasting and broadcasting.

Server-Focused versus Diffused Traffic Flow

Some applications are server-focused; users of the system connect to central servers and interact with them. The traffic flow in these cases is similar to a starburst, with the heaviest traffic surrounding the servers

---

Traffic Flow and Multicast Specifications

Overlaid on the geography, draw a diagram of the flow pattern, showing, for each major class of user and for each direction of traffic flow:

1. Application flows, including client/server and server/server

2. Multicast and broadcast patterns, including any user clustering

3. External multicast servers, reflectors, transcoders, etc.

4. Flow patterns for unusual applications situations, including partial application or network failure and including database update and resynchronization

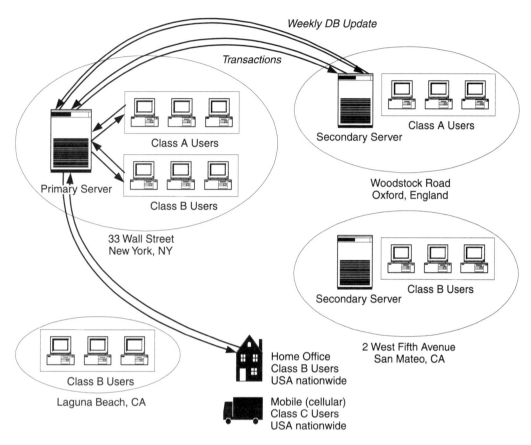

Figure 4.2 Application traffic flow.

and with tapering trunks of traffic leading away toward the users. Often there are groups of servers in different geographical locations, with interserver coordination traffic between servers. This interserver traffic may have considerably different characteristics from the user-to-server traffic. It may be hierarchical, with one super-server at the top of the hierarchy, or it may be a mesh of equals, with servers in different locations splitting the overall load geographically.

In contrast to server-focused flow, an application can have a diffuse flow. (See Figure 4.3.) In that case, all users are equal and connect directly to each other instead of through the mediation of a central server. A typical example of a diffuse flow is that of PC-to-PC packet voice without a central server. Other applications may fall into this category simply because their use is diffused over the network, although the application itself is server-focused. An example of such an application is that of a user

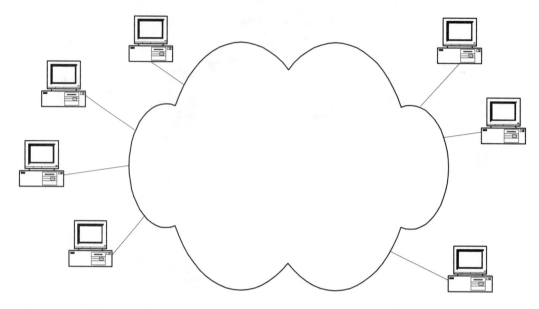

Figure 4.3 Diffused traffic flows.

who establishes a shared workgroup file on his or her office PC. It's technically a server-focused application, with the office PC acting as a file server, but because there are so many of these situations, it appears to the network as if it were a diffused application.

Many applications can take either a server-focused or a diffused form. The classic mainframe-centric application is server-focused, and many new development projects try to break this pattern by using multiple servers in different geographic locations. The development of such a multiple-location server-based system is surprisingly difficult, however, and the network staff must be prepared for the consequences of applications design failure. Such failures are usually caused by unanticipated problems in synchronizing the databases and in management of a distributed system. As problems mount with the new design, the operations staff hurries to point out that maintenance, upgrades, and database synchronization at multiple locations can be a problem. Arguments are advanced that network capacity is cheap; why not bring everything to a central site and end the design and operations headaches? So the network staff must always be prepared in such projects for the sudden reversion to a large, single, centrally located server. Instead of a set of medium-sized network hot spots located around the network geography, there will now be one large hot spot with much more traffic than anticipated for any single location—and that capacity had better be available, and at reasonable cost, because management has now had its fingers burned and doesn't want to consider the idea of distributed locations again.

When a multiple-location, server-based system succeeds, there may still be major networking surprises. Interserver traffic may be far greater than anticipated because users stray out of their normal geographic location but still want to access their database files back home. With the trend toward cross-functional teams and almost constant reorganizations, it's also not unusual for team members to be widely distributed geographically and yet need to share data to a greater degree than anticipated by a geographically partitioned application. The result is increased network traffic as data gets pulled between servers and as remote databases are constantly being updated and synchronized. Servers performing transaction updates are an extreme example of this situation; a single transaction could touch all the geographically separated servers, forcing a flurry of interserver messages as the transaction is applied to all databases, confirmed, and then committed. Changes in database design can also result in massive late-night flows among servers, as the new database designs are implemented and the data is loaded. These massive synchronizing flows may also occur at regular intervals to create backup capabilities at alternate locations, and the actual activation of those backup capabilities in the case of server failure will cause yet another surprising flow pattern, as data for the failed server is now rerouted to the backup.

There are also surprises because an actual network's topology may not match its geography at all, and the cost structure of the network may match neither. Users and application designers may build a multiple-location, server-based system based on wildly incorrect assumptions about network costs. They may, for example, simply assume that geographic proximity means low costs. But the actual network may not have a link between two close geographic locations (i.e., the network topology doesn't match the network geography), and it's usually for very good reasons, such as cost. Because of the pricing structures of the bandwidth suppliers, a direct connection may be extraordinarily expensive; the network designers may decide to use a far longer route through different geographic nodes. The applications designers and users, being presented with a bill for this longer route and being told about the reason, may suddenly decide that their server farms are in the wrong locations. It's better to find out about this potential situation earlier rather than later, before the network hardware and bandwidth are purchased and installed, rather than after the networking facilities are built.

Server-focused flows are usually designed by estimating the traffic on various routes and then building the network backbone appropriately. Therefore, knowing the flow pattern and the locations of the major servers and the major user groups is critical to correct QoS design. But it's also important to consider the routes that the traffic will take in failure situations, as most modern networks reroute quickly. QoS functionality will need to be installed on many, if not all, of the routes that the traffic will take both in normal and in some partial-fail situations.

Diffused flow applications offer a different set of design challenges. First, it may be necessary to install complex QoS capabilities at all points in the network, if the flow is truly diffuse and the application is widely used. Second, there is the possibility that the network may experience much more traffic, and to many more unexpected locations, than you'd anticipated! This is an ideal use of QoS capabilities, of course, as QoS will prevent the widespread use of a popular, bandwidth-hungry application from destroying everyone else's network service—but remember that you may have to install that QoS capability everywhere in the network, at considerable expense.

Especially beware of the diffused, low-profile application that suddenly becomes popular and overwhelms the network. It may be tempting at first to say that an application won't be used much, so there's no need to dedicate special QoS capabilities to it—either to ensure its performance levels or to protect other users from its bandwidth demands. But diffused, widely disseminated applications that don't use central servers may not be easy to control by the administration. Users who like an application can flood the network quickly, and there may not be a simple way of controlling them without trying to strip the application out of PC hard drives or retrofitting QoS capabilities into the network everywhere. It's much easier to locate the person in charge of running a major central server hosting a bandwidth-hog application than it is to pinch off the floods of traffic from 10,000 users worldwide who have suddenly discovered a great application and would love it even more if only they could get additional free bandwidth!

To avoid the problems of uncontrollable diffused applications, the applications designers should consider the use of QoS capabilities even if the application does not appear to need them at first glance. They may also want to consider the use of server-based systems instead of diffused systems. There are areas in which both types of systems are viable; tele-conferencing is an example. Both diffused systems and server-based (also called reflector-based) teleconferencing systems are available. The diffused systems may scale better, if the network capacity is not an issue or if widespread QoS is implemented. Otherwise, the server-based systems may be better.

It's usually best to use the actual user geography when drawing the flow pattern, instead of making it a purely symbolic pattern with no relationship to the actual placements of real users and servers. The pattern can then also serve to indicate user locations; otherwise, a separate set of diagrams should be drawn. All major flows should be shown, as should the minor flows that you suspect may suddenly grow. To make it easier to attach QoS requirements to flows, it should be possible to label the different directions of the flow with different QoS requirements. Different user groups may also have usage characteristics that are so different that they should be handled separately. For example, the flow characteristics of members of the Human Resources department using a Human Resources application will be markedly different from the diffused flow of non-Human Resources employees using the same application once a year to change their home address or medical insurance preferences.

Application Broadcasting and Multicasting

Broadcasting is the term used to describe sending data to all users simultaneously. In broadcasting, an application's data packets are sent to every user on the network, whether or not they use that application or have any interest in it. Broadcast packets from all sources arrive at the user's network connections, and the user's system must then sort through them to find the ones that it wants.

Unlike broadcasting, which transmits to everyone on the network, multicasting transmits to only a limited group—although that group can be quite large. The user can send a message to enroll in multicasts, or the multicast supplier can send multicasts only to those users on a predefined list. In either case, the multicasts arrive only at the users who want them. Compared to broadcasting, multicasting decreases the load on the users' systems and on the network links, although the network devices must do additional work to manage the multicast lists.

Broadcasting and multicasting can be performed purely at the application level without network involvement, as shown in Figure 4.4. The central application can open connections directly to all of the users, or the application can be built in a hierarchical fashion, with some application servers receiving the broadcast or multicast message and retransmitting it to users farther down the hierarchy. In both cases, the network sees the traffic as point-to-point connections, not as point-to-multipoint. The network does see the total traffic, however, which can have a massive impact on the network near the source of the multicast as thousands of point-to-point links converge to their source. The application, too, can be overwhelmed by the traffic, as it must separately open each receiver's link and manage that link.

To decrease the impact on the network and on the application, broadcasting and multicasting services can be provided by the network itself, on request from the users. The user simply invokes the appropriate network service and places the broadcast indicator or the identifier of the multicast group into the outgoing address of the data packets. The load on the sender is minimal, as only one broadcast-marked or multicast-marked data packet needs to be sent into the network.

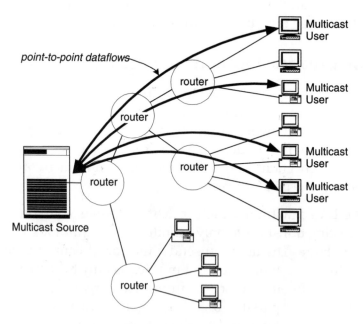

Figure 4.4 Multicasting by the application.

In the case of broadcasts, every network router or switch that receives a specially marked broadcast packet immediately makes copies and sends them out of all the other ports. (Of course, some technologies, such as 10Base-2 shared-media Ethernet, are inherently broadcast.) The number of packets multiplies until there's a copy for each user on the network. This is an explosive growth in the number of packets as the broadcast makes its way through the network routers and switches, but it's still far less than having the application perform the broadcast. That's because the duplicate packets are not all made at the source; instead, they're created as close to the recipient as possible. A branching tree, with its root at the source, reaches out to the receivers. No duplicate packets travel along any network link, and there's no hot spot at the broadcast's source.

There are still a lot of broadcast packets involved in any broadcast, however, and this creates a considerable network load. If the number of broadcasts is large, the network can find that its capacity is being absorbed by the broadcasts, which must find their way down all of the network's paths, no matter how restricted in bandwidth. The users who receive these broadcasts are also burdened by them. They must somehow decide which ones to listen to, a process that requires a certain amount of processing in the user's machine. The load on both the network and the users' systems is therefore considerable. In short, the use of broadcasts by applications as a part of their design strategy is almost always a mistake in any enterprise-size network. It floods the network with data, congests the smaller network links and routers, and places an unwanted burden on the users as they sort through the incoming broadcasts. The only usual exception occurs when virtually all of the users on the network really must receive the broadcast and will continue to need to receive it even if the network is combined with other networks and their users.

Multicasting, especially when performed by the network instead of by the application, greatly cuts the network load when compared to point-to-point links. (See Figure 4.5.) It also eases the task of both the sending and receiving applications, although it makes the job of the network components more complex. In multicasts, the identifier of the multicasting group is placed in the address of the data packets, and each network user chooses the groups to receive. Users are not flooded by multicasts in which they have no interest. Even better, the network routers and switches can learn which users have subscribed to which multicasts, and they can

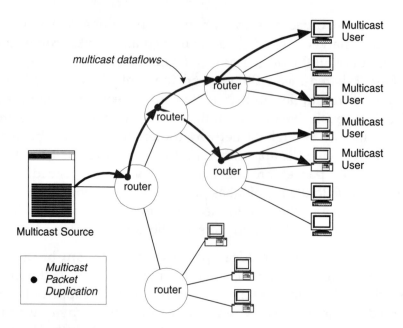

Figure 4.5 Multicasting by the network.

therefore forward network traffic selectively. This is unlike broadcast traffic, which must be forwarded out of each outgoing router or switch port. If a particular multicast doesn't have any subscribers down a particular path, then the router or switch simply doesn't forward that multicast down that path. Multicasting performed by the network decreases the load on the network's links while also decreasing the load on the sender and the receivers.

In both broadcasting and multicasting, it can be difficult to determine whether the intended recipients have received all of the packets without errors. There isn't a point-to-point link, and there usually aren't any acknowledgments from the users. Indeed, in many situations the application itself doesn't know the identities of the users because they enroll in the multicast through the network itself or through separate multicasting retransmitters. The multicast or broadcast application can sometimes receive notification of problems in receiving its transmissions by special features of the multicasting technologies or by asking its recipients to notify it of the network quality—time delay variation, error rate, and so on. Positive notification of each packet's reception by each recipient can be done, but this will result in a flood of acknowledgments returning to the sender, and it isn't usually clear how to handle lost packets. The job of retransmitting lost packets to the relatively few recipients who didn't receive them could easily overwhelm the sending system. Instead, if the error rate is high, or if there are a lot of lost packets or packets that arrive too late, the multicast or broadcast application may simply decide to slow down and hope that the situation improves. In some cases, multicasting sources may transmit more than one outgoing datastream: a high-bandwidth stream for users with high-bandwidth, low-error connections and lower-bandwidth streams for users on more restricted connections. There may also be multicast rebroadcasters, called transcoders, which can take in a high-bandwidth stream and convert it to a low-bandwidth outgoing multicast stream on-the-fly for certain applications, such as video. (See Chapter 3 for further discussion of transcoders and video.)

Because of the difficulties in verifying that packets have arrived, multicast and broadcast applications may ask for special QoS services. They may request unusually low error rates, for example, to decrease the problem of lost packets. If the network's transmission links have high error rates, there may be difficulty in fulfilling this request. The network can try to use specialized hardware that automatically retransmits erroneously received data, but this won't work in all cases. Many multicast applications are time-sensitive and can't wait for the retransmitted data to arrive; delayed data is the same as lost data. Data transmitted with an error-correcting code that permits data recovery (a Forward-Error-Correcting code) can be useful in some situations, though.

The Network QoS Specifications list includes many items that help clarify the needs of broadcasting and multicasting applications, especially with regard to their use of network capacity and their possible need of QoS services. Broadcast and multicast capacity requirements can be substantial, which will affect the type of equipment that must be used in the network; and that will affect the types of QoS services that can be made available.

Broadcasting and multicasting are some of the fastest-growing network applications, and they can have a massive impact on a network. Even if the application itself is able to tolerate large error rates and transmission delay variation, the traffic from broadcast and multicast applications can have a major impact on other network users. This may require the installation of QoS facilities simply to protect the rights of other users who must share bandwidth with these applications. Any broadcast or multicast application that is to be placed on a shared network must, therefore, be carefully examined. As shown in the topics that follow, bandwidth may need to be protected, even for applications that don't, at first glance, appear to need QoS.

Protocols

Protocols are the sets of data formats and interchange rules that programs use while communicating. As discussed in Chapter 3, some protocols make more stringent demands or have more network impacts than others. Our concern here is to list the protocols that will probably be used on the network by the application, along with the extent of their usage in terms of their traffic flow pattern and in terms of the percentage of the application's traffic that uses each protocol.

There are three different groups of protocols. The first is the group of protocols that's most directly used by the network itself; these are the protocols such as Ethernet, Token Ring, TCP, UDP, IP, and NetWare IPX. The different protocols have different QoS characteristics in terms of their QoS requirements to avoid poor performance and in terms of their impact on other flows in the same path. The different protocols also contain provisions for different types of QoS control; ATM, for example, offers a very different set of QoS tools than does simple Ethernet.

The second group of protocols is that set designed to work with QoS at the application level. Typically, these include compression and multimedia protocols, such as the MPEG-2 Transport Streams protocol or RTP and its companion RTCP. Although the facilities for taking advantage of these possibilities are still generally lacking, the application designers should

Protocol Specifications

Overlaid on the flow pattern, note the protocols used and the amount of their use, showing:

1. Network-layer and transport-layer protocols used by the application, including multicast
2. Application-layer protocols that are designed to work with QoS or that are sensitive to QoS

be asked about the presence of these protocols, and they should be recorded along their flow paths in the traffic flow chart.

The third group of protocols contains those application protocols that are known to be sensitive to poor QoS and must therefore be carefully handled. Their impacts on the QoS requirements may not be initially known to the application designer, but asking about them will force the application designers and the network team to consider the QoS effects on all of the protocols used in the application.

Bandwidth Usage Pattern

Bandwidth is the number of bytes per second that can be transmitted with the error rates and availabilities described in its associated specifications. Each application has its characteristic bandwidth use, which it requires to function successfully. Our interest is not in the precise prediction of that bandwidth use, but simply in the prediction of the probable locations of bottlenecks within the network that may need QoS facilities.

Bandwidth needed by the user of an application is interesting if it will be a large percentage of the available capacity of that user's connection into the enterprise network. For example, if the user needs a transaction flow at the same time that he or she needs a real-time video flow, and both of those flows are on a 56-kbps link, then there will probably be trouble—and a need for QoS. In most cases, however, such as that of a user who is connected via Ethernet into the enterprise backbone and is using applications with moderate bandwidth requirements, the end user's bandwidth requirements, by themselves, are not an issue.

Aggregated bandwidth, the sum of the bandwidth requirements of hundreds or thousands of users, is usually of greater concern than an individual's

Bandwidth Usage Pattern Specifications

Overlaid on the flow pattern, note the major bandwidth requirements, showing:

1. Bandwidth variation pattern; average and maximum bandwidth; burst duration
2. Time-of-day and other calendar-related variations

requirements. This aggregated bandwidth demand appears close to the servers or at congestion points in the network, such as at a router positioned at the beginning of a cross-Atlantic link. It can be sufficiently massive to require QoS facilities even if there isn't any congestion at other points in the network and even if there isn't any congestion in the connections to the application users and the application servers.

Aggregated bandwidth for some applications can be difficult to calculate. Nevertheless, a guess—based on measurements, if possible—of the average and maximum flow rates, and of the duration and time of day of the maximum flow rate, should be made to help predict network bottlenecks. Aggregated bandwidth must also be accounted for in both flow directions, as they both add to the total flows through network components and as they are usually very different from each other. In some network designs, these flows may even travel over different paths.

Bandwidth Regulation

The difficulties in predicting bandwidth needs accurately stem, in part, from the way that most applications use available bandwidth: They simply transmit as quickly as possible, using whatever is available. Their transmission rate is governed by their own internal computer bottlenecks, the bandwidth of their connection to the network, the amount of data they have to transmit, and the frequency of transmission. This process is shown in Figure 4.6. The typical application issues a Send command to its operating system's communications interface, the Application Program Interface (API), and when the API indicates that the Send command has completed, it issues another Send command if it has more data to transmit. Sending rate is governed by the speed with which the API indicates that each send operation has completed and the number of overlapping send operations that the API is willing to accept. The API, in turn, is aware of the buffering situation in the operating system's communications software; it will continue to accept Send traffic as long as there's buffer space available.

The communications software must take the data from the incoming buffer, where the application has placed it, and transmit that data into the network. To do so it uses a communications protocol, such as TCP/IP or SNA, and its transmission rate is controlled to a certain extent by that

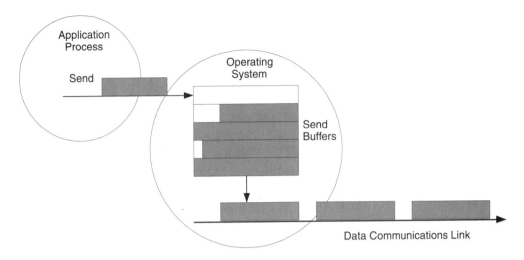

Figure 4.6   Data transmission through an API.

protocol and by the speed of the communications line to which it is attached. The line rate is the primary factor, but the software doesn't transmit a continuous stream at that rate. Rather, it transmits blocks, or packets, of data, then may wait for an acknowledgment from the recipient that the data has arrived correctly. Therefore, *if the protocol uses acknowledgments*, the software at the receiver can regulate the transmission rate by adjusting the rate at which it sends acknowledgments. In some cases, the network may be able to manipulate the acknowledgment rate to manage the transmission rate.

Unfortunately, a number of major protocols do not provide any mechanism for bandwidth management, and among them are the underlying transport protocols usually used in multicasting and in such QoS-sensitive applications as teleconferencing, packet voice, and real-time video. These applications don't have the time to use a protocol that retransmits incorrectly received blocks; the wait for the retransmitted block to arrive would be far too long. But without retransmission, there's no need for acknowledgments; without acknowledgments, the classical way of adjusting the sender's transmission rate is gone. The transmission software transmits continuously at the outgoing link rate, without waiting for acknowledgments or other flow-control signals. If the packets are lost in the first network switch because of a network bottleneck, well, that's not a concern of the protocol. Applications using these transport protocols may use a higher-level protocol, such as the Real Time Control Protocol (RTCP), to obtain feedback from recipients. That feedback can then be used by the application itself to adjust its sending speed by timing the rate at which it issues Send commands to the communications software's API. For example, a multicasting multimedia application could decide that if more than 10 percent of its end users are receiving incomplete data streams, with missing, delayed, and erroneous packets, then it will decrease its transmission rate. This will increase the usability of its data by its end users, and it will also decrease the impact of its transmissions on other users of the shared bandwidth. Without some form of bandwidth control, nonregulated applications may be able to flood a network completely, denying network access to other, more well-behaved, users.

Other transmission rate and bandwidth-control tools are available with some protocols; these are discussed in Chapter 3, "Applications and Infrastructure Issues," in Chapter 6, "Basic QoS Technologies," and in Chapter 7, "Solution Building Blocks." They include the adaptive behavior of protocols when faced with constricted bandwidth channels and the explicit rate control feedback provided by some network interfaces such as that found in Asynchronous Transfer Mode's (ATM's) Available Bit Rate (ABR). These mechanisms allow the network itself to influence the transmission rate by sending signals to the communications software in the user systems. That communications software then adjusts its transmission rate, thereby varying the speed with which it empties its send buffers. The API, noticing the change in the speed with which the buffers are emptied, alters its signals to the applications program, and that program finds that it's waiting longer or shorter periods before being told that its Send command has been successfully completed. Such tools may work with protocols that do not inherently provide bandwidth regulation, as long as the protocol API is able to handle the bandwidth signaling with the network.

It's therefore important for the network QoS designer to know if the applications that will be placed on the network will be good network citizens, with bandwidth demands that are reasonable or that can be regulated by the network. If an application will be using large amounts of bandwidth and won't be using a protocol with acknowledgments, the network QoS designer may have to take steps to protect the network from the application's grabs for bandwidth. Certainly, the network can simply disconnect an application or restrict it to a maximum bandwidth through the use of the queuing and flow control capabilities discussed later in this book. If, however, the application itself has been designed to accept bandwidth suggestions from the network, or to measure network performance and compensate for it by altering its bandwidth use, that can be a more effective and efficient method than the indirect ones that use queuing and flow control. The question of whether an application has flow control built into the application is therefore an important one, and it appears in the Network QoS Specifications list. (The question of whether it is using protocols that are sensitive to flow control is asked in the protocol topic; this topic's question looks for flow control that has been programmed into the application itself, such as cooperation between a sender and a receiver application to measure and adjust transmission rate.)

Finally, some few applications have the ability to mark selected packets for discard by the network if there are bandwidth capacity or congestion problems. Some examples are compression algorithms that produce different types of packets. Loss of the more important packets results in major difficulties at the recipient's end; the less important packets can be discarded by the network without great impact on the end user. This provides a coarse method that the network can use to regulate bandwidth use, especially in applications that don't provide other methods for network control of their bandwidth usage.

Latency and Jitter

Latency is the time that it takes for a data bit to cross the network in one direction, while jitter is the variation in that time. Many applications are not sensitive to latency and jitter; instead, they are sensitive to bandwidth and error rate. Typical examples of these applications are file transfer and electronic mail; they are satisfied if they can successfully transmit a certain file size within a certain period of time. Examples of applications that are sensitive to latency and jitter include interactive voice and video. Delay-sensitive applications such as these usually have a point beyond which late packets are useless to the application and are simply discarded if they arrive. Some delay-sensitive applications cannot tolerate any late packets, whereas others can function well even if a certain percentage of the packets arrive late or not at all.

In some cases, applications may mark packets for selective discard. Those packets are less important than others; they can be discarded by the network if there is congestion or other reasons that the application's bandwidth usage must be decreased. Tagging of packets for selective discard is discussed in Chapter 3 and in the preceding section of this chapter, "Bandwidth Regulation."

Latency

Latency, the one-way delay between sender and receiver, is the result of a number of factors:

Serialization delays, caused by the process of converting a byte or word in a computer's memory to or from a serial string of bits on the communications line. The time needed for serialization is the time needed to write bits onto the communications line or to read bits from the communications line; it's controlled by the line speed. For example, 1500 bytes requires 8 milliseconds to serialize at 1.5 mbps. This delay is added whenever a packet must be read completely into memory from a communications line before being processed, or when it must be read out of memory after processing. Serialization causes delay in most routers and, of course, at the source and destination. Using an external modem instead of an internal modem for a workstation usually adds serialization delay.

Additional delays are caused by byte padding when an 8-bit byte is placed onto an asynchronous line. Asynchronous modems, such as V.34, normally use 10 bits per byte, not 8. A special option of many asynchronous modems, the ITU-T standard V.80, allows transmission of 8-bit bytes in some cases. If V.80 isn't used, then the additional serialization delays caused by those 2 extra bits per byte must be included. Of course, there's also a marked decrease in the effective bandwidth of the line because of the additional overhead.

Electronic delays, the delay caused by communications electronics, such as by the modems in the path. For example, a pair of V.34 modems typically inserts 40 milliseconds or more of one-way delay even when their internal compression and error-correction functions are turned off. (This delay varies by manufacturer.) Allowing the modem to perform internal compression, error correction, and data blocking makes the delays much worse. (Those functions are used by default in most V.34 modems. They improve transmission efficiency, decrease the effective error rate, and allow the modem to change its transmission speed on the communications link while not affecting the speed across the interface to the user's computer [Goodman].)

Transmission delays are governed by the laws of physics. The ITU-T standard G.114 specifies 4 µs/km for coaxial cable and radio, 5 µs/km for optical fiber, and 6 µs/km for submarine coaxial cables. (All of these figures include delays in repeaters and regenerators.) Therefore, it will require 20 milliseconds to travel the 2500 miles (4000 km) between New York City and Los Angeles, or 100 milliseconds to travel the 10,500 miles (17,000 km) from New York City to Melbourne, Australia. A signal beamed up to a geosynchronous satellite and down again, a distance of 44,600 miles (72,000 km), takes approximately 260 milliseconds. VSAT satellites may require multiple hops through the satellite, at 260 milliseconds per hop, to connect two subscribers who use the small VSAT dishes. Transmission delays through the local telephone company for a local call typically take 12 milliseconds one way through an analog exchange or 3 milliseconds one way through a digital exchange; this must be added to the long-distance transmission delay if the signal's travel begins or ends with a local telephone call. These delays do not include any delays because of packet processing at intermediate nodes. *Note that increasing the line speed does not decrease transmission delay!* (It does decrease serialization delay, however.)

Processing delays in the intermediate routers, switches, multiplexers, and other network equipment. These delays can range up to a second or more. Each telephone company exchange adds approximately 1 millisecond to the delay.

These are the one-way latency delays between two points on the network boundary; they do not take into account delays within the user's equipment, such as that used for data compression, encoding, error correction, operating system overhead, application processing, and more. (Some of these considerations are investigated for particular applications in Chapter 3.) Many data communications QoS solutions do not cover all of these areas; for example, a carrier's latency guarantees may not include electronic delays in the modems. To obtain reasonable estimates of end-to-end latency, network designers must calculate a latency budget for the end-to-end path that includes *all* of these factors.

It's also important to note that the delay between a pair of users may be different in the two directions; indeed, that's the normal case in the Internet. The reason is that packet-switched routing may direct the data packets through two completely different paths through the core of the network; such asymmetric routing is often done for administrative reasons. For example, many ISPs make it a practice to transfer a packet to its destination network at the first available opportunity, to decrease the bandwidth that the ISP must devote to carrying that packet. If the destination ISP does the same thing, the packet will follow very different paths in the two directions. Even if the paths are identical, the buffering situations in each router or switch are almost certainly different, leading to different delays. Therefore, *round-trip delay measurements, which are relatively easy to measure, can't simply be cut in half to give the one-way delay.* True one-way delay measurement requires closely synchronized clocks at both ends of the path to provide the needed accuracy.

Users who require low-delay transmission may find that the network cannot supply that requirement without specialized design, such as the installation of circuits for that application alone. As discussed in Chapter 3, the time spent in application processing, data compression, error correction, or other time-consuming user application functions may need to be examined to see if some additional leeway can be obtained by decreasing the processing time in the user systems. Some latency factors, such as the transmission delays caused by the laws of physics, simply cannot be decreased—no matter how fast the line speed or how desperate the need.

Jitter

Jitter is the variation in network delay, and it may be quite large in packet-switched networks. It's caused by the internal operation of network multiplexers, switches, and routers, and it is unavoidable when these devices are used.

Insertion jitter is created whenever a packet has to be neatly placed into a stream of packets, as shown in Figure 4.7. The packet may be ready,

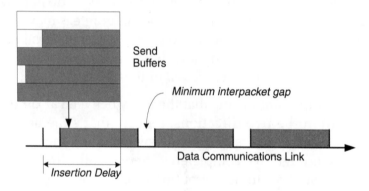

Figure 4.7   Insertion jitter.

but it can't be inserted into the outgoing data link at the moment that it's ready. Instead, it is delayed until the previous packet has completed transmission and the next transmission slot is ready to receive it. This insertion delay for the outgoing transmission slot appears to be random, as it depends on the time that it took to prepare the packet for transmission, other work waiting for the processor's attention, and so on. Jitter is therefore introduced at the source, within the user's system; and it also appears within all of the network components that must remove packets from an incoming datastream, process them, and then place them into an outgoing datastream. Use of long packets, or mixing short and long packets together, increases this insertion jitter, as the wait for a previous packet is then highly variable. Insertion jitter also appears in half-duplex Ethernet and in other technologies where there can be random collisions or delays while waiting for the transmission slot.

Jitter is also created wherever there are queues and buffering in a system, a usually unavoidable feature of routers and of some other communications equipment. Because the number of packets waiting for transmission varies—that's the whole point of buffering, to absorb temporary variations in load—the delay waiting for transmission also varies. That delay variation is jitter. As discussed later in this book, different buffering strategies can be used to decrease jitter, but they may have unwelcome side effects. For example, decreasing the maximum number of packets held in the buffer will surely decrease jitter—for those packets that aren't completely discarded by the router because of lack of buffer capacity when they arrive!

Finally, an extreme form of jitter is introduced whenever a network device must reroute a packet because of congestion or network failure. The packet arrives intact at its destination, but it may arrive much earlier or later than expected because it is taking a different route through the network than was taken by the preceding packets. (Duplicate or incorrectly ordered packets may also appear as a result of such rerouting, but that's a different issue, handled later, in the "Error Characteristics" section of this chapter.)

Designers of real-time multimedia applications don't like jitter because removing it is a problem and because it interferes with the unvarying time offset between sender and receiver that is used by some multimedia applications as an aid to application synchronization. The receiver must maintain a buffer to smooth out the jitter, and, to remove all the jitter, this dejitter buffer must be able to absorb twice the expected jitter. The

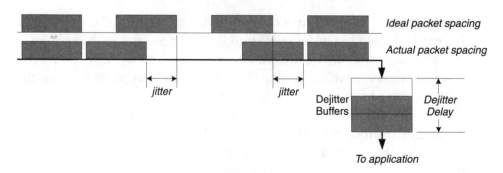

Figure 4.8 Dejitter buffering.

reason is that the buffer must be prepared to accept an early packet immediately followed by a late packet (see Figure 4.8). This buffer adds latency to the application, and the latency may make the entire application perform too slowly, especially if the jitter is large. Worse, the amount of the jitter may be hard to anticipate, so the application may need to use an adaptive dejitter buffer that tries to adjust itself to the jitter that it's seeing in the received datastream. Regardless of how large the buffer is, however, some packets always seem to arrive too late, and they're therefore dropped. There's always a balance to be struck between having the buffer large enough to catch long-delayed packets and having the buffer so large that the added latency ruins the application's user performance. Applications that are very sensitive to latency will therefore cut the dejitter buffer to the minimum, tolerating more lost packets as a trade-off for the decreased delay in the dejitter buffer.

To avoid the need for long dejitter delays, dejitter buffers for speech can be set to only 1x the anticipated jitter. This is less than is needed for perfect speech transmission—some packets will arrive late and be lost—but it's sufficient for humans. If modem signaling tones or faxes are to be sent over the audio link, however, a larger dejitter buffer, on the order of 2x the anticipated jitter, is necessary to increase the accuracy of the decoded signal.

Error Characteristics

Errors occur in many different forms, with differing impacts on different types of applications. Some error types are as follows:

Incorrect bits and errored packets, including inverted bits, extra bits, and lost bits, resulting in discard of the entire packet because of one or more errors detected by the error-detection checksum in the packet.

Lost packets, which are discarded at some intermediate point in the network, because of network congestion, buffer overflow, or packet damage due to noise that corrupts the packet sufficiently so that it cannot be recognized by the hardware.

Extra packets, which are duplicates of previously delivered packets (a situation usually caused during recovery attempts by a failing network component) or are packets that are misaddressed, where the address has been corrupted.

Late packets, which are error-free but are delivered too late to be useful to the application. (In some situations, early packets can also be a problem. They may arrive before there's a buffer ready to receive them, and they must therefore be discarded.)

Note that there's no QoS requirement that packets be delivered in order; it's usually assumed that the packets are sequence numbered and are reassembled into the correct order by the receiving protocol. Older technologies (e.g., SNA, X.25) always delivered packets in order, if they were delivered at all, but the new Internet-based technologies may scramble packet ordering. The time needed to reassemble packets into their correct order, or to wait for delayed packets, may be considered a form of jitter if that reassembly process is hidden from the application.

Different types of applications are affected differently by the four types of errors:

Real-time, low-delay applications, such as interactive voice or video, don't have the time to wait for late packets; they may as well be lost. They also don't have the time to ask for retransmission of a packet with bit errors. These applications are therefore usually built to be tolerant of a certain percentage of packets lost to errors or delays, but they fall apart and can't recover if the errors and delays exceed a certain amount. As discussed in Chapter 3, these applications usually have different types of packets, some of which are more important than others. These packets may be marked so that the network can tell them apart for selective discard.

Bulk-transfer applications, such as file transfer and streaming video, are much more forgiving. They have the time to wait for retransmissions of erroneous packets, and they can wait for late packets. Even they cannot tolerate massive problems, though. As the error rate increases, the effective bandwidth of the transmission path decreases. With enough errors, and enough delays for retransmissions, the file transfer won't complete in a reasonable time, or the streaming video receiver won't be able to buffer enough data to insulate the viewer from the gaps that appear when data is delayed.

Multicast or broadcast applications usually don't have a method for retransmitting lost or erroneous packets; therefore, they're more sensitive to error rates on all of the branches of their transmission tree. These applications are usually designed to tolerate errors, however. Multicast applications that require error-free transmission can use specialized multicast protocols, such as Scalable Reliable Multicast, for that capability.

Applications that absolutely require error-free transmission quality from the network service can use two methods for achieving this, either one of which could also be implemented within the network itself. First, the application or network can use an error-correcting protocol, which retransmits erroneous packets until a good copy is received. Second, if the application cannot wait for the retransmissions, it or the network can use an error-correcting code attached to each packet of data. Such a code allows the receiver to detect and correct most errors without needing a retransmission. The difficulty with these Forward-Error-Correcting (FEC) codes is that they increase the size of the packets, thereby cutting the effective bandwidth of the link.

Error rate QoS agreements often depend on the percentage of erroneous bits over a period of time, sometimes as long as days or weeks. This Bit Error Rate (BER) is commonly used and available, and it may be based on the ratio of good to bad bits for a specified error pattern and a specified transmission length. As such, it's easily measured by test equipment, but it's a measurement that's not as useful as it could be. It's important to consider the patterns in which errors actually occur and the patterns to which the application is actually sensitive.

Telecommunications networks tend to have bursts of errors instead of individual errors that are randomly distributed. The bursts are caused by the underlying technologies and physical processes; they appear both in the basic communications links and in more complex systems, such as the Internet backbone itself. For example, many digital communications problems are caused by clock synchronization difficulties within the network hardware, and these tend to cause bursts of errors. (Another way of saying that is to say that when a digital line is good, it is very, very good, but when it is bad, it is horrid!) Physical processes such as rainstorms, lightning, and sunspots also cause clusters of errors. The Internet itself has been shown to have self-similar (fractal) behavior, not random behavior; that is, errors occur in horrid bursts.

Many contracts for communications links therefore define errors in terms such as error-free seconds, in which a particular second is counted as being erroneous regardless of whether 1 or 10,000 errors occur within it. A thousand errors in 1 second is counted as 1 error in such contracts. For example, the ITU-T G.821 specification for International ISDN error rates [ITU G.821] specifies that "fewer than 10 percent of one-minute intervals will have a BER worse than 1×10^{-6}, fewer than 0.2 percent of one-second intervals will have a BER worse than 1×10^{-3}, and fewer than 8 percent of one-second intervals will have any errors at all (i.e., 92 percent error-free seconds)." This type of error definition is quite helpful, as it's often a reasonable measure of the impact of errors on the application. After all, applications can usually ride out individual errors, or small bursts of errors, without difficulty. The application will probably not even know how many errors occurred within a particular packet; most network interfaces will not deliver a packet to an application if it contains any errors at all. Therefore, for such situations, a packet containing even a single error is useless. An unfortunate result is that for applications with large packet sizes, a seemingly low Bit Error Rate can result in the loss of a large number of bytes of data if those errors are distributed evenly over the flow, so as to destroy the maximum number of packets.

To provide a more realistic representation of the impact of errors on an application, the error definition known as Packet Loss Ratio, or Block Error Rate, is used. These give the percentage of packets, for a specified packet length, that contain one or more errors. Similar error definitions may include both the length of the error, in terms of time or bytes, and the frequency of the error. The Network QoS Specifications therefore contain an item that defines error explicitly; a rate stated in terms such as a packet loss ratio of acceptable to unacceptable packets is preferred.

The Network QoS Specifications also ask if the application can handle packets that contain errors. Some applications may be able to accept packets with a certain number of bit errors, as their decoding and decompression algorithms may be able to compensate for the situation. The difficulty is that many network interfaces will not present erroneous packets to the application. The communications stack in the operating system may be designed to evaluate the packet checksum automatically and delete erroneous packets without giving the application the option of receiving it anyway. For example, TCP never presents erroneous packets, whereas UDP can be configured to ignore checksums.

Availability

The formal definition of network Availability matches the network user's intuitive definition: the percentage of time that the network is available for use. Technically, Availability is defined as the Mean Time Between Failures (MTBF) divided by the total time that the network could have been available (MTBF + Mean Time To Repair). A network that fails rarely still gives the users headaches if each failure takes three days to fix!

After the agreement on the meaning of Availability, however, the problems with definitions begin. It's important to define the time periods during which the application is sensitive to availability, the user's willingness to count bursts of errors and problems as if they are one problem, and the parts of the network that must be functioning for the network to be considered available.

Some applications run 24 hours a day, 7 days a week (so-called 24 × 7); most, however, do not. Unless they're running on specialized systems, such as those from Tandem Computers (now a division of Compaq), they're down for regular maintenance, for database reorganization, for repair of failed disk drives and other components. Many run only during the business day or are sensitive to failures only during the business day. It's therefore necessary to specify the time periods during which the application is sensitive to network availability. Note that some applications may have different degrees of sensitivity. The application's users may be willing to pay more for availability guarantees during the business day, but they may also want above-average availability during the evening hours of the work week. Some groups of the application's users may be more sensitive to availability than others, as they may be using different parts of the application. For example, the availability of the network for entering transactions is probably more important than the availability of the networks for customers to view their order status—and the former group may be located in a small geographic area, for which high-availability QoS can be supplied at moderate cost.

The next availability issue is that of error bursts resulting in availability problems. At what point is a burst of errors sufficiently intense that the network is declared unusable by the application? This is an important question, as it will need to be included in the Network QoS Specifications and will probably be a part of any services contract, such as a service-level agreement (SLA).

Most applications consider a network unavailable if they cannot establish a new connection, possibly after a certain number of attempts (call blocking). They also consider a network unavailable if a signal is received from the network to close existing connections (disconnection). But long bursts of errors may cause enough trouble that the application decides it cannot continue and therefore terminates the connection by itself. The network is therefore, from the point of view of the application, not available. It is this more complete definition of availability that should be used in the QoS requirements.

Before deciding that the network must supply a certain availability, however, the application designers should look at their design to see if some changes could make it less sensitive to communications failure. Such communications failures will occur; after all, it's extremely difficult and expensive to remove all of the causes. Any link in the network chain—communications facilities, switches, routers, corroded LAN connectors, operator failure, air conditioning failure in the network computer rooms—can cause failure of the circuit. And any transmission depends on the laws of physics and on human frailty; everything from sunspots, to rain, to software bugs and hardware glitches, to power failures, and to operators who make mistakes, don't realize it, and then go out to lunch—any of these can cause problems. For an application that requires 24×7 availability, 99 percent availability means that the network will be dead for 100 minutes per week; for an application that's sensitive to availability only during the 40-hour work week, 99 percent availability means that 24 minutes per work week will be lost and the amount of dead time at other hours of the week is irrelevant.

The application designers who need to increase their application's tolerance of network availability problems have a number of possible approaches. Even without explicit consideration of the issue, most applications can tolerate complete loss of connectivity for at least a couple of seconds, and some will tolerate it for minutes or more. For example, Internet-based file transfer applications may wait five minutes or more before declaring that the link is unusable. With design attention paid to the issue, file transfer application restart and recovery procedures, coupled with consideration for the increased bandwidth demands if a delayed file transfer must be completed before a deadline, can make such types of applications less sensitive to network availability.

Applications involved in real-time processes, or those that directly interact with people, are usually less tolerant of network problems; among other reasons for the lack of tolerance is that people simply won't wait for long network delays. They cancel the operation or take some other action well before a few minutes have passed. To decrease sensitivity to availability in such cases, the application designers must consider moving some processing to the client application running in the end user's machine. Buffering of transactions at the end user's location, decreased need for end-user interaction with the server, and use of a hierarchy of servers with high-availability connections between end users and their closest servers are all possible approaches to decreasing overall availability needs. The application designers may then find that instead of requiring 100 percent availability, they can begin to define their needs in terms of the maximum amount of time that they can buffer data within their end users' machines, or they'll find that they need high availability only in certain restricted geographic locations, for only certain periods of the day.

The last consideration in the definition of availability is the choice of which parts of the network must be functioning for the application to consider the network available. The application designer probably thinks that the network is available if all of the parts of the application, including the end-user components, can communicate simultaneously. That's one possible definition, and a good one, but it may be difficult for the network managers to monitor on a network-wide basis for the service-level agreements of all of the network's user applications. Alternative definitions may therefore be considered, such as a definition depending on the ability of the application's core servers (if it is server-centric) to connect into the network backbone, coupled with the ability of a specified percentage of the end users (possibly a statistically sampled percentage) to connect into the same backbone. For diffused applications, similar statistically sampled connection success rates could also be proposed. These statistically sampled measures may be based on monitoring software that is installed in a percentage of the servers and in a percentage of the end-user systems, or they may be based on internal network management tool measurements or on measurements by proxy systems that represent the end-user experience. The latter technique is especially useful in cases where the end users will not accept monitoring software in their systems; a common example is that of Internet-based users. Proxy systems, such as those supplied by Keynote Systems (www.keynote.com), are often used for availability and performance monitoring in such cases.

QoS Control and Guarantees

Although most of the information about an enterprise's philosophy on this topic is explored in Chapter 2 and documented in the "Enterprise-Wide Requirements and Constraints" summary list at the end of that chapter, it's still useful to gather information about each major application separately. In some enterprises, the managers of individual applications may be able to negotiate their own QoS control methods and performance guarantees with the network organization; in others, specific applications may be controlled by groups within the enterprise that have unique requirements or that have a power base that permits separate negotiations with the network organization—with outsourcing to external network suppliers if those negotiations aren't satisfactory.

Applications can control their QoS directly, through their Application Program Interface (API), or the QoS can be set up by network administration and assigned to particular users as identified by their network addresses, their protocol characteristics, and so on. These issues are discussed first, followed by the issues involved when more than one administrative group controls the network. Finally, there's a brief discussion of the QoS performance guarantees that a particular application may require from the network administration.

QoS Control

The most common method for controlling QoS is for the network administrator to assign QoS services through the use of network configuration parameters internal to the network. The network administrator assigns network priorities and other QoS parameters by configuring the routers, switches, and other network equipment to identify flows by their packet header information. That header information includes the addresses of the sender and receiver, the particular network port used (which usually indicates the application), the protocol, and, possibly, a priority group. This method works well when, for example, all applications using the SNA protocols need to receive special handling in the routers to avoid timeouts. It can also identify flows that are all heading to or from a few large-scale servers; the network equipment is instructed to give special treatment to flows with a particular destination or source address and port number. The main drawback of this method is that it requires considerable amounts of work and time to configure all of the network components involved. Only recently are automated tools becoming available to make the configuration task simpler.

In contrast to administrator-assigned QoS, it's possible for applications to use an API to assign QoS to themselves. The main advantage of using an API for QoS control is that the individual program can request different levels of QoS dynamically, depending on what it's doing with a particular flow and depending on the user's needs. For example, a file transfer application could ask the user for a priority rating for each transfer, and it could then pass that information through the API to request above-average communications bandwidth for high-priority file transfers. Without such an API, there would need to be some other way for the network to identify high-priority file transfers, such as running two copies of the file transfer package at two different network addresses or ports, with one package handling regular priority and the other handling high priority. This is easy to do with a simple file transfer package, but it can be difficult if there are multiple different QoS options to be considered and if the application is complex.

But most APIs can't handle QoS requests, and even when they can (WinSock 2.0, the ATM APIs, and Sun Microsystems's Solstice Bandwidth Reservation are examples), the applications rarely use those functions of the API. Allowing the application to control QoS through an API also has one major danger: All users may request the highest priority, thereby making the priority scheme unworkable. "If upgrades are free, everyone will fly first class." For that reason, most network administrations either disallow API requests for QoS, or they validate those requests through the use of a network-controlled policy server.

Policy servers, which entered production use in 1999, allow the network management to control the use of APIs to request QoS. They also make the job of configuring and managing QoS much easier. The policy server is configured to identify users and applications, usually through integration with the security system, and it then refers to a directory listing that tells it which QoS levels the user and application are allowed to use, under which circumstances (time of day, day of month, etc.). The policy server then configures the network devices and validates all QoS requests that are received by the network from the APIs. Special software is required in the network devices to send and receive policy information from the policy servers.

The granularity of the QoS control also has to be considered. Granularity refers to the fineness of the control, both in terms of distinguishing individual flows so that they can be individually controlled and in terms of the fineness or coarseness of the QoS control that's placed on those flows. Some QoS technologies permit individual control of flows, with each flow precisely identified and separately handled through the entire network or through major portions of that network. Other technologies group the flows into QoS classes in which all the flows in a class have identical or very similar requirements, greatly simplifying the job of the equipment in the network core. It's important to note if the application's flows can be grouped in this manner, or if there's something so unusual about them that they will have to be specially identified and treated separately. For example, consider whether there is an absolute need to be given priority over other flows or whether there is a strange combination of QoS requirements (though this will probably be determined later, in the design stage). It's also important to consider whether the users will need to make frequent changes in the QoS level furnished to their application.

Administrative Domains

Within an enterprise, different groups may control different portions of the network; for example, one group may control the network's WAN backbone, while the LANs and MANs within local areas may be controlled, and possibly funded, by local organizations. It's important to note that there may be funding boundaries as well as control boundaries; the QoS solutions will need to work across administrative borders and may need new equipment for which all groups must find funding.

If data traffic passes through networks that are not controlled by the enterprise, such as through public networks or network pathways (tunnels) through another organization's network, those situations must be clearly indicated on the geography diagram. QoS control of such situations may require special consideration. For example, interfaces with the outside organization's QoS capabilities may be needed, or it may be necessary to arrange for separate, parallel paths through that organization's network, with different groups of QoS characteristics assigned to each path. By using separate, parallel paths, the outside network wouldn't need to be able to communicate about QoS; all the traffic sorting would be done before the traffic is given to the outside network for transport. (See Figure 4.9.)

It's also important to note boundaries between outside networks. It may be necessary to arrange for QoS information to cross those boundaries, even though they aren't contiguous with the enterprise. The enterprise network administrators may need to become involved in the agreements that are made between outside services, or, at least, they may need assurances that their service providers have made arrangements for QoS compatibility with other service providers in the enterprise's data flow path.

The issue of controlling the end user's software and network interfaces must also be understood. Many QoS solutions require the installation of software in the user machine; some also require specific connection hardware. Even if software or hardware doesn't need to be installed, the network administration may need to control the user machine's configuration, and it may be necessary for the network management systems to interact with the machine to debug programs or to monitor network performance.

Security issues certainly interact with QoS. Security may affect the QoS information that can be sent through the network. It can also affect flow paths and therefore the routes along which QoS facilities must be installed. Security is also involved in the move toward standardized databases that hold both security and QoS information for traffic control. Here, we're primarily interested in any flow path alterations and control issues caused by security. For example, there may be gateways that are network hot spots, where many traffic flows converge and must pass through security barriers; such hot spots may need QoS facilities to keep

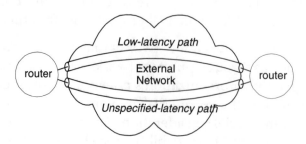

Figure 4.9 Using tunnels with different QoS specifications.

the traffic flowing smoothly. Or security restrictions and firewalls may hamper the interchange of QoS information among network components.

Finally, there is the issue of political boundaries. Some countries have regulations about the transport of data across their borders that may affect flow paths and, therefore, the placement of QoS facilities.

All of these considerations about administrative domains may affect the QoS designs, and, therefore, the flows should be carefully examined to see if they should be modified. The boundaries of the administrative domains, and any necessary flow modifications, should be shown on the charts that were developed for the Flow Pattern specification.

Guarantees, Alternatives, and Audit

QoS control can be fine or coarse, ranging from precise guarantees of latency, jitter, error rate, bandwidth, and other characteristics, all the way to simple prioritization with no other guarantees. Prioritization is simpler to implement than absolute guarantees, but when the workload on the network peaks, all prioritized flows suffer—although the flows with higher priorities probably suffer less than the others. At this stage in the process of collecting QoS requirements, it's time to go back over those requirements and see how strict they are. Could they be met most of the time by prioritization? Will the users understand if their performance degrades at times of heavy workload?

In some cases, the network administrators may find themselves competing with outside suppliers of connectivity. These suppliers often offer fixed-rate leased lines, such as T1 or E1 links, or their equivalent Constant Bit Rate (CBR) facilities. Although the user's application might be better served by latency guarantees, administrators forced to compete with bandwidth guarantees (the result of CBR links) may find that they have to provide bandwidth QoS even when it's not the best technical solution for the user. Some of the new QoS technologies, discussed in Chapter 7, try to provide the equivalent of such CBR facilities within packet-based backbones.

Along with prioritization and guarantees of network QoS performance come audit requirements. Users who demand QoS guarantees, and who probably will also have service-level agreements, will want their service levels audited. There are a number of different mechanisms for this; a few were discussed in this chapter's section entitled "Availability," and more are discussed in Chapter 7. The question here is whether an audit is needed at all, and whether detailed usage and performance information must be collected for all users or for a sample of the users. Such information can be expensive to collect if all of the users must be monitored. Sampling of performance from a few user locations equipped with monitoring software, or from proxy agents that represent users and run standardized transaction scripts, can be a more reasonable way of collecting the information, especially when coupled with usage statistics from the network or from policy servers.

Summary

Taking the results from Chapters 2 and 3, in this chapter we finally derive the network-level QoS specifications. We specify the application geography and topology, looking for areas where we may be using LAN or WAN technologies and for areas that may have poor QoS facilities available. We evaluate the need of the application for diffuse traffic flows, and for multicasting and broadcasting; then we look at the bandwidth involved. We also quantify the requirements for latency and jitter, and the chapter explains the origins of network-level latency and jitter as a complement to Chapter 3's discussions of higher-layer latency. Finally, we look at error and availability requirements, and we discuss the various types of control over the QoS that the users and administrators might want.

Network QoS Specifications for Applications

Application Name:

Flow and User Group Identification:

Contacts:

Development Status and Plan:

Rollout Plan (capabilities, locations, dates):

Each application may have different groups of users and data flows with different QoS requirements and specifications; these should be specified separately.

Geography:
Draw a diagram of the geography, showing:

1. Geographic clustering that could use a LAN or MAN

2. Long-latency links (e.g., satellite)

3. Restricted-bandwidth links (e.g., using wireless LANs, Ricochet, dial-up, etc.)

4. High-error links (e.g., mobile)

Traffic Flow Pattern, including Multicast/Broadcast:
Overlaid on the geography, draw a diagram of the flow pattern, showing, for each major class of user and for each direction of traffic flow:

1. Application flows, including client/server and server/server

2. Multicast and broadcast patterns, including any user clustering

3. External multicast servers, reflectors, transcoders, etc.

4. Flow patterns for unusual applications situations, including partial application or network failure and including database update and resynchronization

Protocols:
Overlaid on the flow pattern, note the protocols used and the amount of their use, showing:

1. Network-layer and transport-layer protocols used by the application, including multicast

2. Application-layer protocols that are designed to work with QoS or that are sensitive to QoS

continues

Bandwidth Usage Pattern:

Overlaid on the flow pattern, note the major bandwidth requirements, showing:

1. Bandwidth variation pattern; average and maximum bandwidth; burst duration
2. Time-of-day and other calendar-related variations

Bandwidth Regulation:

1. Mechanism (if any) for application to respond to feedback about available bandwidth
2. Mechanism (if any) to tag packets for selective discard if bandwidth is restricted

Latency and Jitter:

1. One-way latency and jitter requirements, beyond which data is useless
2. Percentage (if any) of data packets allowed to fail the latency and jitter requirements

Error Characteristics:

1. Definition of Error, possibly including acceptable Bit Error Rate, Packet Loss Ratio (including packet size) Note: this may be different for different flows in a multicast.
2. Dependence (if any) of acceptable error rate on the particular packets that are lost
3. Ability of application to recover useful data from packets containing errors

Availability:

1. Time-of-day and other calendar-related sensitivities
2. Definition of Unavailable (error rate and pattern threshold, call blocking, etc.)
3. Definition of Connected (end-to-end, to the network backbone, etc.)

QoS Control and Guarantees:

1. QoS characteristics to be controlled by network administrators only

2. Need for frequent changes in QoS furnished to application

3. Willingness of users to accept relative priorities instead of strict QoS guarantees

4. QoS characteristics, if any, to be directly controlled through application API; of those, characteristics to be validated through network policy servers

5. Method for identifying the flows in this particular case to the required level of granularity (protocol ID, address pairs, port numbers, class ID, API commands, etc.)

6. Overlaid on the flow pattern, the administrative and security domains through which the flows must pass

7. Willingness of users to allow installation of network control software within user machines

8. Accounting mechanism (fixed per-seat rate, variable based on usage, SLA, etc.)

9. Required proof that QoS is being provided (none, statistical sample, proxy measurements, direct end-to-end measurements, etc.)

10. Penalties for unacceptable performance

11. External alternatives under consideration and the rationale (e.g., procurement of dedicated bandwidth from public carriers)

CHAPTER 5

Requirements Methodology

T he preliminary work of describing user, enterprise, application, and infrastructure requirements was done in the preceding chapters. Those chapters included detailed definitions, examples, and sets of questions that should be used while interviewing users and application designers to develop the network QoS requirements. Chapter 2, "Enterprise-Wide and User Requirements," Chapter 3, "Applications and Infrastructure Issues," and Chapter 4, "Network QoS Design Specifications," helped build the knowledge that network designers need by discussing the network QoS requirements in detail, so the network designers know what they're aiming for—what they need to learn from the application designers and users, and why. The chapters looked at the common application processes and functions that require network QoS facilities, such as speech and video compression, to help network designers learn enough about them to be able to ask reasonable applications-level questions and translate the answers into information that's useful to them while, at the same time, helping the application designers and users to make good choices about their use of network services.

This chapter now integrates all that work into a single methodology to produce the final network QoS requirements. (Those requirements were outlined in three summary lists at the end of the preceding chapters: "Network QoS Specifications for Applications" at the end of Chapter 4, "Infrastructure Considerations and Constraints" at the end of Chapter 3, and "Enterprise-Wide Requirements and Constraints" at the end of Chapter 2.) By tracing the requirements from the user's needs, through the various applications and technologies used to satisfy that need, we'll build a structure for evaluating any user application and reducing it to technical requirements on the underlying network. At the end of this requirements process, we'll have a concise, technical statement of the QoS capabilities that the network must provide. We can take that statement into the next part of the book, in which we evaluate the various QoS technologies to see which ones will help us meet those requirements and at what costs. We can then work with suppliers to make reasonable cost/benefit decisions about providing QoS capabilities.

A major part of the design methodology involves the discussions among managers, users, user application specialists, and network specialists about the trade-offs that must be made in the choice of user applications. It's critical that the networking specialists understand enough about the technologies underlying the user applications to be able to follow, and sometimes guide, those discussions.

The problem is that until their application is placed in production, or until a network architect discusses the issue with them in a meeting, many users and application specialists may not even be aware of the impact that the network can have on their application. They may not have realized that they have to dig down into some of their own assumptions and some of the assumptions of the application designers to find the parameters that will optimize the fit with the network. Applications that have worked well on dedicated LANs may have parameters that can be modified to optimize their operation on shared WANs, but the application designers may never have used them. Custom-designed applications may be designed for high-speed LANs simply because the designers were unaware of the requirements of WAN technologies, and they wouldn't find out their error until the cost of changing the design is exorbitant. Therefore, it's the job of the network architect to bring these issues to light for consideration.

Users, application developers, and network specialists should work together to refine the choices of particular applications or application families, because those choices can have a major impact on the network's cost and structure. In many cases, the exact application does not need to be known, but discussions about the available applications or application families and their characteristic network requirements, cost, and performance trade-offs will help users focus on the network and cost implications of their initial requirements list. As the user and technical groups work together, the technical network requirements and the trade-offs among various application families should become clearer.

The network QoS requirements, as developed from the user requirements, applications requirements, choices of application communications protocols, and the network topology of the applications are all then weighed against costs and the overall enterprise principles and environment. The final cost/benefit evaluation needed to decide about the level of QoS to be furnished to each application can then be performed. In some cases it may be found that the cost for providing QoS is so high that the enterprise is unwilling to make the investment—but that can only be determined after the cost is known. Therefore, it's best if this methodology can be followed in detail for the major applications that may need QoS, and an abbreviated version of it should also be useful in performing quick evaluations of smaller applications.

In many cases, of course, an enterprise is simply too large or too complex for this methodology. In such cases, this chapter can serve as a guide during the design of a methodology to handle the enterprise's particular situation. Many very large enterprises may evolve a QoS architecture that consists of islands of QoS capabilities interconnected by simple Class of Service (CoS) technology. This methodology can help as those localized QoS designs are developed and as the considerations for the Class of Service interconnections are devised.

The detailed flow of the methodology begins with three parallel tasks, labeled A1, A2, and A3 in the sidebar "Applications Requirements Methodology" that follows:

- The network architects must solicit input from the enterprise managers about the overall enterprise environment and about project planning, budget restraints, and cost-recovery methods.

- They must understand the existing network facilities and the opportunities and costs of network component reuse and expansion.

- The architects must meet with network end-users, present and future, to learn about their current and proposed applications.

The first two tasks are described in the "Enterprise Requirements" section of Chapter 2 and the "Infrastructure Considerations and Constraints" section of Chapter 3. The third task, however, takes the greatest effort and needs further discussion.

Applications Requirements Methodology

A1: Network architects meet with enterprise managers to understand and document relevant enterprise principles and to discuss project planning, budget constraints, and cost-recovery methods. (Chapter 2)

A2: Network architects document the technical considerations and constraints on network redesign, including adaptability of existing networks and cost considerations for changing and adding to the existing network infrastructure. (Chapter 3)

A3: Advisory groups of users help determine the probable network applications and give us the user's view of acceptable performance. (Chapter 2)

B: Users meet with applications and network specialists to refine the choice of application, or application family, to the extent necessary to make network QoS technology decisions. Network designers document application designs and network design considerations, including user locations and user-oriented QoS requirements (availability, guarantees and control, specialized measures). (Chapters 2 and 3)

C: The choice of applications family and the topology of the application results in additional technical requirements, which are caused by the demands of the particular applications and by the demands of the protocols used by those applications. These network requirements are discussed with applications designers and documented. (Chapters 3 and 4)

User Requirements

User expectations help form some of the first network requirements, and these may be independent of the particular applications used. We therefore begin by finding and working with the network users. Typically, an advisory board is formed, composed of the major users of the network. They should be chosen from all the user departments, both to ensure that all of the critical applications are included and to avoid later political problems caused by users who weren't consulted and who are justifiably upset. Although the people on the advisory board may not represent all of the user groups, they should be sufficiently knowledgeable about the organization to be able to find those groups, wherever they are hidden. Members of research, marketing, and HR groups may know of unusual network applications that may be critical to the long-term growth of the company but that, at first glance, aren't as obvious as the main-line manufacturing, sales, financial, and personnel applications.

Certainly, all the users of important network applications should be included in the network design conferences, if only through written user surveys. A small, but important application can suddenly cause major issues if a new design doesn't support it! Review of all existing network protocols can bring some of these applications to the surface. For example, many manufacturing plants may use equipment that depends on network protocols that are obsolete today, but often the manufacturing equipment can be retrofitted only at enormous cost. Older DECnet, LAT, polling, and similar protocols are typical examples of this situation. They may have rigid network QoS requirements that must be met if the protocol is to work. Unfortunately, ways of encapsulating the protocol within a modern protocol may not solve the problem if end-to-end time delay is an issue and technical workarounds cannot be found. All of these older protocols must be found; the applications requiring their use must be located; and their data transport needs must be understood.

Because we need to plan for future network applications, it's also important to locate users who aren't on the network yet. In today's fast-changing world, much of the enterprise's future growth may depend on new uses of the network infrastructure that simply aren't on the network today in any form whatsoever. Many of the applications that most need QoS facilities are precisely those that are not yet on the network—possibly because they can't function reliably without QoS. Applications such as packet voice, teleconferencing, and distance learning may be waiting in the wings, ready for use on the network when QoS facilities appear—or when enough other enterprises use them that everyone assumes the corporate network is ready, whether or not it actually is. The time to find the users of these future applications is before their near-term plans depend on them, while the networking managers can still affect the choices of application and the user groups can fully understand the implications of their decisions in terms of network costs and performance.

The research, marketing, and HR groups can be very helpful in finding future users, and they can represent those users in the discussions. At the same time, they will become more knowledgeable about network-based possibilities themselves. These groups are usually responsible for future planning of products and services that will use the network in innovative ways, and their members may go to conferences and read business journals that contain the seeds of ideas that will, over the years, become network applications. Remember that these groups may hide as very small units within larger organizations, such as sales or manufacturing.

But a change in the sales organization's way of doing business by using Web-based or client/server applications will have major impacts on the network.

The enterprise's telecommunications groups are also important future users of the network backbone. They will certainly be aware of users who are discussing new voice and video applications, and they can be valuable sources of information about alternatives to QoS strategies on a shared multiservice network. For example, they are in a position to be able to help evaluate the actual cost of using temporary ISDN links for teleconferencing instead of installing QoS facilities to enable teleconferencing over the enterprise's multiservice backbone. They'll also be aware of changes in telephone company tariffs and service offerings, so they are valuable participants in later discussions about the cost trade-offs of QoS alternatives.

Once we've found the users and potential users of the network, we can begin to work with them to understand why they want to use the network and to understand their expectations. The users can tell us what they're doing on the network now, and what they'd like to do if the technology is there and the cost is reasonable. They can also explain what their assumptions are about performance and cost. And they may be able to tell us the advantages that new network uses will bring to the enterprise—which will help justify the expense of new QoS and network equipment and services. This process is discussed in detail, with the necessary background information, in Chapter 2; it is summarized here.

In this step, we first derive those hard QoS requirements that we can obtain simply by working with network users, before we begin to dig into the insides of the applications and its designs. We can do this because certain applications, such as person-to-person voice communications, have some network requirements that aren't dependent on the particular application or network technology used. These hard requirements probably won't change as discussions with application designers and network architects progress, and we should be able to quantify them and thereby begin our list of network requirements.

Typical hard QoS requirements that should be found at this stage are as follows:

- End-to-end latency as seen by the application users; e.g., for interactive voice or video.

- Bandwidth for batch transfer over a time interval; e.g., a guarantee that one megabyte can be successfully transferred over any five-hour period.

- Bandwidth for online data processing over a time interval; e.g., a guarantee that end-to-end throughput of 20 kbps will be available between the hours of 8 A.M. and 7 P.M. local time.

- Availability over a time interval; e.g., the network will meet its transport requirements for at least 98 percent of the 10-minute intervals during the work day and will never fail its availability requirement for more than six consecutive intervals.

- Control of QoS characteristics by the application's users; e.g., allowing users to obtain a better grade of service (latency, bandwidth, availability) through a command on their application's user interface or by contacting network management.

We also need to know the answers to some standard administrative questions that any network manager asks when new users or applications are introduced. These answers will be needed when we're evaluating the various QoS technologies.

- What are the geographic locations of the users and the application servers? Are some of these users or servers in geographic locations that have restricted or unusually expensive choices in communications links? How are the users and servers grouped topologically; can they be clustered on LANs?

- Are there requirements for mobility? Will there be dial-in users? Will there be untethered (radio or equivalent) users? Will the users expect the same performance while mobile? What are the performance and error characteristics of the mobile technologies, if they've been chosen? Where, geographically, will these mobile users be located?

- What are the alternatives that are being considered? Are users allowed to go outside the enterprise to buy network capacity, and, if so, how is that capacity offered? (Will the in-house networking people be competing with fixed-capacity leased lines or with a more sophisticated, variable-bandwidth product?)

- What are the billing procedures, and how much money is available? What accounting method is required, or expected? Are users expecting to pay a fixed rate, or are they expecting a variable rate based on usage or on a service-level agreement for bandwidth and performance? What are users expecting to pay? Do users expect that networking costs will decrease over time, regardless of additional technical or geographical requirements? Are they willing to pay a premium for premium services?

The user requirements listed thus far are listed as hard requirements that will probably not change and can probably be found by discussions with nontechnical users. Many of the requirements that are developed during initial discussions with users are softer, however. They depend more on the particular applications used or on trade-offs between cost and quality. Soft requirements may change, or we might find that there's some difficulty in defining them precisely. The goal when working with users at this point is to list the possible trade-offs for the soft requirements. The list will help structure the discussion when we meet with the application designers who can help to focus the decisions and reach some conclusions about the QoS requirements.

An example of a soft requirement is driven by the possible cost sensitivity of packet voice communications. Some users may be willing to trade voice quality and user-perceived end-to-end latency for cost reduction. Their requirement for end-to-end latency as seen by the user may therefore vary depending on the cost of providing low-latency connections and compression equipment; it's a soft requirement to be taken to the next phase of the requirements process for discussions with applications technologists. Such users should list the possible voice quality versus cost trade-offs that they are willing to consider.

Another example is driven by the need for students in a Distance Learning classroom to communicate with their instructor. The instructors and course developers, who are the users of the distance learning classrooms, may start with a requirement for full-motion, two-way videoconferencing between students and instructors. After all, that permits the greatest amount of interaction. Unlike hard requirements, however, users could decide that this requirement could be modified and still permit distance learning to function. The users might be influenced by cost considerations to move away from full-motion, two-way videoconferencing and toward the use of an audio teleconference for student responses, possibly with a computer whiteboard capability. The hard requirement for latency remains, but the requirement for the bandwidth to support video is a soft one. The users should consider the cost that they're willing to bear to provide increasing levels of student communications.

The typical soft QoS requirements that are found at this stage are the result of user wish-lists of features; they're in the same areas as the hard QoS application requirements, but they have additional considerations associated with them. The easiest way to find soft QoS requirements is simply to ask users what they'd like to have if transmission were free and instantaneous, then work toward the opposite situation, that of expensive and slow, to see what happens to the hard requirements.

Applications Requirements

The next step, labeled B in the sidebar, is to try to make some of the softer user requirements more accurate by discussing the user applications with applications technology experts, as summarized here and discussed in detail in Chapter 3, with some supporting information in Chapter 4. The experts introduce a dose of reality into the user expectations, and they may also know of alternative applications that can provide the users with the result they want for lower cost or with less impact on the network. It's at this stage that the first considerations of network cost versus user expectations are made. The goal is still not to define the final network QoS technical requirements; rather, it's to help the users develop a reasonable set of expectations for the performance and cost of the applications that they are going to place on the network.

Users, application technologists, and network specialists must all participate in these meetings. The users know what they'd like to have, and the application technologists know some of the technical implications of those requests. Their knowledge of which design concepts have worked successfully in other installations can be very valuable at this stage. The network specialists understand the overall design of the enterprise's networks and can work with the applications technologists to choose a set of reasonable applications technologies to suit the user's needs. The final applications may not be chosen, and all the requirements may not be completely firm, but these discussions will move the user's vision of the applications performance closer to what will eventually be implemented. This will help set the user expectations appropriately—always a good step—and it will at the same time provide a firmer basis for subsequent development of the technical QoS requirements specifications.

The previous examples of soft requirements—voice latency considerations and distance learning's desire for full-motion, two-way video—

are also good examples of requirements that undergo some firming at this stage. Voice application technologists could demonstrate the actual effect of increased latency on voice communications, and they could provide the results of industry experience with the acceptability of such increased latency in various work situations. They could discuss the various types of voice compression and their implications in terms of network requirements and user reactions to the voice quality provided. Similarly, distance learning applications specialists could show the various methods used for student interaction with instructors, some of which may be new concepts to the enterprise's instructors and course developers. Gross estimates of cost, complexity, and student acceptance may be all that's needed to help narrow the broad range of options for distance learning, making the subsequent job of the network designer much easier.

To help get the greatest benefit from these discussions, the network specialists guiding them should be sure to raise the following application issues related to QoS, in addition to any other issues important to the organization:

- Possible alternatives to high-bandwidth, low-latency communications needs

- The willingness of users to accept degraded application performance over high-latency, high-error-rate, or low-bandwidth networks, the probability that these situations will be encountered in the enterprise's normal use, and the ability of the application to adapt to these situations

- The willingness of users to accept prioritization instead of strict QoS guarantees

- The expectation of the users for application availability, and the ability of the application to provide that availability if the underlying transport is having availability problems

- The industry experience with the application in networks similar to the enterprise's network; for example, in networks with the same latency and bandwidth characteristics

- The management of the application; e.g., the need for massive file downloads to perform application client updates, or the need for specialized end-to-end monitoring and management through the network to provide quick-response problem solving in a complex client/server environment.

In the process of discussing these issues, application technologists can work with the network specialists to refine or relax the evolving user-level QoS specifications based on their knowledge of the standard techniques for building certain classes of applications. We aren't primarily interested in the details of the application, but, instead, we're really interested in the application's network demands. For example, transaction applications with powerful client-end processing may be able to accept and buffer transactions even when the network is unavailable. The application technologists may be able to relax the requirements for high availability connections if discussions with the users reveal that their particular needs could be satisfied by such industry-standard buffering methods. This relaxation in requirements can be made even if the final application platform is not yet chosen, as it could be put into the application specification without greatly restricting the possible platform choices. The result might be a requirement for availability that has a particular cost range associated with it, based on the anticipated cost of the buffering solution, rather than being a rigid requirement that cannot be changed for any reason.

The applications specialists may also discover that the users are asking for something that's impractical from an applications viewpoint, or that's soon to be obsolete, or that is better solved by a completely different family of applications. That may start a whole new chain of user thought, leading to a completely different set of network QoS requirements. It's better to discover that at the early stages of network design than at later stages, when major design choices may have been made to accommodate an application that will never be built.

Network Requirements

The preceding steps were designed to produce a set of realistic, reasonably stable end-user requirements. Having determined those end-user requirements as much as possible, it's now time to turn to the QoS requirements that those applications will place on the network. This is step C in the sidebar, summarized here and discussed in detail primarily in Chapter 4, with supporting information from Chapter 3.

The applications technologists, who were focused on the user needs in the previous step, must now focus on the network-related needs of their applications. Now they'll work with the networking specialists to develop a set of technical requirements that will describe what the network must provide as a base for their applications, to enable those applications to meet the user expectations. The hard and soft QoS requirements that the users placed on the applications must now be converted into application designs and network-level QoS requirements. In many cases, the application designers will be working with the networking specialists to find ways to handle the requirements from the users without requiring complex applications software or expensive underlying networks.

It's important to note that the application designers need more than just a list of network services and costs. Many different services can be offered by a network, and some of them place far greater loads on the network infrastructure than others. In some cases, two different network services might be equally easy for the applications designer to use, but one might save huge amounts of time, money, and aggravation for the network designers and operators when compared to the other. Similarly, two different network services that are equally easy for the network designer to implement might have completely different implications for application design. Choosing one of them arbitrarily, without the assistance of the applications designers, would be a wasted opportunity. The application designers and the network specialists must work together, moving both the applications design and the network design toward each other. The goal is to get people to look at design assumptions and alternatives before implementation problems force them to do so, before they've built a system based on assumptions about application or network performance that can't be met.

Cooperation on application and network design has many advantages. Potential problems can be found early, as networking specialists have usually seen what has happened to many applications as they were rolled out across the corporate networks, and as they have a better idea than the application designers of what the new networking technologies will, and won't, do. Network and applications designers won't be unpleasantly surprised when new applications move from the development labs onto the enterprise network. Applications designers may learn about some of the counter-intuitive quirks of standard network communications systems, before their own design is caught in a trap by some so-called feature that occurs rarely, and never (of course!) during system development, but which may be deadly to production systems.

Application designers may also learn of networking options that they didn't know existed and that simplify their job considerably. Through cooperative design, the application and network designers will probably be able to build systems that compensate for each other's weaknesses without exorbitant expense. For example, cooperative design could help by building applications that use local storage and preliminary processing to compensate for poor or often-interrupted communications links in developing countries. The alternative in such situations is usually the use of expensive redundant communications links, satellites, or other facilities.

For the networking specialists, these design sessions are the chance to influence an application's network design in the early stages, before it becomes cast in stone and difficult to change. Asking the correct QoS questions early in the development cycle should get everyone thinking deeply enough so that most QoS-related answers won't change as the application goes through its implementation cycle. The network designers will therefore have the information needed to plan realistically.

But the network staff has another job, besides that of assisting the applications designers as they design and build their applications. The network staff also has to build the list of network QoS requirements shown in the summary list at the end of Chapter 4, "Network QoS Specifications for Applications." That list summarizes the network QoS facilities that the applications will require, and it summarizes them in a way that will be useful as the network designers evaluate and price the various options for building the architecture and topology of the network.

As we can see, network designers must be knowledgeable both in the design of the QoS facilities of the networks themselves and in the design of applications that use networks. They have to understand the applications and the user needs well enough to create the list of technical QoS requirements that will guide the network design, and they must be also be aware of all the network service options that the network could be built to support. Understanding the common ways in which applications use (and misuse) networks is a major part of that knowledge.

Summary

This chapter takes a brief break from the technical content of the rest of the book to look back over the requirements phase and develop a methodology that will lead the reader through the process of developing QoS specifications. It outlines a plan for talking with enterprise managers, network users, and applications designers, working with them to develop their ideas for network use at the same time that they're contributing to the QoS design. It's important to understand all of the major existing applications, and their requirements; in some cases, the most rational step may be to isolate some of these applications from the network if their demands would be too great. It's equally important to dig out information about upcoming network applications, as these may have a massive impact on the network. Many of these new applications may be very small, hidden in corners of the organization when the QoS design is first being performed. They can cause a lot of trouble if the network architect isn't prepared, and if the application designers don't take the network capabilities into consideration when building them.

CHAPTER 6

Basic QoS Technologies

This chapter is a tutorial about the underlying technologies used to provide the Quality of Service solutions discussed in the next chapter. Technologies discussed here include the application program's QoS interface, other methods of signaling for QoS, queuing techniques, and traffic shaping technologies.

The first section of this chapter discusses signaling and marking technologies, which are used to request a specific level of network service. These requests can be explicit, through the use of the Application Program Interface (API) to the operating system or the use of special-purpose fields in the outgoing messages. They can also be implicit, through the use of preconfigured network addresses, physical ports, and other methods outside the control of the programmer.

Allowing programmers and users to request their own QoS level can result in chaos; that's the reason why sophisticated networks include an admission control and policing function, which is discussed in the second section of this chapter, "Admission Control and Policing."

The third section, "Statistical Behavior," discusses the statistical behavior of Ethernet and Internet traffic, in preparation for the fourth section, "Queuing and Scheduling," and the fifth section, "Traffic Shaping," which discuss queuing techniques and traffic shaping technologies, respectively.

Signaling and Marking

QoS signaling and marking are used to tell the network what type of special handling, if any, to apply to a particular flow. QoS handling is signaled when packets enter the network, and, in some cases, packets may be explicitly marked in their headers to indicate the QoS to be applied as the packets make their way through the network devices and links. This QoS marking can be applied by network devices when the flow enters the network, or it can be set by the user before entry as a form of explicit signaling.

There are two types of QoS signaling: implicit and explicit. Implicit signaling uses information that wasn't originally intended for control of QoS, such as network addresses and protocol identifiers. With implicit signaling, the network manager has complete control over the allocation of service. End users and application programmers don't have any direct control over the QoS that they receive, as they can't signal it through an API. Instead, they must make arrangements with the network administrator to configure the network to give them special handling when they use specific network addresses, protocols, or physical ports.

Explicit signaling allows end users and application programmers to request specific levels of QoS directly, through an API that the programmer can manipulate. The network manager's task in verifying the allowed QoS levels is more complex in this case than in the case of implicit signaling, where there's no direct user control. Both implicit and explicit

What Is a Flow?

A flow is a sequence of packets between a specific sender and a specific receiver. In some network systems, such as X.25, Frame Relay, and ATM, a flow is the same as the virtual circuit that's explicitly created when the connection is initiated. In other systems, such as IP, a flow may be implicitly defined as a packet sequence in which all packets share the same identifying information. That identifying information is usually the source and destination addresses, ports, and protocol identifier (sometimes called a five-tuple) because all those identifiers, taken together, uniquely identify a flow of data between two network users. In IPv6 and in some other network systems, there may be a special flow identifier or set of associated hop-by-hop circuit tags to provide that unique identification in a system that otherwise doesn't have virtual circuits.

signaling are discussed in detail, followed by an introductory discussion of flow identification and marking.

Implicit Signaling

The simplest type of signaling technology for the network administrator is implicit signaling, and it is still the type most commonly used in IP-based networks. In implicit signaling, the application programmer and the user have no direct control over the requests for special network handling. Instead, the network administrator configures the network devices to assign various priorities or QoS classes to flows depending on flow characteristics such as addresses and protocol type.

An early example of implicit signaling in IP-based networks was caused by the need to give SNA traffic priority over other types of traffic going through routers. Without that priority, the SNA traffic could be delayed, causing the IBM SNA devices to assume that there had been a disconnection in what they thought was a dedicated line. They'd then close their communications session, causing a lot of problems. To avoid these difficulties, implicit signaling was used to detect SNA sessions.

One way of providing implicit signaling is to give special handling to data arriving or departing on certain network physical ports. This can be useful if certain network links are dedicated to specific QoS levels. For example, two routers could be interconnected by two separate links: one an inexpensive, high latency link, and the other an expensive, low latency link. The traffic that absolutely requires low latency could be directed to the low latency link, and at the same time, the router could give that traffic preferential treatment. The receiving routers would also be configured to realize that traffic arriving over the low latency physical link should get preferential treatment through the router's queues and should be routed out of other low latency physical ports whenever possible.

Configuration of signaling that depends on physical ports can be time-consuming and error-prone if there are a large number of network devices involved. Each link that needs special treatment must be configured on each network device, and there are many opportunities for mistakes. The network managers must design special QoS paths through their network, and those paths must be carefully mapped to physical ports on all devices in the path. Early examples of this type of configuration appeared in IBM's hierarchical SNA designs; later examples appeared on IP routers with simple priority queuing based on physical port of entry to the router. Both could be nightmares for configuration in large networks, and large programs were eventually designed to preplan routes thorough the networks and to generate lists of configuration commands for all of the switches or routers.

A simpler method for QoS implicit signaling uses the address fields in the packet headers. The router or other network device is configured by the network administrator to examine the address fields and make a decision based on them. For example, a router could give preference to any packets destined for a certain network address, or to any packets originating from a certain network address. In some cases, both addresses could be used to define a flow to be given special handling. These address-dependent methods are very convenient if the destination address is dedicated to a high-priority application, or if the source address is that of a corporate executive who demands top performance. If the priority of the application cannot be deduced from the address, however, different methods are needed.

One slightly different method is that of using the address port instead of the address itself. The address port is different from a physical port. Instead of being a physical connector into a network device, it's an additional subaddress that's appended to the end of the network address—similar to an extension number used when telephoning into a large company. It's used by the destination to select the appropriate application, and it can be used by network equipment to distinguish among different users and applications at the same network address. Most protocol systems have some method for providing a subaddress, although the name of that subaddress can be different in different protocols. The IP-family uses the term port, but other protocols call similar fields a socket, or a subaddress, or a virtual circuit identifier. In some cases, there's a standard port number associated with a particular application, regardless of where the application is located. For example, the IP-family uses port 23 for the telnet application. With standard port numbers, the network equipment can be configured to recognize applications needing specialized network services regardless of where they are located. In such cases, it's the port number, not the network address, that is used to recognize and set up QoS handling. This is very useful in environments where new users and servers are constantly being installed. It's much easier to configure network devices to give special handling to any flow using a specific, fixed port number than it is to constantly reconfigure all of the network's devices whenever a high-priority end user or server address is added or changed.

It should be noted, however, that the address port may not be sufficient to identify a particular application even if the application's port numbers are fixed. Many modern networks are multiprotocol, and each protocol usually has its own set of port numbers. The packet header's protocol identifier must therefore be used in conjunction with the port number to produce a unique identifier for each application. The IP-family is a good example of this; there are different sets of port numbers for TCP and for UDP, both of which ride within the IP headers. Identifying the telnet application, which uses TCP, actually requires a combination of identifying both the TCP protocol and the TCP protocol's Port 23.

In multiprotocol networks, just using the protocol identifier may be sufficient for identifying flows that need special handling. If a particular protocol is having problems with cross-network latency, jitter, or packet loss because of that protocol's special sensitivity to such things, then it may be possible to configure the network equipment to identify that particular protocol's packets for special handling based on the protocol identifier in the packet's header. Some protocols can sometimes be identified by the range of addresses that they use; multicast is one example of this.

None of these three methods was originally designed to assist in assigning QoS to flows; therefore, they cannot be used blindly, without careful examination of the capabilities of the network equipment and of the peculiarities of the protocols and flows. A couple of examples will illustrate the problems.

First, many networks don't use fixed port numbers for particular applications, or those port numbers are used for only a few of the flows that are involved in the application. The File Transfer Protocol (FTP) from the IP-family initiates its connections on a fixed set of port numbers, but the actual file transfer usually takes place on temporary port number picked for that one transfer alone. Unless each router is able to watch the transfer being established (an impossibility, as the route may shift during establishment and as the overhead is impractical), the routers will be unable to identify the actual ports used for the data transfer. They could give special handling to the initial setup, which almost certainly doesn't need it, and then fail to give special handling to the bulk data transfer, which does.

Another problem arises in networks that don't have end-to-end information embedded in their headers. Many networks conserve packet header space by performing a setup phase at the start of each flow. The setup phase places routing information into all of the transit routers and other network devices. The packet itself carries only minimal identification, and even that identity may change from hop to hop. The routers or other network devices therefore can't look into the header itself to discover the ultimate destination address, protocol, or port number. Instead, that information would have to be stored into each network device at the time that the network route is established.

Finally, even if the end-to-end information is embedded in the header, and the flows needing special treatment can be reliably identified by that information, it can still be a major effort to collect that identity information and configure it into the many network devices that need to know. New applications, users, and servers constantly appear, with their own new network protocols, ports, and addresses. New devices are inserted into the network, and those devices need to be configured with the information about the QoS needs of all of the flows that may go through them. Configuring only the devices in the direct path between a source and destination is not sufficient; modern networks usually have rerouting capabilities, so the QoS information also needs to be sent to devices that could be in an alternate route.

Recently, as discussed in the next chapter, new methods are being designed to track flows and to configure flow QoS information to the involved network components. These methods, generally part of policy-based networking, use the QoS information discovered during connection setup along with network management databases to send QoS commands to all of the network devices in the flow's path. Highly sophisticated versions may combine QoS with security and firewall capabilities. These can identify a new flow when it is initiated, refer to a centrally controlled database system to determine the security and QoS rules that apply, track any temporary port numbers or other identifiers used by the application, then set up a route across the network and configure all the involved network devices for both security and QoS. Simpler versions may use an existing QoS facility or priority field in the packet header to carry some QoS information, but, instead of allowing the application to use the facility or set this field (a topic explored in the next subsection), they examine the flow, determine the appropriate QoS level, and then use the facility or set the header field themselves. This keeps the network management in control of the network QoS, while using some of the facilities originally designed for the application programmers themselves.

Explicit Signaling

Explicit signaling uses QoS signaling facilities that are built into the application programmer's Application Program Interface (API) specifically for the purpose of signaling QoS requirements. These APIs then couple with protocol features that are also designed for QoS signaling. This is unlike the implicit signaling methods described previously, in which non-QoS features are being used for QoS. Even legacy protocols, such as SNA and Token Ring, included facilities for explicit QoS signaling

Examples of the new programmer APIs are the Microsoft Windows WinSock 2.0 and the Sun Microsystems Solstice Bandwidth Reservation Protocol API, both of which support explicit QoS signaling for IP's Resource Reservation Protocol (RSVP), discussed in detail in Chapter 7, "Solution Building Blocks." RSVP allows the programmer to request different types of QoS when initiating the connection, and the network is allowed to accept or reject that request. The programmer APIs for QoS also function for non-IP protocols, such as ATM.

These APIs can be quite complex and can allow the programmer a lot of control of the QoS requested of the network. For example, the WinSock 2.0 API includes the ability for the programmer to specify requested data rates, latency, jitter, cost, and many other factors that can apply to both IP QoS and ATM QoS facilities. For some of these QoS factors, the requested QoS can be changed by the programmer at any time, although the network doesn't have to grant those requests.

Flow Identification and Marking

Marking, also called coloring, is used to indicate the QoS level to be applied to packets as they make their way through the network. It's done by setting an indicator in the packet header, and that indicator may be set explicitly, by the programmer, or implicitly, by network hardware as a result of examination of other packet characteristics. (This implicit marking is usually done by network edge devices, so that the heavily loaded network core devices have to look at only the QoS mark to determine how to handle the packet.)

Many protocols have used the QoS marking technique, including protocols such as Token Ring and the IBM SNA family, but the best example for our use is the marking technique used by the IP protocol family.

Internet Protocol version 4 (IPv4), the current version of IP, was specified by RFC 1349 as having a Type of Service (TOS) byte in its header. This byte contained two separate fields: the precedence field and the type-of-service field. (The original IP specifications, such as RFC 791, defined the priority and type-of-service fields slightly differently.) The precedence field contained three bits, for a total of eight possible values. Based on the U.S. Department of Defense's priority system, it included military priority levels (Routine through CRITIC/ECP) and even higher levels for network control messages. The type-of-service field, in contrast, did not imply importance or priority. Instead, it was to be used to specify the sensitivity of the traffic to different types of QoS. The type-of-service field contained four type-of-service bits; these indicated to the network whether it was to minimize delay, maximize throughput, maximize reliability, or minimize monetary cost. Although it appears that the bit patterns could be combined to create, for example, a packet that needed maximum reliability at minimum cost, this was not allowed. Only one type-of-service value could be chosen.

The main IP RFCs discuss the TOS byte and the actions that should be taken by users and by network equipment. RFC 1349 has a long list of suggestions for type-of-service field settings depending on the application, and RFC 1812 discusses how the routers should handle the various requirements. Some modern routing protocols (for example, OSPF and IS-IS) can handle the construction of different routing tables for different sets of QoS characteristics; they can therefore, in theory, use the type-of-service field to select the particular route to be used.

Nevertheless, the TOS byte was and is almost never used. The normal TCP/IP API doesn't allow the user to set the precedence or the type-of-service field, and most routers therefore ignore it by default. In some cases, network edge equipment or routers can be installed that examine incoming packets from the users, filter them based on some criteria such as network address, protocol, and port, then set the TOS byte for use by the core network equipment and routers. Once the field is reliably set, it is often possible, with some effort, to program a router to examine the TOS byte and take some action as a result.

The original IPv6, the new generation of the IP protocol, contained a priority field with some similarities to that in IPv4. There was a 3-bit priority subfield, with network control traffic as the highest priority, and then there was an additional bit to distinguish between traffic that was sensitive to congestion and able to respond to feedback about bandwidth and traffic that was insensitive and unable to respond. The former included TCP flows; the latter included real-time audio and video. The former type of data was given priorities in accordance with their need for quick interaction (e.g., telnet ranked above HTTP, which ranked above newsgroups); the latter type of data was given priorities in accordance with their sensitivity to packet loss.

The original IPv6 also contained a 24-bit Flow Label field, which could be used to identify individual flows for special handling. The idea was that flows that needed unusual handling would set this field to a non-zero value, and all of the routers that handled the flow could use that value as an index into a hash table of prestored instructions for that flow.

The IPv6 priority field underwent some changes as the protocol was re-designed, and it eventually evolved into an 8-bit Traffic Class field in the RFC 2460 version of IPv6. (It grew by four bits, taking those bits from the Flow Label field in the original IPv6 specification. The Flow Label then became a 20-bit field.) The Traffic Class field was only loosely de-fined, as it was simply a placeholder for the Differentiated Services Byte (DS-Byte).

The Differentiated Services Byte (DS-Byte) is a recent development that replaces the TOS byte in IPv4 and the Traffic Class field in IPv6. RFC 2474, "Definition of the Differentiated Services Field (DS Field) in the IPv4 and IPv6 Headers," is the formal definition of how this new 8-bit field re-places the earlier priority and Type of Service field, so that its use is now uniform regardless of whether the IPv4 or IPv6 protocol is being used. The DS-Byte is discussed in more detail in Chapter 7, but it's useful to mention here that it is not a strict prioritization field. Instead, it allows the definition of many different types of QoS, called Code Points. For example, some of these announce different sensitivities to packet loss, while others provide QoS facilities that make the packet-switched sys-tem appear to be a constant bit rate leased line.

With the coming of the DS-Byte, it's now more probable that programmers will actually begin to use explicit signaling in the IP world. RFC 2460 requires that "the service interface to the IPv6 service within a node must provide a means for an upper-layer protocol to supply the value of the Traffic Class bits . . ." and the new programmer APIs, unlike the previous ones for IP, are being built to allow this.

Admission Control and Policing

As mentioned at the beginning of this chapter, the fact that a programmer, and therefore an end user, can specify QoS levels may lead to difficult situations in the network. If QoS APIs are given to programmers, and, therefore, to end users, the network managers must build a structure that will allow for validation of QoS requests as they arrive. No network can afford simply to grant all QoS requests without checking that the requester is entitled to the resources that are being demanded and that the network is able to grant the use of those resources without affecting previous QoS guarantees. And after the network has agreed to provide an enhanced level of service, it's important to monitor the user to be sure that the amount of traffic being fed into the network doesn't exceed the agreed-on traffic profile. It's the role of admission control and policing to perform those functions.

Admission control evaluates each incoming network service request by looking at the identify of the requester, the traffic load that's going to be imposed on the network, and the service that's being requested. The user can often be identified by his or her network address, but there are many cases in which many users can flow through a single network address, or one user can appear at many addresses. So more sophisticated systems, possibly integrated with security applications, can be used to provide positive user or user group identification. The traffic load is specified by the user during an explicit QoS request, and it typically includes such traffic specifications as the average data rate and the maximum data rate during a data burst and the maximum length of that burst. And finally, the QoS service requested usually includes the category of service (such as constant bit rate or variable bit rate, guaranteed service or prioritization), the required maximum latency and jitter, and the maximum error or packet loss rate (which may include both the error pattern and the associated rates).

The admission control system looks at all of the components of the request and then decides if the request should and can be accepted. The user or user group may not be allowed to make the request, or all of the capacity allocated to that user or user group may have already been allocated. The network itself may not be able to accept the request because of existing commitments or because the network infrastructure is incapable of satisfying the request in any case. Most admission control systems have a centrally controlled database, which may have topologically distributed components, to keep track of user capabilities and the current state of the network's commitments to all users. If the request can't be accepted, the user is normally given the reason for the rejection and may be allowed to modify and resubmit the request.

If a user is accepted and the connection is allowed to proceed, the network must still monitor the user's flow to ensure that it isn't exceeding the traffic specifications submitted as a part of the original network service request. That function is known as policing, and it normally occurs in the edge device where the traffic flow enters the controlled part of the network. The policing system knows about the original traffic specifications, and it may discard or mark packets that exceed that specification. The policing device may contain a specially designed input buffer, configured to match the submitted traffic specifications, and excess entering traffic will simply overflow the buffer and be lost, thereby preventing the network itself from being affected by too much unanticipated traffic. Or the policing device may keep track of the used data rates and turn on a special packet flag in packets that exceed the submitted traffic specifications. That flagged traffic will be carried by the network if there is excess network capacity, but it will be the first traffic discarded if there's a capacity problem anywhere in the network. For that reason, such flags are commonly referred to as discard eligible flags.

In sophisticated network systems, the user may have a traffic specification parameter that allows multiple levels of discard eligible flagging. These different levels of discard eligible flags could differentiate, for example, between crucial packets such as MPEG I frames and less important packets, such as MPEG B frames. The network can then have different levels of response to congestion at some internal node, discarding first all the least important frames, then moving to the next level of discard if congestion hasn't been sufficiently relieved, and so on. Both the end user and the network itself would then be setting the various discard eligible flags, to indicate preferences for discard if there's congestion and to police the traffic specifications.

Statistical Behavior

Almost all of the traffic analysis underlying data communications networks depends on knowing the statistical behavior of the arriving traffic and how that affects the queues inside network devices. Therefore, before starting the next section, on queuing and scheduling, we must look very briefly at the statistical behavior of the traffic that we're trying to handle. For detailed explanations, see, for example, *High-Speed Networks: TCP/IP and ATM Design Principles* [Stallings], from which much of this section is derived.

We'll first look at random arrival of traffic and the results on queues. Random arrival means that there is no correlation among the times that individual traffic packets arrive, and those arrivals are truly random. *In random arrival, the time that each packet arrives is completely independent of the time that any other packet arrives.*

Random arrival is a very convenient assumption that greatly simplifies the mathematics, and it's used to model the arrivals of transactions from a large number of human operators, the arrivals of new remote login connections at servers, and many other situations. However, if the real situation is that arrivals tend to be evenly spaced instead of truly random, then calculations based on random arrival will overestimate the system queuing delays. On the other hand, if the real situation is that arrivals are bunched in groups instead of being truly random (for example, groups of large packets and groups of short acknowledgments), then the calculations based on random arrival will underestimate the system queuing delays.

Our intuition is usually very misleading when we think of the results of random arrival on queuing delays. For example, let's assume that a bank teller can handle precisely one customer every minute, and precisely one customer arrives every minute, with absolutely *no* variation. In that nonrandom world, there would be no queue at all and no delay for service. At the very moment that a customer appears in front of the bank teller, the teller has just become ready to handle that customer. And that customer will leave just before the next customer arrives. There's no rest for the bank teller, but there's no waiting for the customers.

Now let's introduce a tiny bit of randomness: A customer arrives a second early! Because there's *no* resilience in the system, a queue appears.

We can hope that there will be an exactly compensating bit of randomness in a minute or so—a customer who's a second late—and the queue will vanish, but real randomness isn't so convenient. In fact, introducing randomness has a massive effect on the queue size and the resulting delay waiting for a bank teller.

William Stallings, in his book referenced earlier, has a few examples of the effect of randomness on queues. If the arrival rate is half of the rate at which bank tellers can handle customers, bursts of arrivals dissipate rather quickly. There's a lot of resilience, because the system can absorb peaks by spreading out the load to subsequent time intervals. The queue is zero for most of the time, although there are some startlingly large peak queue lengths (more than 500 waiting customers!) as groups of customers arrive (possibly from a commuter train) and then are swiftly handled by the spare capacity of the bank tellers. The average queue length is 43, but that's a bit misleading because of those huge peaks. More than 75 percent of the time, the queue length is zero.

As the arrival rate increases, however, the system's resilience greatly decreases. Excess capacity at times of low demand can't be stored for future busy periods, while times of peak demand can force a queue to grow endlessly, storing trouble for the future. When there's an incoming burst of customers that's greater than the bank tellers' service capacity, the system has to wait longer and longer periods before there's a long-enough below-average arrival rate to allow the bank tellers to catch up with their workload. For example, when the arrival rate is 95 percent of the bank tellers' capacity, there are very few periods during which the queue length is zero, and the average queue length is greater than 1800 waiting customers. When the arrival rate is 99 percent of the bank tellers' capacity, there are virtually no periods during which the queue length is zero, and the average queue length has increased to more than 2500.

Graphs of the relationship between queue length and the server capacity show a distinct knee in the curve at approximately 80 percent of the server's capacity, as shown in Figure 6.1. These graphs have been used for years to predict the delays through server systems and to plan for capacity increases. Without using these graphs, intuition leads most of us to predict linear increases in response time as average system load increases, as shown by the dashed line in Figure 6.1. It's queuing analysis based on random arrivals that is responsible for the common guideline that reminds us to ignore our intuition and plan for increasing the

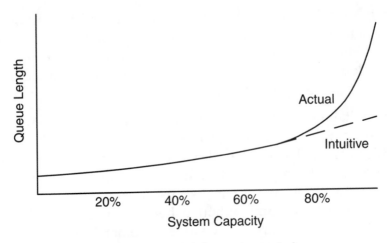

Figure 6.1 Intuitive versus actual queue length for random arrivals.

capacity of the servers when system load approaches 80 percent of the theoretical server capacity.

Although random arrival is very convenient mathematically, it's unfortunately not accurate as a description of actual network behavior in many cases. In the last few years, it has been discovered that the traffic pattern on Ethernet LANs and on the Internet has self-similar, or fractal, qualities instead of being truly random [Sahinoglu].

Self-similar traffic shows the same pattern regardless of changes in scale. If we look at a one-minute period on the Ethernet, we'll see the same traffic pattern as if we looked at a one-hour period. When the traffic pattern doesn't become smoother as we look at larger and larger time periods or greater and greater traffic aggregations (i.e., the total traffic on a major internode trunk as contrasted with the traffic on an individual link to a user), then we have a self-similar pattern. It's impossible to look at a self-similar pattern and decide what the scale is.

Fractal geometry is the well-known example of this behavior; enlarging the scale of a map showing a coastline doesn't decrease or increase the jaggedness of the coast. Many natural objects have fractal characteristics, and modern computer graphics systems use fractal geometry to simplify the drawing of trees, leaves, and other natural objects.

Mathematically, data traffic has self-similar characteristics. It doesn't smooth out as we go to smaller and smaller scales, and the traffic pattern at small scales is very similar to the traffic pattern at large scales. (It has been argued, however, that data traffic becomes less self-similar, and more random arrival, at very large scales and degrees of aggregation.)

Self-similar data traffic can be modeled by advanced probability distributions such as the Pareto distribution. This distribution has a heavy tail; that is, it has much more variability than a purely random-arrival distribution. In a random-arrival distribution, the probability of extreme values occurring decreases greatly as the values increase. If the average value of a measurement is 1, then the probability of a value of 100 appearing is small, the probability of a value of 1000 is very small, and the probability of a value of 10,000 is extremely small. With a heavy-tailed distribution, those probabilities of the values of 1000 and 10,000, while small, aren't nearly as small as with the random-arrival distribution.

Traffic on Ethernet and on the Internet has been measured by researchers and has been shown to have heavy-tailed distributions and self-similar behavior. This isn't surprising, because there are a lot of very long file downloads mixed into short packets and short acknowledgments. This huge variability in file size is a characteristic of heavy-tailed distributions. Such characteristics have also been found inside compressed video traffic, as action scenes (resulting in a large amount of data) are intermixed with more static scenes, and this is similar to the pattern of intermixed inter- and intra- compression blocks and frames.

Some important implications result from the self-similar nature of data traffic. The first is that the required queue length, and therefore the average queuing delay, for self-similar traffic is much longer than for random-arrival traffic. The knee of the curve for self-similar traffic, as shown in Figure 6.2, is to the left of the knee of the curve for random-arrival traffic. The knee appears at approximately 50 to 60 percent of the server's theoretical maximum capacity, instead of at approximately 80 percent. As Stallings says, "If high levels of utilization are required, drastically larger buffers are needed for self-similar traffic than would be predicted based on classical queuing analysis." ([Stallings], p. 200)

Another important implication of self-similar behavior is that combining traffic streams doesn't quickly result in smoother traffic patterns. It's only at the very greatest levels of traffic aggregation, if then, that random-arrival statistics can be used. At lower levels of aggregation, designers must plan for the larger buffers that are characteristically required by self-similar traffic.

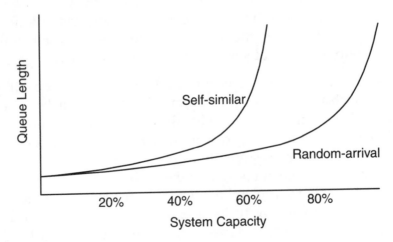

Figure 6.2 Self-similar versus random-arrival traffic queue delays.

Queuing and Scheduling

Now that we've learned a bit about the statistics of data communications traffic, we can begin to examine the various queuing and scheduling methods that have been developed for handling that traffic as it arrives at network devices during times of restricted capacity.

First-In, First-Out Queuing

The default method of queuing incoming traffic when there's temporarily insufficient outgoing bandwidth is first-in, first-out (FIFO). When a packet arrives for an outgoing port that is already busy handling a previous packet, then the newly arriving packet is placed in a queue to wait. There's only one queue for each outgoing port, and packets are stored in the queue in order of arrival. No attention is paid to packet size, priority, or any other criteria. The outgoing port always takes the longest-waiting packet first when it picks a new packet for transmission. Equipment vendors have worked for years on FIFO techniques, and the result is that FIFO is very efficiently implemented.

Although FIFO implementations are efficient, and they are the default for most router configurations, FIFO is not ideal for all situations. FIFO works best when it's used to handle short queues and situations where the packets are of similar length and priority. As queues build, FIFO's disadvantages become more apparent.

The most obvious problem with FIFO is that it doesn't handle priorities. Important flows are delayed behind unimportant ones; there's no way to move high-priority traffic to the head of the queue. If there's a constricted link, then FIFO queuing ensures that a sales rep doing a backup of his 6-GB hard drive during business hours can bring all order-entry traffic in his office virtually to a standstill while that backup travels to the central data center for storage. The backup process will feed a steady, uninterrupted stream of long packets into the link, and all other traffic will have to slip between them.

Another major problem is that FIFO does not discriminate among packets of different lengths. Short packets on Internet backbones usually benefit from low-latency transmission more than long packets, as those short packets are usually protocol acknowledgments, interactive speech packets created by vocoders, and interactive transactions. But FIFO can delay those short packets behind long file transfer packets that don't need the high level of service that they're obtaining. For example, just one 8000-byte file transfer packet could hopelessly delay a 40-byte speech packet, rendering it useless. A result of this is that the average packet delay is longer than if short packets were sent to the head of the queue. For example, one long packet can delay a dozen short packets; average per-packet delay would be much less if those short packets, which don't require much bandwidth, could somehow be moved ahead of the long packet.

Because of the intermixing of long and short packets and because of the lack of prioritization, FIFO introduces considerable jitter into data traffic. This isn't a problem for file transfers and for most transactions, but it's a major problem for interactive audio and video, which need to have large dejitter buffers at the receiving end to remove that jitter.

Finally, we know that FIFO doesn't look at packet priorities, but that doesn't mean that FIFO ensures that all flows have equal access to services. It doesn't care where the packets came from, and greedy flows, which transmit long packets frequently, get a higher share of the available bandwidth than better-behaved flows. A poorly implemented TCP stack, which doesn't back off when there's congestion, will run away with almost all of the available bandwidth when other, better-behaved stacks back off.

Priority Queuing

Using pure FIFO in routers worked reasonably well for many networks, but there was trouble as people began to use gateways to route legacy traffic through packet-switched networks. The legacy traffic, such as IBM's SNA, thought that it had a leased, circuit-switched line; it didn't understand that there could be long, multisecond delays in the delivery of individual protocol blocks. The legacy protocol thought that any delay meant that the link had failed, and it disconnected the endpoints. To avoid this problem, priority queuing was introduced.

Instead of having a single FIFO queue, in priority queuing each output port has a number of FIFO-type queues, one for each priority level. As packets arrive for transmission, the output port looks at the packet's priority and places it in the appropriate queue. When the output port needs a new packet for transmission, it always picks the next available packet from the highest-priority queue. Only if the highest-priority queue is completely empty does the output port look at the next-higher priority queue to find a packet for transmission. This certainly helps the latency performance for the high-priority packets, and it can also improve jitter characteristics if all of the packets at the highest level are of the same approximate length.

Priority queuing isn't perfect, however, and it has some costs in addition to the obvious one of the additional processing needed. As priority queuing is based on FIFO technology, albeit there is now more than one queue per output port, the problem of short packets being delayed behind long ones and the problem of unfair access to services within one priority aren't solved. These FIFO-style difficulties occur within each priority level, exactly as they appeared in the pure FIFO situation. Short packets are delayed behind long ones, resulting in higher average packet delay than if they could go to the head of the line. And greedy stacks can grab bandwidth from better-behaved stacks, as priority queuing doesn't look at individual flows to ensure that all flows have equal access to services within their priority level. Additionally, the effective bandwidth available to TCP flows depends on many factors beyond the control of the priority queuing mechanism, such as total network round-trip delay, bandwidth constrictions at any point in the path, and packet losses resulting in the protocol's cutting its transmit rate.

There are more problems for the lower-priority flows. Priority queuing can cause them to be completely starved, and it will almost certainly increase jitter for them. Bandwidth starvation is worse than it first appears because completely starving a flow cuts off its acknowledgments and flow control signals. The flow collapses, and the endpoints may assume that the connection has completely failed. In effect, the problem that priority queuing was designed to solve—excessive delay in packet delivery—has simply been transferred to lower-priority packets. If these packets can handle the situation, this may be acceptable; if not, there's trouble. If there are a large number of high-priority packets, the situation for lower-priority packets is quite grim. Their access to bandwidth is very quickly constricted, and the seemingly random blocking of access to that bandwidth caused by higher-priority packets results in a massive increase in the jitter for the lower-priority packets.

Fair Queuing

Priority queuing tries to solve the problem of FIFO's inability to differentiate among priorities; fair queuing tries to solve the problem of FIFO's inability to differentiate among flows to ensure equal access to service. Fair queuing tries to keep greedy protocol stacks from grabbing more than their share of the bandwidth; it isolates traffic flows from each other.

In fair queuing, the network device keeps track of individual flows, possibly by examining packet addresses, port numbers, and protocol types. The output port then takes only one packet at a time from each flow, in round-robin fashion, thereby ensuring that no one flow can monopolize the output link. Badly behaved protocol stacks can try to push a lot of packets through the system, but the only result is that their own personal queue will get larger.

There are some problems, however. The first problem with fair queuing is that processor power is needed to classify packets into flows and to manage all the individual queues. The second problem is that after all that work, the bandwidth fairness depends on all packets being the same size. Using fair queuing, a flow with large packets gets more bandwidth than a flow with small packets.

Weighted Fair Queuing

Weighted fair queuing (WFQ) is a very sophisticated form of queuing that is designed to improve the performance of small-packet flows, such as speech and interactive transaction processing, compared to high-volume, large-packet flows such as file transfers. It also enhances the way that fair queuing prevents a single flow from starving other flows. One of the major problems with bandwidth starvation is that it prevents acknowledgments and flow control messages (such as window sizes) from traveling back to the source. WFQ gives low-volume traffic priority over high-volume traffic, which helps move these small packets through the system rapidly.

The operation of weighted fair queuing requires considerable processor power. Whenever it needs to transmit a packet over an outgoing link, an output port examines all packets waiting for transmission and picks the packet that will arrive first at the destination. (A weighting factor that reflects packet priority is also applied, so the actual computation is a bit more complex than indicated here.) In effect, this often moves small packets to the head of the queue, decreasing average packet latencies for them while not greatly affecting the average packet latencies for the larger packets.

A major advantage of weighted fair queuing is that it can be used to place a boundary on the possible queuing delays of individual service categories. Entry to the category must be controlled, but, given that control, it has been proven that WFQ can provide the latency guarantees needed by real-time speech and multimedia traffic. The computations and packet transmission scheduling performed by WFQ guarantee that one flow cannot starve others, and they also allow the network administration to provide latency guarantees.

A major disadvantage of WFQ is that it requires a lot of processor power and has therefore often been restricted to relatively low-speed links (1.5 mbps) or to output ports with specialized processors. It also has more jitter for the highest-priority packets than does priority queuing (see RFC 2598).

Class-Based Queuing and Weighted Round-Robin

Class-based queuing (CBQ) is an attempt to provide fair allocation of bandwidth without requiring massive amounts of processing power in the network devices. Its goal is to provide a method for sharing the available bandwidth among classes of users in accordance with agreed-on allocations among those users. Each class of user is guaranteed a certain minimum bandwidth, and any excess bandwidth is allocated according to rules set up by the network administration. Specific implementations of CBQ have been designed with an entire hierarchy of classes, with, for example, excess capacity redistributed within each branch of the hierarchy as much as possible.

The CBQ system tries to ensure that the average bandwidth allocated to each class over a specified time period is in accordance with the instructions from the network administration. It does this by using a weighted round-robin scheduler, somewhat similar to simple fair queuing, but with the change that the scheduler can take more than one packet per turn from each class's queue. It keeps track of the bandwidth allocated to each class and the number of bytes already sent within the time interval that it's using for bandwidth control. It then takes enough packets from each queue to obtain the number of bytes that the particular queue is allowed during the time interval.

If the scheduler is forced to take more bytes than it wants, because of packet sizes, then it decreases the number of bytes it will take the next time around. This works well on high-speed lines with few traffic classes, as is typical of network backbones. However, if the scheduler visits each class relatively infrequently, because the outgoing line is slow or there are many classes, then there can be temporary unfairness. The scheduler may be forced to take a huge packet from a class, and, as the other classes won't get a chance to regain their fair share until a number of scheduler cycles later, a long time can elapse before the average bandwidth allocation is correct again.

CBQ can also use prioritization as well as bandwidth allocation, trying to ensure that high-priority flows receive precedence over lower-priority flows while also trying to meet the bandwidth requests.

Class-based queuing is a significant advance over FIFO, priority, and fair queuing. It works best on high-speed circuits, where the time to transmit even long packets is quite brief. It can require more processor power than the simpler forms of queuing, although it needs less than WFQ.

Traffic Shaping

When a queue overflows, packets are lost. As very long queues would be expensive and would greatly increase jitter, it's useful to have some mechanism to shape the incoming traffic. The traffic shaping system has two tasks: to force incoming traffic to conform to an agreed-on traffic flow specification and to smooth traffic flow, reducing the chunkiness of data and the need for large queues. We'll look at two categories of traffic-shaping techniques: one category of general traffic-shaping techniques and another category for the specialized techniques used for TCP flows.

General Techniques

The simplest way of shaping traffic is by using the leaky bucket technique and its variant, the token bucket. These are discussed first, followed by the use of class-based queuing as a traffic shaper.

Leaky Bucket

The leaky bucket can be used to create a constant-rate traffic flow from a varying rate flow, as the input rate to the leaky bucket can vary, but the output rate of the leaky bucket is a constant. The capacity of the bucket determines how much excess data can be buffered before data packets must be discarded. Leaky buckets are constructed by using a FIFO queue of the required bucket capacity. For example, if the user of a network service has agreed to a traffic flow specification of 50 kbps, with a maximum burst of 75 kbps for one second, then the output of the leaky bucket is set for a constant bit rate of 50 kbps and the leaky bucket's FIFO must be able to absorb the excess 25 kbits of data.

Leaky buckets are also used to mark or discard incoming flows that exceed a traffic flow specification. When the bucket is filled, additional arriving packets either are marked, typically with a Discard Eligible marking, or are immediately discarded. Packets marked Discard Eligible will be discarded later, if there's congestion within a network device and some packets must be discarded to relieve the congestion.

A problem with the simple leaky bucket is that it cannot take advantage of temporarily available additional bandwidth. Its output is always at a constant rate. The token bucket, discussed next, handles that situation.

Token Bucket

Leaky buckets always produce data at a steady rate, regardless of network conditions. Token bucket systems, in contrast, respond to signals from the network that indicate the amount of capacity available at any given time. Incoming flows can be sorted into different classes, and each class can have its own set of tokens, allowing the network to control the bandwidth allocated to each class.

There's no rule requiring token bucket systems to transmit at a steady rate; they are allowed to burst to the maximum speed of their link as long as they have permission to transmit. A token bucket system obtains permission to transmit data by receiving tokens from the network. Each token allows the token bucket to transmit a certain number of bytes of data. If the network is congested, it will give the token bucket fewer tokens, decreasing the effective data rate; if the network has excess capacity, it will increase the number of tokens given to the token bucket, allowing more data to enter the network. The output from a token bucket can be very bursty if the token bucket has accumulated a large supply of tokens that it can use instantly when a data burst arrives. In some cases a token bucket is followed by a leaky bucket, to prevent a token bucket that has accumulated a large number of tokens from allowing a large burst of traffic to pass through without smoothing.

Because it is good at describing bursty traffic, token bucket terminology is sometimes used to specify traffic flow characteristics, even if token buckets aren't being used to manage those characteristics. For example, the IETF's Integrated Services architecture, described in Chapter 7, describes flows by using a specification, called a Tspec, that's based on token bucket terms.

Class-Based Shaping

Class-based queuing, discussed previously, can be also used to shape traffic by allocating bandwidth to different traffic classes. Data traffic cannot expand its bandwidth use beyond that allowed by the class-based queuing unless spare capacity is available in the system and the queue itself helps smooth out the peaks in the flow.

TCP Techniques

Two specialized techniques were designed for use with TCP: Random Early Detection (RED) and its variant, Weighted RED (WRED), and Rate Control.

Random Early Detection

As discussed in Chapter 3, "Applications and Infrastructure Issues," TCP has a global synchronization problem. Whenever a TCP flow loses a packet, it assumes that there is congestion and drastically cuts back its transmission rate. If a buffer in a router overflows, it's very possible that most of the flows going through that buffer will each lose a packet, and therefore each of those flows will cut their transmission rate. This is very disruptive to all of those flows, and the aggregate data rate is usually cut far more than is necessary to relieve the congestion.

The Random Early Detection (RED) technique was designed to avoid this problem by noticing when a buffer is becoming dangerously full and then by selecting a flow for sacrifice. Because it keeps the buffer from over-flowing and thereby losing many packets from many different flows, RED prevents the global synchronization problem. It sacrifices only a few flows to protect the integrity of many more.

RED operates by examining the average queue length and comparing it to two thresholds. At the higher threshold, RED discards incoming pack-ets because the congestion is already serious; this is the same as the be-havior without RED. But between the two thresholds, congestion is appearing but not yet serious. RED has a complex formula that it uses to decide when to discard a packet, but the effect is to increase the prob-ability of discard as the queue length increases to the upper threshold. The result is that more and more packets are selected for sacrifice as the queue length grows. As the aggregate data rate decreases further with each sacrificed packet because of TCP's reaction to packet loss, the queue size will eventually begin to decrease. This will bring the total queue length out of the danger zone and back below the lower threshold.

RED depends on the correct functioning of modern TCP stacks; it needs the stack to respond to data loss by decreasing its transmission rate. Early TCP implementations don't have that behavior, and neither do most non-TCP protocols. Indeed, other protocols may react badly to RED, as they may immediately retransmit discarded packets, increasing the data rate instead of decreasing it.

Weighted RED is a variation of RED that, instead of picking a flow at random, uses a priority mechanism to pick a low-priority flow for discard.

Rate Control

Rate control [Packeteer] is another technique designed specifically for TCP traffic shaping. Unlike all of the preceding techniques, rate control is considered by some to meddle with the operation of TCP in a way that violates the spirit of the TCP specification. Nevertheless, it is in widespread and successful use.

Rate control depends on TCP's sliding-window flow control. As described in Chapter 3, each TCP acknowledgment tells the sender the number of bytes that can be transmitted without overflowing the receiver's buffer; that number is called the window size. Rate control intercepts this window size and alters it, increasing the number of acknowledgments, decreasing the window size in each acknowledgment, and spacing out the new acknowledgments to smooth the returning flow. An example will make this clearer.

As shown in Figure 6.3, our example begins with the receiver sending an 8000-byte window to the transmitter. The transmitter could then, by

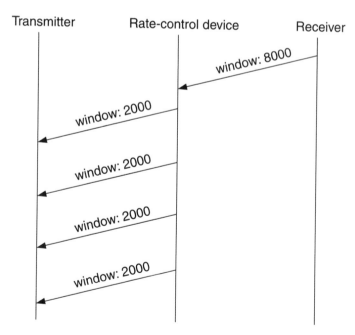

Figure 6.3 TCP rate control example.

the rules of TCP, immediately send one or more packets totaling 8000 bytes. (I'm assuming we're past the Slow Start stage.) The rate control device, inserted into the flow, intercepts the original acknowledgment containing the 8000-byte window and deletes it. It then constructs four new acknowledgments, each containing a 2000-byte window, and sends them to the transmitter. The new acknowledgments are separated in time to ensure that the returning flow will be smooth.

The transmitter is unaware of the fact that these acknowledgments don't come from the receiver, and it responds to them as if they did. Responding to the four separate acknowledgments, the transmitter sends four separate sets of one or more packets, each with a total of up to 2000 bytes. The flow is therefore smoother than if it had received the original, 8000-byte window and responded to it in a burst.

Rate control works only with TCP, as it needs to be able to manipulate the acknowledgment window. It depends on being able to find and alter the contents of that window, and on being able to generate fake acknowledgments that the transmitter cannot distinguish from real acknowledgments. Although this does work, it's a more risky strategy than depending on queuing. It also violates the protocol layering design, as it injects a network-level device into the functioning of an end-to-end protocol. In its favor, however, it must be said that TCP rate control provides a very fine-grained, explicit control of individual flows without losing any packets. Queuing-based traffic control, in contrast, loses the occasional packet because of buffer overflow or because of RED as the TCP flows settle into their proper data rate.

Summary

Chapter 6 is a tutorial on the basic QoS technologies. It starts with a discussion of how flows can be marked for QoS and how QoS requests can be signaled into the network. Implicit signaling is under the control of the network administrator, not the programmer or network user. It makes use of network characteristics such as station address and protocol type to indicate the kind of QoS desired, and it's the most common type of signaling used today. Explicit signaling allows the programmer (and, therefore, the user) to signal the desired QoS through an API or by marking the data packets. This is most common in ATM networks, but it's beginning to appear in other networks as well. When explicit signaling is used, the network administrator must have some mechanism to police the incoming traffic. Otherwise, programmers could just push all their traffic up to the highest priority and flood the network.

The chapter then looks very briefly at the statistical nature of Ethernet and Internet traffic, preparing for later discussions of queuing and of QoS technologies in Chapter 7. It shows that most people's intuitive understanding of queuing is very wrong, and it then goes on to show how Ethernet and the Internet exhibit self-similar behavior, which is worse than random behavior when applied to queues.

The chapter discusses five basic types of queuing: first-in, first-out (FIFO), priority queuing, fair queuing, weighted fair queuing, and class-based queuing. FIFO is the simplest, but it can trap high-priority packets behind slow file transfers. Priority queuing helps those high-priority packets, but it can starve lower-priority packets of bandwidth. In an attempt to handle these difficulties, the other methods were developed with varying degrees of success. Weighted fair queuing has been shown to be able to guarantee latency, when coupled with admission control; class-based queuing is often used to allocate bandwidth on network backbones.

Finally, we look at traffic shaping using queuing techniques and using rate control, which meddles in the operation of TCP to smooth the traffic.

CHAPTER 7

Solution Building Blocks

This chapter gives a focused overview of all of the major building blocks for constructing an enterprise-wide network that can handle QoS. Technologies discussed here include the following:

Overprovisioning, the simplest solution for some networks, but with some important pitfalls

Isolation, often used for situations in which many flows with strict QoS requirements must be combined, or when traffic with different QoS levels must cross the public networks and retain their QoS

LAN QoS, including LAN prioritization and bandwidth reservation

Frame Relay, which is a popular method for interconnecting widely separated geographic locations, but which has limited QoS capabilities

Asynchronous Transfer Mode (ATM) and associated technologies, which are available in both private and public networks and which provide the most sophisticated QoS tools, but which may be more than is needed in some situations

IP Type of Service (TOS) and Filtering, the technology that has existed for years on IP-based networks and is in widespread use, but which can be time-consuming to configure and manage

Integrated Services and RSVP, the most flexible and sophisticated of the new IP-based QoS technologies, but which has some scaling problems in large networks

Differentiated Services (with a note about **Multi-Protocol Label Switching, MPLS**), the newest of the IP-based QoS technologies—less flexible than Integrated Services/RSVP, but much easier to scale

Traffic Shaping, a technology sometimes used in stand-alone situations to control IP traffic chunkiness

QoS Policy Management and Measurement, the technologies that measure QoS and give managers the centralized policy-based networking tools they need to control network utilization

These building blocks are discussed in order, and the major building blocks are all organized with the same structure:

- Introduction to the history and uses of the QoS technology
- Outline of the technology's internal architecture
- Detailed description of the QoS facilities provided
- List of standard QoS characteristics and the ways in which this particular technology handles them, including:
  - Bandwidth control
  - Discard control
  - Latency and jitter control
  - Prioritization control
  - Error control
  - QoS signaling and policy control
- Remarks about integration with other QoS technologies

The QoS characteristics are summarized in "QoS Characteristics of Major Network Technologies" at the end of the chapter.

Note that there isn't a section on availability within these discussions. It's not that availability isn't an important consideration—after all, it was a major topic in the first half of the book. Rather, it's that high-availability design is generally separate from QoS design. If high availability is needed, any of these underlying technologies can be used—but the techniques to provide that design are the subject of a different book.

Overprovisioning

In some situations there's no need for the complexity of QoS technology. A typical example is the research or video lab located in a single room and using Gigabit Ethernet technology. As long as there is plenty of capacity, and there's no need for a hierarchy of Gigabit Ethernet hubs or the need for a wide-area link that might create congestion at aggregation points, overprovisioning is a simple, relatively inexpensive solution. But overprovisioning requires work; it's not an effortless solution. And it is inefficient and has scaling difficulties.

Overprovisioning is not effortless because an overprovisioned network, by definition, is one that has a lot of excess capacity. It can be surprisingly difficult to ensure that the excess capacity is always there, however. As discussed before, in Chapter 6, "Basic QoS Technologies," Ethernet and Internet traffic is self-similar, not random, and it therefore can hit capacity problems much earlier than networks based on random behavior. Indeed, an Ethernet or Internet network that's at 50 percent utilization may already be on the edge of having major problems. As network usage grows, the network engineer responsible for an overprovisioned network must always keep it far ahead of the capacity demands. There's no way to ensure that crucial network traffic will be able to flow smoothly despite unanticipated congestion while waiting for a network upgrade; the network must always be upgraded *before* trouble appears. Unfortunately, because bandwidth demands grow constantly and because a new, bandwidth-hungry application can suddenly appear out of nowhere and be instantly installed on the network by hundreds of users, massive congestion can appear overnight. Without QoS, there's no way to deny network access to the new application; the entire network suffers and all of the users—guilty and innocent—complain.

There are also unavoidable inefficiencies involved in overprovisioning. Low-priority junk e-mail and the highest priority real-time video traffic receive the same service. This may not be a problem in a network owned by a small group, but in most larger networks the groups using the network for e-mail will start complaining about bearing the cost for an overprovisioned network that has to support another group's real-time speech and video traffic.

Finally, overprovisioned networks have difficulty scaling, especially if wide-area links are involved. Any aggregation point in the network is a place where the self-similar nature of Ethernet and Internet traffic may cause temporary congestion, resulting in unanticipated packet loss. It may not be frequent, but it will happen. Worse, introduction of a wide-area link almost certainly will result in a bottleneck and resulting packet loss. It's not cost-effective at this time to provide the same bandwidth on wide-area links as is available on LANs, despite the recent increases in transmission speed over fiber. After all, it's not the speed over fiber that's usually the limiting factor; it's the speed of the switches and routers at either end and the charges from the long-distance telecommunications suppliers. Without QoS, there's no way to handle traffic streams differently at that bottleneck, protecting some critical streams from packet loss or trading off packet loss for lower latency and jitter.

Isolation

One of the simplest ways of handling QoS is to isolate flows or groups of flows from one another. This time-honored method has been used for many years for handling different legacy protocols, and it is still an excellent method for use today in some QoS situations.

Multiplexing is one of the oldest forms of isolation. In its purest form, that of Time Division Multiplexing (TDM), shown in Figure 7.1, bytes from the flows are intermixed in an unchanging pattern, and underutilized capacity in a flow is wasted, not distributed to the other flows. (The flows are separated into their original flows by a companion multiplexer at the remote end.) This ensures that there will always be the capacity to carry the maximum load on all traffic streams without the need to delay, or buffer, any of the arriving traffic. Multiplexing is often used to carry datastreams that have strict latency and jitter requirements, as it is the equivalent of a totally separate leased line for each datastream.

Note that the more sophisticated forms of multiplexing, such as Statistical TDM, may not be able to make strict guarantees of latency and jitter. They usually work by first packaging the incoming datastream into packets and then using packet technology to intermix datastreams. Statistical TDMs are used when the arriving datastreams sometimes burst above the total aggregate capacity of the link, and they handle that situation by buffering the packets that they create—resulting in latency and jitter problems.

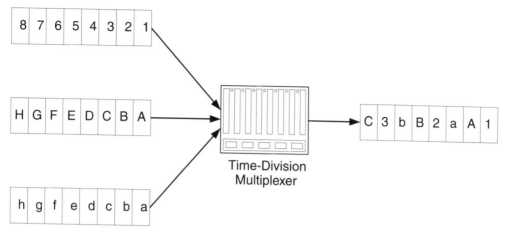

Figure 7.1 Time-division multiplexing.

One of the most important uses of the isolation technique by an enterprise appears when it's necessary to carry different QoS levels across a public network that isn't controlled by the enterprise. Except for ATM, signaling of QoS levels into the public network is in its infancy, so it's much easier to establish parallel paths across the network, as shown in Figure 7.2. The enterprise's boundary routers at both ends of the path are then configured to put certain QoS levels on one of the paths and other levels on another path. Packets arriving at a boundary router are classified according to QoS level, and they're then sent out of the appropriate physical port onto the appropriate public link. The different parallel links can use different technologies, if necessary, to deliver different levels of QoS. For example, one link could use a satellite, while another link could use a leased terrestrial line, and a third could use Frame Relay.

Isolation is also commonly used to support videoconferencing. Instead of trying to use QoS facilities across the data network, the videoconferencing

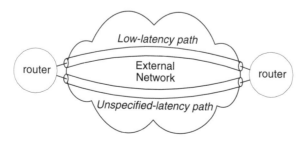

Figure 7.2 Using parallel paths with different QoS specifications.

equipment is configured to connect using dial-up ISDN links. That guarantees the QoS needed by the videoconference while avoiding the expense of providing QoS guarantees on a data network that may not be ready to provide them.

LAN QoS

LANs are a shared resource; a pair of stations can overwhelm the LAN with traffic, denying connectivity to all other stations on the LAN. But most LANs use Ethernet, and Ethernet originally didn't have any method for indicating frame priority or for performing congestion control. All frames were equal; there was no way to give frames containing low-latency speech packets priority over frames containing pieces of a file backup. Token Ring and FDDI (Fiber Distributed Data Interface) did have priority or bandwidth-reservation fields in their frames, but they provided few classes of service. Most installations didn't make them available to users at all. Some vendors produced unusual LANs that had some prioritization or bandwidth guarantee facilities, but they have had little success in the marketplace.

Recently, there has been much more interest in devising a standard method for marking LAN frames with priority levels. In response to that interest, there is now a new, standard method for indicating the priorities of LAN frames. This method, originally called IEEE 802.1p, has been incorporated into the IEEE standards 802.1D and 802.1Q.

Architecture

The original Ethernet didn't have any priority field, and that was an understandable omission because the original Ethernet was a system that had no central control or orderly method for allocating LAN access. All of the user stations shared a single, thick cable (nowadays, that cable is replaced by a shared Ethernet hub), and any station wanting to transmit simply waited for a pause in the traffic and then tried to inject its signal on the shared media. It was first come, first served. There was no easy way to select among competing users with different priorities, because there was no central control that made decisions. The only way to give some users preference over others on the LAN when using standard Ethernet was to manipulate the Ethernet parameters, such as the delay between retransmission attempts. If a user tried to transmit and was blocked by traffic that was already on the Ethernet LAN, that user was supposed to wait a certain interval (set by the Ethernet specification), then try again. If the user ignored the specification and retransmitted very quickly, he could, on average, get better service than other users. These manipulations were nonstandard, however. Some attempts were made at developing proprietary or standardized methods for allocating Ethernet bandwidth, such as the IEEE 802.9a standard and 3Com's PACE Class of Service, but these have not been widely adopted.

Unlike the random behavior of standard Ethernet users, all grabbing for the LAN whenever they feel like it, Token Ring and FDDI users wait patiently for explicit permission to transmit. It is therefore possible to provide a way for the control mechanism to allocate access according to service level.

- Token Ring has a user priority field in the header and a very orderly way of giving users access to the LAN. The priority field provides eight priority levels, although these are not usually available to the end user.

- FDDI is similar to Token Ring, and it has a way for stations to reserve bandwidth and a way to prioritize the capacity that remains after the bandwidth reservations. But few installations have used these priority and bandwidth-reservation systems.

Recently, the need for QoS service levels has increased, and the IEEE committees have added a priority mechanism that can be used across all LANs. If Ethernet had remained with its original shared-media or shared-hub technology, it would have been difficult to add prioritization. Fortunately, switched Ethernet, which has virtually replaced shared Ethernet in major networks, provides a way to handle the situation.

In switched Ethernet, all users connect directly into a switching hub. The cable between the user station and the hub isn't shared, so the hub itself is the only place where more than one user station can transmit at the same time and where congestion can occur. One of the great advantages of switched Ethernet is that the hub can allow multiple pairs of user stations to communicate simultaneously, as shown by Figure 7.3, because the hub can switch each user's packets separately. If two user stations are simultaneously trying to send a packet to a third station, which is especially likely if that third station is actually a link to another Ethernet

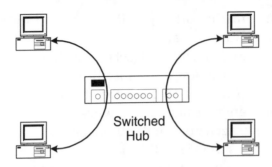

Figure 7.3 Switched Ethernet.

switching hub, then there can be conflict. The Ethernet switching hub can accept both packets, but it will have to queue them for transmission. Prioritization can be used to manage the packets when they're placed in the queue, and congestion control can be used to regulate the flow of incoming packets if the queue is reaching its maximum capacity. In the original, shared Ethernet, all packets were at the same priority, and there weren't any queues. If the system wasn't completely idle when you tried to transmit, you were blocked.

QoS Facilities

Some LANs always had rudimentary prioritization, bandwidth allocation, and congestion control facilities; others did not. We'll look first at the older LAN technologies and then at the latest developments, the Subnetwork Bandwidth Manager and IEEE 802.1p technologies.

Token Ring

Frames that must traverse multiple interconnected Token Rings will usually select the path with the best performance, avoiding congested areas, and Token Ring was designed with eight priority levels. The Token Ring technology can use the priority level to handle queuing within a Token Ring station and also to select the highest-priority frame waiting on the ring for transmission. Theoretically, bandwidth guarantees can also be made on Token Ring. The highest priority level must be used, and only one frame should be sent per token. It is then possible to calculate the maximum possible latency and jitter from the ring's characteristics. In practice, though, the majority of Token Ring systems do not allow users to choose their priority.

FDDI

FDDI provides a way to reserve bandwidth and to prioritize traffic. Traffic on an FDDI system can be divided into synchronous traffic and asynchronous traffic. The synchronous traffic has priority, and it's possible to reserve dedicated bandwidth for it. Most FDDI systems, however, don't provide these facilities.

Classical Ethernet

The original Ethernet LAN specification didn't include prioritization, bandwidth allocation, or congestion control, although there were some vendor-specific solutions for Ethernet prioritization and bandwidth allocation. For example, 3Com's PACE Class of Service provided two levels of priority. There were also some unusual standards, such as Isochronous Ethernet (isoEthernet), IEEE Standard 802.9a, which can reserve up to 96 64-kbps channels on the same physical LAN in addition to the standard 10Base-T channel. None of these has had much success in the marketplace, however.

Congestion control was handled by collisions in the original Ethernet design. Either you could get control of the LAN, or you couldn't; there isn't any buffering in a shared-media or shared-hub LAN. Only a few bridges are allowed, and those bridges have virtually no buffering facilities. If the destination bridge or LAN isn't ready for the frame, the frame is lost. With the arrival of switched Ethernet, that situation changed. There are now switching hubs that include buffering, and Ethernet speeds are increasing, so more data is lost when frames are discarded. The IEEE 802.3x standard therefore provides a rudimentary congestion-control method for switched Ethernet.

IEEE 802.3x is the standard that introduced full-duplex Ethernet. Older Ethernet was half-duplex, an obvious situation if you think about it, because only one station can transmit on the cable or shared hub at one time. With the new switched hubs, it became possible for more than one station to transmit simultaneously. The connection between a user station and the switching hub station has only the station and the hub on it, and the connection between them uses the 10Base-T standard, which has two data paths, on two separate pairs of wires. It is therefore possible for both the user station and the switching hub to transmit simultaneously. The only place where contention can occur is inside the switching hub, and the switching hub can use buffering to manage the situation.

Switching hubs needed a way to choke incoming frames if their internal buffers were filling up. If half-duplex Ethernet is used, there's an easy solution. The station that doesn't want to receive any more frames simply transmits some meaningless frames into the shared LAN, blocking anyone else from transmitting on the segment. But that wouldn't work on a full-duplex Ethernet LAN, so IEEE 802.3x allows the switching hubs to produce a control frame called a Pause Frame to perform congestion control on full-duplex connections. The Pause Frame tells the recipient how long it must wait until beginning to transmit again. The switching hub can transmit multiple Pause Frames that supercede each other, with each Pause Frame giving a new pause interval. The interval can be either a time to wait or zero, which means that the waiting can end immediately. The Pause Frame has a special address in it to prevent forwarding by Ethernet switches and bridges. Therefore, Pause Frames are restricted to a single link; they don't pass through a series of Ethernet switches and bridges to arrive at the ultimate originator of a traffic stream.

Pause Frames in Ethernet have the same problems that choke packets have in general: they're too coarse. If the other end of the link is another switching hub, all the frames coming from that hub will be stopped. There's no control over the types of packets that are delayed, because priorities and QoS classes are not considered by Ethernet congestion control mechanisms.

Subnetwork Bandwidth Manager

The Subnetwork Bandwidth Manager (SBM), originally an extension to the Resource Reservation Protocol (RSVP) system (discussed later, in the "Integrated Services and RSVP" section), acts as a resource broker for the LAN even if some of the network devices on the LAN don't know anything about QoS and the SBM. It communicates with end users, who can use an extension to the RSVP signaling system (the SBM protocol); it also communicates with wide area routers that interconnect to the LAN, to interact with the routers' QoS systems. The SBM keeps track of the resources used on the shared LAN facilities and accepts or rejects requests to provide enhanced QoS to individual users. The SBM ensures that a low-latency class, to pick an example, will not be overwhelmed with traffic. Of course, there has to be policing of all flows at the entrance to the LAN to make this work.

802.1p

In 1998 the IEEE developed a priority standard for Ethernet and incorporated it into the basic LAN standards that apply to all LANs. The new priority standard, initially named 802.1p, is now integrated into one of the primary LAN standards, 802.1D-1998, which specifies the operation of the bridges that interconnect LAN segments. (Switched hubs technically act as if they were bridges, so they fall under the 802.1D specification.) It is also included in 802.1Q-1998, which was originally developed to standardize the identification of Virtual LANs (VLANs). Briefly, VLAN technology allows user stations on separate segments of a large, enterprise-wide switched LAN to function as if they were physically on the same shared-media segment. The most obvious result is that they all hear the same broadcasts, as if they were on the same physical LAN segment or on the same shared hub. Different manufacturers devised different methods for tagging packets with their Virtual LAN segment identifier, so that the switched hubs used in a VLAN system could keep track of them and distribute broadcast and other frames appropriately. When the IEEE standardized the VLAN identifiers in the 802.1Q standard, it provided a field where a priority field could be inserted. The 802.1p standard uses that field.

The new 802.1D-1998 specification provides a three-bit field for priority, called user_priority. There are therefore eight possible priorities. The IEEE standard says that these must represent non-overlapping priorities, but it doesn't say much else about what those priorities mean to the networking equipment. The priority field must be included when equipment copies a frame from an incoming port to an outgoing port, if the outgoing port can handle priorities. If an outgoing port connects to equipment that can't handle priorities, such as a port that connects to an older Ethernet device, then the network equipment must use the older Ethernet header format without the new header fields.

The meanings of the priority levels in the new standard are still under discussion. One option, as discussed by the IETF Integrated Services over Specific Link Layers (ISSLL) Working Group (http://www.ietf.org/html.charters/issll-charter.html), is to map them to the QoS classes in other QoS systems, such as those used by IP's Integrated Services or Differentiated Services. The mapping could be handled by the Subnetwork Bandwidth Manager.

LAN QoS
QoS Characteristics

Existing LANs have no user-accessible QoS control in most installations, outside of some specialty products. Future LANs will probably include some QoS levels that will be controlled through integration with enterprise-wide QoS facilities and the major WAN facilities, such as with ATM and with IP's Differentiated Services.

Bandwidth Control

LANs currently provide a few methods for reserving bandwidth, but they are not often used at this time. The Subnetwork Bandwidth Manager is a recent development that may become widely used.

- Token Ring stations can reserve their highest priority for traffic that must have access to the LAN with a guaranteed maximum time between accesses, but this can be done only for the highest priority. Most existing Token Ring installations do not provide user control over priorities.

- A FDDI system can reserve dedicated bandwidth.

- Some unusual LANs, such as Isochronous Ethernet (isoEthernet), [IEEE 802.9a], can reserve up to 96 64-kbps channels in addition to the standard 10Base-T.

- The Subnetwork Bandwidth Manager can implement the same guarantees provided with Integrated Services and RSVP (discussed in a later section, "Integrated Services and RSVP").

Unless they use switched hubs, LANs have few buffers inside the network, so they have generally depended on users' higher-level protocol for congestion control. There have also been tricks that LAN hub developers could use to slow incoming traffic temporarily on half-duplex LANs, such as generating fake outgoing Ethernet traffic to keep the ports busy. Full-duplex Ethernet LANs couldn't use these tricks, so a new Pause Frame was developed to handle congestion control. It is coarse in operation and should be used only to handle brief periods of congestion.

Discard Control by Users

LANs don't provide any method for users to indicate their preference when a LAN must discard frames because of congestion or other problems.

Latency and Jitter Control

LANs currently provide few methods for latency and jitter control; the Subnetwork Bandwidth Manager is a recent development that may become widely used.

- Token Ring stations can reserve their highest priority for traffic that must have access to the LAN with a guaranteed maximum time between accesses, but this can be done only for the highest priority. (Other Token Ring priorities have no such guarantees.) This could provide LAN access with a latency and jitter specification resulting from the Token Ring specifications for token circulation; no other latency and jitter values are possible.

- An FDDI system can reserve dedicated bandwidth. This would allow guarantees of maximum latency.

- Some unusual LANs, such as Isochronous Ethernet (isoEthernet), [IEEE 802.9a], can reserve up to 96 64-kbps channels in addition to the standard 10Base-T.

- The Subnetwork Bandwidth Manager can implement the same guarantees provided with Integrated Services and RSVP (discussed in a later section, "Integrated Services and RSVP").

Prioritization Control

LANs currently provide some methods for prioritization:

- Token Ring stations have eight priorities, but users usually can't set them.

- FDDI systems have a method for reserving constant bit rate bandwidth, and there's also a method for prioritizing the remaining FDDI traffic with up to eight priority levels.

- Some unusual LANs, such as nonstandard Ethernet, provide methods for prioritization. 3Com's PACE Class of Service Ethernet is an example, providing two levels of service. These solutions have virtually no market share.

- The Subnetwork Bandwidth Manager can implement a priority system.

Error Control

Some error control is provided in Ethernet LANs. Ethernet frames contain a frame check sequence to detect errors, but damaged frames are silently discarded. Other LANs, such as Token Ring, provide a mode in which damaged frames can be automatically detected and retransmitted.

QoS Signaling and Policy

In general, LANs are a part of a larger QoS solution, and the trend is for them to be integrated into those solutions. To that end, the Subnetwork Bandwidth Manager, COPS (discussed later, in the "QoS Policy Management and Measurement" section), or a similar facility is used to control LAN QoS instead of a dedicated, LAN-only solution. There are, however, some LAN-only solutions, such as 3Com's PACE Class of Service Ethernet or the use of Token Ring priorities, but they are uncommon.

Integration with Other QoS Technologies

LAN QoS facilities are only recently becoming integrated with other QoS facilities, primarily through the use of the Subnetwork Bandwidth Manager and the new 802.1p field. There will also be edge devices that will map LAN 802.1p QoS levels to QoS facilities in ATM.

Frame Relay

Frame Relay is a widespread link-level technology that is available from public carriers around the globe. It uses a frame similar to HDLC, and it allows a system to intermix packets for many different destinations onto a single outgoing link. The addresses for the destinations are given by an abbreviated address field, the Data Link Connection Indicator (DLCI), and the Frame Relay system agrees to deliver the frames in order at the destinations—although it makes no guarantees that all frames will be delivered. A big difference between Frame Relay frame formats and HDLC formats is that there's no control field. Frames are not numbered, and there's no frame acknowledgment mechanism.

Frame Relay is almost always used with Permanent Virtual Connections (PVCs); that is, the destination addresses are configured beforehand by the network administrators, and the DLCIs for those addresses are preset into the system. The Frame Relay specification allows for the use of Switched Virtual Connections (SVCs), in which DLCIs are dynamically assigned to whichever Frame Relay destination address the user wants, when he or she wants it, but public carriers do not generally offer that service. Frame Relay therefore isn't often used to make connections to systems that are outside an enterprise's network or standard set of correspondents. Instead, Frame Relay can be a reasonable replacement for leased lines in cases where flow is sporadic and the mileage charges for a leased line are high. In contrast to leased lines, for which a user pays a fixed rate that's usually based on mileage, the cost for Frame Relay is usually based on usage and is not sensitive to distance.

The Frame Relay system has some QoS facilities, but they're rudimentary. There are some basic flow control mechanisms, and there's a simple way of tagging the relative importance of frames if the system has to find some to discard. However, there's no standard method for guaranteeing latency, priority, error characteristics, or other QoS parameters.

Architecture

First, we should note that Frame Relay user interfaces can be built on top of any type of network. Although pure Frame Relay technologies are available from many vendors, some public carriers have chosen to reuse existing network equipment to provide the Frame Relay function, and there are other possibilities as well. All that's required of the network is that it deliver frames in order, if it delivers them at all. There are no latency or other QoS requirements. Therefore, the fact that you may have had excellent latency, jitter, or error rate characteristics with a particular public Frame Relay supplier for a particular link is no guarantee that if you install a similar link in another part of the world or with another supplier, you'll have the same level of service. Indeed, it's also possible that the excellent service you're receiving will deteriorate over time as more users are added to the public carrier's system. But, by and large, Frame Relay offers reliable, cost-effective service for transactions and bulk transfer worldwide. That said, let's look at the interface to public Frame Relay.

The Frame Relay system expects a packet in a defined format, as shown in Figure 7.4. This is similar to the HDLC frame, with its starting and ending flags and with a Frame Check Sequence (FCS) for error detection. The DLCI address bits are contained in a variable length address header field (two to four octets), and they're assigned to destinations either administratively (through manual configuration) or by a separate exchange of protocol packets on a separate virtual circuit, with DLCI = 0, that is dedicated to the call switching function. The former case, the administrative assignment of DLCIs to destinations, is the one that's generally used. The resulting circuits are called Permanent Virtual Connections (PVCs); the other system, rarely used, is for Switched Virtual Connections (SVCs).

It's important to notice that there are no sequence numbers, acknowledgments, receive windows, or rejection notifications in Frame Relay. The network will deliver packets in order, but there may be long delays and some packets may disappear completely. The network can discard packets

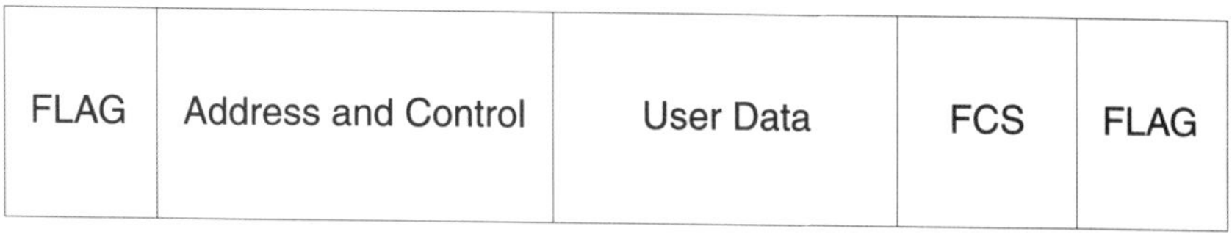

FLAG	Address and Control	User Data	FCS	FLAG

Figure 7.4 Frame Relay format.

whenever it wants to, and it doesn't have any way to tell you about that! If you exceed your contractual data rate (your Committed Information Rate, CIR), the network may discard any packets that exceed that rate. The network will also silently discard any packet with a failing FCS, and it doesn't tell you, give you the option to receive the packet anyway (e.g., for a higher-level protocol that might be able to recover from small errors), or ask for a retransmission. It's the responsibility of a higher-layer protocol to number packets, to detect missing packets, and to arrange for retransmissions if necessary.

QoS Facilities

Frame Relay has some simple congestion control facilities. It can tag frames that exceed the agreed-on Committed Information Rate (CIR), and it can recognize frames that are tagged by the user as being relatively unimportant. It also has a way of notifying the users when congestion in the network is building to the point where it may have to start discarding frames.

The Frame Relay frame has a bit, the Discard Eligibility (DE) bit, that's normally set to zero. (All of these control bits are in the Address and Control field of the header.) If this bit is set to one, it means that the frame is less important to the user than the other frames. If the network becomes congested, it will try to discard frames with the DE bit equal to one before it discards frames with the DE bit equal to zero. The user can set the DE bit, but that is almost never done. The application's interface may not have a way to set that bit, and setting the DE bit when other users are almost certainly not setting theirs will probably lead to worse service for the user setting the DE bit.

The usual way the DE bit is set is that the Frame Relay switch at the entrance to the network sets the bit automatically if the user's data rate exceeds the CIR. Users pay for Frame Relay services based on a formula that includes the CIR, and some users discovered early in the development of Frame Relay that paying for a CIR of zero bits per second worked in many cases. The Frame Relay system set the DE bit to one in all of the entering frames, but the new, uncongested network almost never needed to discard frames. That's rarely the case now, and the user should be prepared to pay for whatever bandwidth is normally needed. Occasional bursts above the CIR may still be necessary, but some of the frames may not arrive at the destination. Remember, the Frame Relay network won't signal when this happens; it will just drop the frames silently.

The network isn't completely silent when it has some congestion problems, however. There are two other bits in the frame header that the network uses to signal congestion: the Forward Explicit Congestion Notification (FECN) and Backward Explicit Congestion Notification (BECN) bits. As queues build within the Frame Relay network, and before frame discard is necessary, network switches will automatically send FECN and BECN to the datastreams with queue problems. The FECN arrives at the destination, and the BECN arrives at the source. The network hopes that the sender will decrease its data rate or that the receiver will use some higher-level flow control mechanism to signal to the sender to decrease the sender's data rate. Unfortunately, most senders and receivers ignore the congestion notification flags, if they can receive them at all over their API. Higher-level protocols such as TCP are completely unaware of congestion flags and take no notice of them. Some routers are aware of them, however, and may be configured to decrease their transmission data rate when congestion notification arrives.

If the data rate continues to increase after the FECN and BECN have been sent, the network eventually starts discarding frames with the DE bit set. With luck, those frames are from TCP transmissions that are already exceeding their agreed-on CIR, and the loss of a frame will force the transmitting TCP stack to cut its data rate drastically—equivalent to the result of Random Early Detection (RED) in routers. If the lost frames are from protocol stacks that simply retransmit without decreasing their data rate, loss of frames may make the situation worse. Ultimately, if the data rate continues to increase, the queues overflow and all frames are lost.

There aren't any other QoS-related facilities inside the basic Frame Relay system, and there's no way to signal QoS needs other than by using the DE bit or by some nonstandardized way of assigning QoS levels to different PVC DLCIs when arrangements are initially made with the Frame Relay administration. Some Frame Relay networks provide a method for prioritization of individual DLCIs, but the latency and jitter guarantees that are associated with that prioritization may be weak or absent altogether. Some vendors provide prioritization within the Frame Relay Access Device (FRAD) that connects the user to the Frame Relay system, but that doesn't affect prioritization once the frames enter the network [Newman, Minoli 1998a]. The Frame Relay Forum's standard, "Service Level Definitions Implementation Agreement," [FRF.13] sets the standard for measurement metrics, but it doesn't specify the time period. Be sure that your average latency measurements aren't 30-day averages if you need to have short latency and jitter guarantees for applications such as real-time voice traffic! Fortunately, work is underway within the Frame Relay Forum to enhance the QoS guarantees of Frame Relay.

Integration with Other QoS Technologies

The Frame Relay QoS facilities are very limited, and few other systems work with them directly. There are some examples of integration, however:

- Some routers can optionally respond to the congestion control signals by altering their transmission rate.

Frame Relay QoS Characteristics

Frame Relay has rudimentary QoS control. It provides some methods for coarse control of bandwidth and for frame discard, but no standard methods for prioritization, latency, or error control.

Bandwidth Control

Frame Relay's service is that of constant bit rate with a burst allowance. The subscriber pays for a certain Committed Information Rate (CIR) and may burst above that rate. In some cases, there can be a different CIR for each direction. All packets above the CIR are tagged with Discard Eligibility (DE) by the Frame Relay network; they can be discarded silently if there's congestion. There is no way to request a change in CIR dynamically on a PVC.

Before packets are discarded, the Frame Relay network sends notifications to the senders and receivers by turning on the Forward Explicit Congestion Notification (FECN) and Backward Explicit Congestion Notification (BECN) bits in the frame headers. Users should decrease their transmission rate when these bits are on, but most users and transmission stacks are unable to react. Some routers can decrease their transmission rate when they receive these congestion notifications; this must be specially configured. There is no other flow control method in Frame Relay; for example, there's no acknowledgment window giving the number of bytes that can be transmitted.

Discard Control by Users

The subscriber can set the Discard Eligibility bit in the Frame Relay frame header to indicate that the packet is less important than other packets. Most subscribers never set this bit, however, and that results in a disadvantage to any user setting the bit. That

- The Frame Relay Forum (www.frforum.com) standard, "Frame Relay / ATM PVC Network Interworking Implementation Agreement," [FRF.5] and the standard, "Frame Relay / ATM PVC Service Implementation Agreement," [FRF.8] specify the interconnection of Frame Relay and ATM's AAL-5 (ATM Adoption Layer 5) interface. These specify two types of interconnection: Frame Relay can be carried over ATM and restored to Frame Relay formats and behaviors at the other end of the connection, or Frame Relay can be connected to an ATM system and thereby talk directly to an ATM user. As part of the interconnection, Frame Relay's DE header bit can be

user's frames will be discarded first if there are any congestion problems in the network; they'll be grouped for discard with frames that have exceeded their CIR.

Latency and Jitter Control

Latency and jitter control are not provided in standard Frame Relay, although some vendors and public carriers may offer nonstandard latency and jitter guarantees that can be administratively associated with specific PVCs.

Prioritization Control

Prioritization control is not provided in standard Frame Relay, although some vendors and public carriers may offer nonstandard prioritization that can be administratively associated with specific PVCs or can be implemented within FRADs to manipulate queuing [Newman, Minoli 1998a].

Error Control

Some error control is provided in standard Frame Relay. The system places a 16-bit Frame Check Sequence (FCS) at the end of each frame, and it automatically discards any frame that has been corrupted and therefore fails its FCS check. There is no way for users to accept a corrupted frame.

Frame Relay does not automatically retransmit incorrect frames, and it does not notify the user that a frame has been lost or explicitly discarded. It does attempt to deliver frames in sequence, although there are no explicit sequence numbers.

QoS Signaling and Policy

Except for the Discard Eligibility bit, there is no QoS signaling or policy control in Frame Relay. There may be nonstandard methods for associating different QoS levels with different DLCIs (implicit signaling), but there's no provision for that in the standards.

mapped to and from the ATM Cell Loss Priority (CLP) header bit. The FECN and BECN bits in Frame Relay are carried through an ATM network for the case where Frame Relay is carried over ATM, but they are not normally mapped to ATM's Explicit Forward Congestion Indication (EFCI). If ATM congestion is experienced, that congestion can be mapped to Frame Relay FECN and BECN bits. The Frame Relay Forum is working on standards for new Frame Relay QoS facilities and for the interoperation of those facilities with other QoS technologies, especially with ATM and with IP's Differentiated Services.

- As discussed previously, TCP will discover that there's congestion by noticing that some frames have been discarded. TCP flows that have exceeded their CIR will probably lose frames first, as those frames will have automatically been marked with the DE bit when they entered the network. Those TCP flows will therefore be the first ones to decrease their transmission rate, which is a result that we probably want. Other protocols, which aren't looking for implicit rate feedback, may simply retransmit discarded frames, making the problem worse.

If Frame Relay must be used to provide QoS, it's best to rely on nonstandard methods for assigning different QoS levels to different groups of PVC DLCIs. This is similar to the isolation method of QoS, discussed earlier in this chapter. Different vendors have different methods for doing this, and they have different QoS guarantees for the performance that can be provided. Using these methods for providing the performance needed by SNA systems and other classical transaction-oriented systems is well accepted [Nolle]; using them for providing the low latency and jitter needed by interactive voice is very new and depends heavily on special characteristics of the underlying systems.

ATM

Asynchronous Transfer Mode (ATM) is the result of ITU work on the Broadband Integrated Services Digital Network (B-ISDN) that was intended to be the general-purpose, high-speed, connection-oriented data switching platform for telephone companies. ATM, which is the transport for B-ISDN, provides facilities for building constant bit rate circuits (the equivalent of leased lines) as well as variable bit rate circuits. It also provides a way of handling bursty transmissions and a way of providing many different Quality of Service levels. The work of standardization is now done primarily by the ATM Forum (www.atmforum.com).

ATM is widely used by telephone companies and by some ISPs, which like the fact that they can use it to create the equivalent of leased lines between any two points in the ATM network. It's a simple way for them to reconfigure their connections between routers. ATM is also used by institutions such as medical research centers that need ATM's heavy-duty Quality of Service facilities immediately. (Because ATM was designed with QoS from the start, its facilities are far more flexible and reliable than are those in the IP world at the time of this writing.) Native ATM services are available in some regions of the world from the public carriers, where they can be used to interconnect enterprise ATM backbones while maintaining ATM Quality of Service levels.

Originally, its designers hoped that ATM would replace both WANs and LANs, bringing seamless connectivity from desktop devices, through a mixture of local and wide area networks, and then to servers. All this would have end-to-end Quality of Service facilities with telephone-company reliability and manageability. It hasn't turned out that way, and ATM now seems to be primarily a WAN technology. Some high-powered servers connect directly to ATM, but virtually all desktop devices connect first to an Ethernet LAN and then pass through an edge device to connect to ATM. Special technologies, called MPOA (MultiProtocol over ATM) and LANE (LAN Emulation), are used to make that connection easier.

Architecture

ATM is a connection-oriented technology. Instead of placing the full network address at the beginning of each data packet, as is done with IP, an ATM network first sets up a connection, called a Virtual Connection, and creates an abbreviated address. It then uses that abbreviated address in the short headers at the beginning of each ATM cell. The cells follow each other through the network, all using the route that was established when the connection was first created. The ATM network supports both Permanent Virtual Connections (PVCs), for which the abbreviated addresses are permanently associated with destinations through an administrator's console, and Switched Virtual Connections (SVCs), which allow users to connect to any address and which create temporary abbreviated addresses. SVCs are dynamically created by signaling through the end-user's API.

ATM switches were designed from the ground up to handle Quality of Service and high speeds. Internally, the ATM system uses 53-byte cells that contain 48 bytes of data. The relatively short cell size prevents long cells from delaying others in queues, and the uniform cell length and fixed header formats simplify high-speed buffer management and cell switching. The routing technology used by modern ATM switches is very aware of the QoS requested by a new connection. It automatically tries to find a route that will satisfy all the QoS demands, and it can probe different routes until it finds a satisfactory one, taking into account the current conditions in the network and the network's existing promises to users. Once it finds that route, it stores the routing information in the ATM switches, where it is used by the cells running along the virtual connection.

Each initial connection request for the virtual circuit is checked by ATM's Connection Admission Control (CAC), which looks in its database to see if the user is allowed to make the connection at the requested QoS level and for the requested traffic characteristics (requested average and peak data rates, etc.). If it is, and if the network has the capacity to honor the request, then the connection is established; if not, then the user can try again later. Once the connection is established, the traffic characteristics and QoS levels cannot be changed.

After data begins to flow through the virtual connection, the ATM network continues to monitor the connection to look for data rates that exceed those specified when the connection was established. This traffic policing function is called Usage Parameter Control (UPC), and it uses the leaky bucket algorithm and other methods to detect incoming traffic that exceeds the agreement. That traffic can then be tagged for discard if congestion occurs, using the Cell Loss Priority (CLP) field in the cell header.

Four alternative ATM Adaptation Layers (AALs) provide standard ways for interfacing ATM's fixed-length cells to other data formats. Depending on the AAL used, the AAL and its associated processing can automatically break incoming frames into segments for transmission over ATM cells and reassemble them at the destination as well as handle flow control, manage errors, recreate end-to-end synchronous data clocks if necessary, and perform other functions. Their details don't concern us; we need to note only that some applications are designed to run over a preferred AAL type. For example, the H.310 teleconferencing standard is designed for AAL5, whereas applications originally designed for synchronous transmission over leased lines prefer AAL1. TCP/IP normally uses AAL5, as that AAL has very little additional overhead.

- AAL1 is designed for constant bit rate traffic. It makes ATM appear to be a standard digital leased line, including a very stable clocking frequency. This AAL is often used by public carriers to create the equivalent of leased lines connecting any two points within the carrier's network.

- AAL2 is designed for variable bit rate traffic that needs an accompanying, very stable clocking frequency. This would seem to be the ideal AAL for compressed video or voice, but it was a very new, untried standard that was just entering production use when this book was written.

- AAL3/4 (yes, it's a strange name—it was created by combining AAL3 and AAL4) carries variable bit rate traffic. It's designed to carry pieces of data frames that have variable lengths, and it can multiplex together data from different sources that are traveling together over the ATM network. It therefore has the header fields that are needed by the AAL processing software to reassemble those frames correctly at the destination. AAL3/4 has the strongest error control facility of all the AAL types.

- AAL5 has the least overhead of the four types; it simply delivers frames in order and without errors. It does not provide a built-in multiplexing facility.

In addition to the AAL interfaces, ATM provides a number of specialized technologies to carry non-ATM traffic over an ATM backbone. These include MPOA (Multi-Protocol Over ATM), LANE (LAN Emulation), and various other technologies, such as those to interconnect with Frame Relay and those to carry IP over ATM. They are all discussed later in this section.

QoS Facilities

Before looking at the categories of ATM service, we need to look at the details of both the ATM traffic specifications and the ATM QoS specifications.

When an ATM connection is made, the user specifies the characteristics of the traffic that will flow over the connection, the QoS guarantees that are needed, and the type of transport service required. These are set before the connection is established; they're specified by signaling for SVCs and by manual setup for PVCs. The ATM network's routing protocol uses that information to select the appropriate route through the network and reserve the necessary facilities. We'll look at them in order.

Traffic Descriptors

Not all of these traffic descriptors are needed for each connection; different ATM service categories need different ones.

Peak Cell Rate (PCR) is the maximum rate that the user will transmit cells. For constant bit rate (CBR) circuits, this is the only rate allowed.

Sustainable Cell Rate (SCR) is the average cell rate over a long period.

Minimum Cell Rate (MCR) is the minimum cell transmit rate needed by the user. This is needed by many protocols to keep the connection alive and send end-to-end signaling and flow control messages. It can be set to zero.

Maximum Burst Size (MBS) is the maximum number of cells that will be transmitted by the user in a single burst at the Peak Cell Rate. The average cell rate must not exceed the Sustainable Cell Rate.

Cell Delay Variation Tolerance (CDVT) gives the variation in cell delay that is created by the network interface at the entrance to the ATM network.

Conformance Definitions are the specification of the traffic policing rules that the network will use. The network may mark nonconforming cells for discard if there's congestion, or it may simply drop them at the network's entrance.

QoS Parameters

As was true for the traffic descriptors, not all of these parameters are used by all of the ATM service categories. The older ATM networks allow users to choose only certain values of these parameters that have been preselected by the network administrators; current ATM networks may allow users to choose any value.

Maximum Cell Transfer Delay (maxCTD) is the sum of the latency and the maximum acceptable jitter across the entire ATM network, including all switching nodes and all links. It's the maximum time that a cell will take between entering the network and leaving it; cells delivered later than maxCTD are assumed to be useless to the application.

Peak-to-Peak Cell Delay Variation (CDV) is the jitter at the exit of the network.

Cell Loss Ratio (CLR) is the ratio of lost cells to total transmitted cells.

Each ATM cell header contains a **Cell Loss Priority (CLP)** flag that can be equal to zero or one. Cells with CLP = 0 are considered to be more important by the network, and the network's Usage Parameter Control (UPC) will set a cell's CLP = 1 if that cell exceeds the agreed-on traffic descriptors for that connection. The user can also set CLP = 1 before the cell enters the network. The network switches cannot distinguish between cells that have CLP = 1 because they were that way originally and cells that were set to CLP = 1 by the network.

The network can accept two different Cell Loss Ratio (CLR) values for each connection, one for those cells with CLP = 0 and one for those cells with CLP = 1. Of course, the CLR value for the cells with CLP = 0 must be at least as demanding than those for the cells with CLP = 1.

ATM networks also provide three standard error measurements. They are the **Cell Error Ratio (CER)**; the **Severely Errored Cell Block Ratio (SECBR)**, which is the equivalent of a Block Error Rate; and the **Cell Misinsertion Rate (CMR)**, which counts cells that have bad headers, are in the wrong place in the datastream, or belong to another datastream altogether.

ATM provides a way of detecting cell header errors, and ATM Adaptation Layers 3/4 and 5 (AAL3/4 and AAL5) provide Cyclic Redundancy Checks to detect errors in the payload. ATM Adaptation Layer 1 (AAL1), used for constant bit rate traffic, detects only incorrectly ordered cells; it does not detect bit errors inside the cells.

ATM Service Categories

Current ATM networks, with UNI (User-Network Interface) 4.0, provide six categories of transport services that are tuned to different user needs, and each ATM service includes a set of QoS parameters. The six categories are as follows:

Constant Bit Rate (CBR) provides the equivalent of a leased line and is used by applications that have that type of steady traffic flow or that need the constant, unvarying timing synchronization pulse provided by a CBR circuit. Examples are telephone calls using G.711, teleconferencing using H.320, and real-time video using MPEG-1, which is very sensitive to jitter and appreciates the steady clock of ATM CBR. Other video systems also run well over ATM CBR; it's not the most efficient carrier for compressed video as far as the network management is concerned, but it's certainly the easiest to configure and connect to existing video and teleconferencing systems. The traffic specification is simple; it's just the bit rate. The QoS specifications include maximum latency and jitter.

Real-Time Variable Bit Rate (rt-VBR) provides a constant, unvarying timing synchronization pulse, of the type appreciated by real-time video traffic, while also allowing variations in the data rate. This is a good match for compressed video, in which intra-coded video (e.g., an MPEG I Frame), which has a high data rate, is intermixed with inter-coded video (e.g., an MPEG P Frame), which has a much lower data rate. The traffic specification for rt-VBR consists of the average cell rate, the peak cell rate, and the maximum size of a burst that's transmitted at that peak cell rate. The rt-VBR QoS specifications are the same as those for CBR. Maximum latency and jitter are important to rt-VBR users, as late cells are usually useless.

Non-Real-Time Variable Bit Rate (nrt-VBR) does not provide a constant timing synchronization pulse and does not provide a guarantee of latency or jitter. It's a good match for streaming video, which will be buffered at the receiver before being played back. Streaming video doesn't go directly to a video monitor screen, and it doesn't fall apart if it loses timing synchronization as do some types of real-time video. Frame Relay traffic, which has average and maximum transmission rate specifications similar to those used by nrt-VBR traffic, and which usually doesn't have a latency or jitter guarantee, is a good match for nrt-VBR if it must be routed over or interconnected with ATM. The nrt-VBR traffic specifications are the same as for rt-VBR.

Unspecified Bit Rate (UBR) is a best-effort, non-real-time service, providing no constant timing synchronization pulses and no guarantees of QoS or even of minimum available throughput. In most ATM networks, UBR is used to carry the IP and LAN traffic that isn't carried over a CBR service. IP and LAN higher-layer protocols are accustomed to long latencies, large jitter variations, and lost frames; they can handle these situations—although they may not be happy about it—when they appear on UBR connections. UBR traffic specification is simple; it's just the expected maximum data rate. In general, ATM networks don't police UBR traffic. Because UBR traffic is the least important traffic on the network, it won't hurt any other traffic type's performance. If there is any network congestion, the UBR traffic is always the first to be discarded.

Available Bit Rate (ABR) is a very interesting non-real-time service that is designed to provide explicit rate control feedback to applications. It's similar to UBR in that it doesn't provide a constant timing synchronization pulse and is designed for applications that don't need latency or jitter guarantees. It does, however, provide minimum bandwidth guarantees (minimum cell rate, MCR). The ATM network agrees to provide at least that minimum bandwidth between sender and receiver, and it will try to provide up to the maximum rate asked for in the traffic specification's Peak Cell Rate (PCR). The network can adjust the allowed cell rate (ACR) at any time by sending a special ATM ABR control cell that's called the Resource Management (RM) cell. The ATM network provides a guarantee of low packet loss *if* the user agrees to keep his or her transmission rate below the ACR signaled by the RM cells. First-generation ATM switches can periodically ask the sender to adjust the sending rate either up or down, if necessary, in standard steps. Second-generation ATM switches can simply tell the sender the precise maximum rate at any time.

Guaranteed Frame Rate (GFR) is a recently developed non-real-time service designed for IP traffic that doesn't need a constant timing synchronization pulse or guarantees of latency or jitter. The user specifies the maximum frame size (MFS) and minimum required bandwidth (minimum cell rate, MCR) in the traffic specification. The network agrees that if the frames meet those specifications, then it will guarantee low packet loss. This is very similar to Frame Relay's Committed Information Rate (CIR). GFR traffic can burst over the specified minimum required bandwidth, but there are no guarantees in that case—the same as with CIR.

Integration with Other QoS Technologies

Virtually every other QoS building block has plans for integration with ATM, and a number of facilities are already available. The primary ones are these:

- **Nailed-up connections** use PVCs between bridges or routers.
- **LAN Emulation over ATM (LANE)** uses SVCs to bridge LANs across ATM.
- **MultiProtocol over ATM (MPOA)** uses SVCs to bridge LANs and to route IP and IPX across ATM.
- **Classical IP over ATM (RFC 2225)** routes IP over ATM.
- **Frame Relay Interworking (FRF.5 and FRF.8)** interconnects Frame Relay and ATM.

All of these facilities are affected by the ATM Service Category used to carry the traffic. The one most commonly used is UBR, but it offers few

ATM QoS Characteristics

As we've seen, ATM has very sophisticated QoS control, and that control is available today, in proven production technology.

Bandwidth Control

ATM provides all types of bandwidth control. The user can select constant bit rate (CBR), variable bit rate (VBR) with possible maximum and minimum rate guarantees, or an unspecified bit rate (UBR) with no guaranteed bandwidth at all. There are six different types of ATM services, and they're discussed in detail in the section "ATM Service Categories."

Discard Control by Users

ATM subscribers can set the Cell Loss Priority (CLP) flag in each cell to indicate whether that cell is as important as the others. Cells with CLP = 1 are less important than those with CLP = 0. The network may also set a frame's CLP = 1 if it falls outside the agreed-on traffic characteristics for the connection. Some ATM services allow the user to request one Cell Loss Ratio (CLR) guarantee for cells with CLP = 0 and another CLR for cells with CLP = 1.

Latency and Jitter Control

The real-time ATM services, CBR and rt-VBR, allow users to specify the maximum acceptable end-to-end transport delay, which is equivalent to latency + jitter. They also require the user to adhere to his or her traffic characteristics agreement, set up at the beginning of the connection, which specifies the maximum jitter in the entering traffic. If that maximum input jitter isn't exceeded, the real-time ATM services will guarantee the maximum exiting jitter.

guarantees. Problems occur when UBR cells are dropped, as loss of a single cell destroys the frame that it's in. The other cells in the frame are still carried, uselessly, to their destination—increasing the congestion. Guaranteed Frame Rate (GFR) was devised to handle this problem.

When used to carry TCP connections, there can be an additional issue. In most cases when TCP loses a packet, it assumes that there's congestion and that it must cut its transmission rate drastically. It then returns to its initial transmission speed very gradually because it's worried about encountering the congestion again. An ATM network that's congested eliminates that congestion immediately, however, by discarding cells. Therefore, TCP's gradual return to full speed is unnecessary and wastes

Prioritization Control

In ATM, each connection can have strictly defined QoS parameters for latency, jitter, error rate, and bandwidth.

Error Control

ATM provides, in addition to the Cell Loss Ratio (CLR) specification that can be negotiated for each connection, a standard set of error ratios: the Cell Error Ratio (CER); the Severely Errored Cell Block Ratio (SECBR), which is the equivalent of a Block Error Rate; and the Cell Misinsertion Rate (CMR), which counts cells that have bad headers, are in the wrong place in the datastream, or belong to another datastream altogether.

ATM provides a way of detecting header errors, and ATM Adaptation Layers 3/4 and 5 (AAL3/4 and AAL5) provide Cyclic Redundancy Checks to detect errors in the payload. ATM Adaptation Layer 1 (AAL1), used for constant bit rate traffic, detects only incorrectly ordered cells; it does not detect bit errors inside the cells.

QoS Signaling and Policy

ATM has both implicit and explicit signaling. Implicit signaling is the default for both PVCs and SVCs; it's set up by the network administration. Explicit signaling can be made for SVCs when the connection is established; it's done through the standard ATM User-Network Interface (UNI). UNI version 4.0 allows complete flexibility in setting traffic characteristics and QoS parameters.

ATM networks have extensive built-in facilities for admission control and traffic policing, along with centralized administrative systems to enforce security and QoS policy depending on the particular connection attempt being made. There are also major ongoing efforts to integrate ATM signaling and policy control with that of LAN and IP signaling and policy control.

bandwidth. Fortunately, ATM offers many service categories that can be used to ensure that cells will rarely be discarded if the TCP traffic remains within its traffic descriptors.

Nailed-Up Connections

The simplest way to interconnect two non-ATM networks over ATM is to take advantage of ATM's Permanent Virtual Connections (PVCs). The various routers and LAN bridges are simply interconnected by ATM PVCs, the same as if they were interconnected by leased lines. The ATM administrator sets up the PVCs and gives them the needed bandwidth and QoS characteristics; no signaling is done by the network's users. (See "Multiprotocol Encapsulation over ATM Adaptation Layer 5," [RFC 1483] for the encapsulation specification.)

The advantage of this technique is simplicity, and it is widely and successfully used to provide the equivalent of leased-line interconnections. For more complex situations, however, there are some disadvantages. One disadvantage is that the non-ATM network traffic cannot connect to native ATM users. For example, a workstation user on an Ethernet that's bridged across the ATM network by PVCs cannot use that ATM network to connect to a large server system that has a native ATM UNI connection. When using Ethernet bridges that are interconnected by nailed-up connections, the workstation is not aware of the ATM network in any way. It thinks that it is on a simple bridged Ethernet network.

A second disadvantage is that the different classes of traffic that might be on those interconnected networks cannot signal their QoS classes and QoS requirements to the ATM network. If LAN QoS is being used on some Ethernet LANs that are interconnected by nailed-up connections, two workstations on different Ethernet LANs cannot use their LAN QoS signaling to tell the ATM network to give their connection special QoS handling. The only possible workaround is to use the Isolation technique, described earlier, to create two or more parallel PVCs through the ATM network, each with a different, fixed, ATM QoS level. The Ethernet edge devices at the boundary of the ATM network would then look at the LAN QoS signaling and place the Ethernet packets on the appropriate PVC.

A third disadvantage is that ATM's multicasting facilities aren't used. If a non-ATM station wants to multicast, it must use a separate point-to-point connection to each destination. It can't use ATM's built-in multicasting facilities.

A fourth disadvantage, which is a more general case of the multicasting problem, is that ATM switching isn't used by the non-ATM networks. Each non-ATM network is interconnected by a PVC; there's no way for the ATM network to look at the non-ATM network's packet headers and do packet routing. If there are a large number of non-ATM networks, this can result in a very large number of PVCs if the non-ATM networks are to be interconnected by a full mesh.

LANE

LAN Emulation (LANE) [ATM-1997a, ATM-1999] overcomes the first three disadvantages of nailed-up connections. It allows LAN-attached workstations to communicate with servers that have native ATM UNI connections; it allows signaling of QoS from the LAN into the ATM network; and it uses ATM's built-in multicasting facilities to emulate LAN multicasting. LANE can bridge Ethernet/IEEE 802.3, Token Ring, or FDDI network segments over ATM, although it can't be used to connect Ethernet to Token Ring. It can be used with all the common protocols that operate over LANs, such as NetBIOS, AppleTalk, Novell's IPX/SPX, and IBM's APPN. LANE's architecture is shown in Figure 7.5.

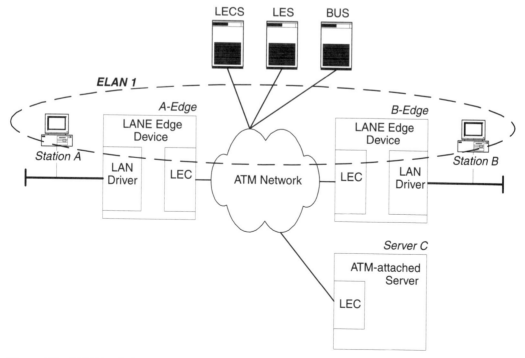

Figure 7.5 LAN Emulation (LANE).

LANE allows the ATM system to emulate Ethernet/IEEE 802.3 or IEEE 802.5 (Token Ring) LANs; FDDI LANs can use LANE through Token Ring or Ethernet emulation. Normal LANs can interconnect with ATM's Emulated LANs (ELANs) without realizing that they are based on ATM. Normal LANs can bridge across ATM networks by using ELANs, and users on normal LANs can use LANE to connect directly into ATM-attached servers and workstations that have LANE capabilities. Both transparent bridging, commonly used with Ethernet, and source-route bridging, commonly used with Token Ring, are supported. The LANE system can emulate many separate LANs simultaneously, but, as is true for normal LANs, the different emulated LANs can't interconnect without going through a router.

To do all this, the LANE system provides some special resources:

LANE Clients (LECs) operate within the ATM-attached servers or within the edge devices that connect normal LANs to the ATM network. They emulate an Ethernet/IEEE 802.3 or Token Ring/IEEE 802.5 interface. The LECs receive LAN frames, convert LAN addresses into ATM addresses, prepare the frames for transmission over the ATM network using the AAL5 format, and then transmit the LAN frames over the ATM network to the LEC (or LECs, in the case of multicasting) at the other end. An LEC can handle any number of attached LAN addresses, but they must all be on the same ELAN.

LAN Emulation Configuration Server (LECS) is the first resource used by a new LEC when it enters the network and needs to learn where the other LANE resources are. The LECS handles the network's policy rules for assigning new members to emulated LANs. A new LEC can find the LECS automatically; it's a feature of the LANE standard.

LAN Emulation Server (LES) handles address mapping. When a LAN station sends a frame into its attached LAN, it's using a LAN address—the 48-bit Media Access Control (MAC) address or a Route Descriptor for Token Ring. The LAN Emulation Server tells the LEC the address mapping between LAN and ATM addresses. The LES also handles multicasting registration, which is necessary to allow LECs to subscribe to multicasts.

Broadcast and Unknown Server (BUS) handles multicasting, broadcasting, and frames that are being sent to destinations that aren't already known by the LES. It distributes multicast and broadcast frames to the LECs that want to receive them. (For example, broadcasts are restricted to members of a particular ELAN.) It also is the default destination for LAN traffic going to unknown LAN addresses; the BUS sends those packets to all the LECs.

LANE operation can be shown by using Figure 7.5. Let's assume that Stations A and B are on the same ELAN. When an Ethernet frame destined for Station B is transmitted from A, it enters the attached LAN and is received by all stations on the LAN, including the LANE gateway, commonly called an edge device. That edge device, A-Edge in the figure, uses the LAN Emulation Server (LES) to discover the ATM address of Station B's edge device, B-Edge in the figure. The LES sends the address to A-Edge, which stores it in its cache. A-Edge then either uses an existing direct ATM virtual circuit to B-Edge or establishes a new one. A-Edge sends the Ethernet frame to B-Edge, which places it onto the attached Ethernet network where it is received by Station B. Subsequent frames from Station A use the cached address in A-Edge and the established ATM virtual circuit to go directly to B-Edge without any further overhead.

If Station A wants to transmit a multicast or broadcast, the Broadcast and Unknown Server (BUS) becomes involved. It will locate all the appropriate members of A-Edge's ELAN and will replicate and transmit frames as needed, possibly using ATM's built-in multicast facility. The BUS is also involved if the LANE system doesn't recognize the destination LAN address, as could be the case where the destination is on the far side of a LAN bridge. In that case, the LEC can't forward the frame directly to the destination; it sends it instead to the BUS, which forwards it to all LECs and hopes that they'll forward it through all attached bridges—exactly as if this were happening on a normal LAN.

Workstations or servers that have direct ATM connections (Server C in Figure 7.5) use a built-in LANE Client (LEC) to communicate with LAN-attached destinations on the other side of the ATM network. There is a standard API for this, and that API includes the ability to specify ATM traffic descriptors, the choice of ATM service category (UBR or ABR), and QoS along with the LAN address information. Edge devices also use this API internally; therefore, a bridge device can be built to do any desired mapping from other QoS systems—such as IEEE 802.1p LAN QoS—to LANE and ATM QoS.

The first version of LANE, LANE v1, was inefficient in its use of virtual circuits, didn't handle multicast well, and didn't have QoS capabilities. LANE v2 improves all these areas and also supports more than one of each type of server to improve scalability and availability. LANE v2 doesn't provide for inter-subnet interconnection among different emulated LANs, however. That requires a router or the Multi-Protocol Over ATM (MPOA) facility, discussed next.

MPOA

Multi-Protocol Over ATM (MPOA) [ATM 1997b] is a Layer Three system that was developed to allow inter-subnet connections between ATM devices without the use of a router. If the source and destination stations are both on the same ELAN, then MPOA simply uses its included LANE v2 functionality. If they're on different ELANs, MPOA can create inter-subnet shortcuts through the ATM switch fabric, thereby interconnecting a station on one ELAN directly to a station on a different ELAN without using a router. MPOA handles both IP and IPX protocols.

In an MPOA system, the MPOA Client (MPC) replaces (and contains) the LANE v2 LANE Client, as shown in Figure 7.6. The MPC is a Layer Three

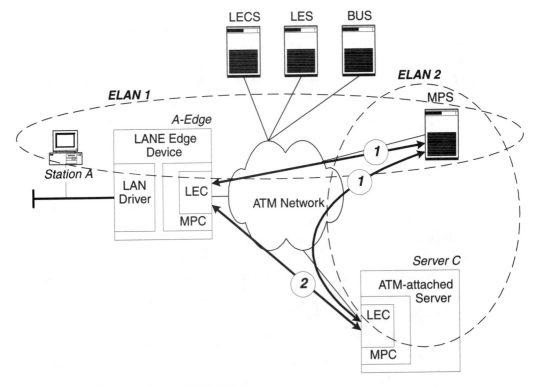

Figure 7.6 Multi-Protocol Over ATM (MPOA).

device; it can examine Layer Three addresses and handle some routing functions. There is also a new device that handles routing protocols, communicates with non-ATM routers, and can also forward packets: the MPOA Server (MPS). We'll see how these devices work by looking at an example of how MPOA connects stations that are on different IP subnets.

When the MPC realizes that the source and destination stations for an incoming packet are on different LANs or subnets, the MPC initially connects them through the packet-forwarding function of the MPS. The MPC sends the data packets across an ELAN to the MPS, and the MPS then forwards the packet to the appropriate destination ELAN (the arrows labeled *1* in Figure 7.6). This is the same as would be done with normal LANs and routers: When different LANs or subnets are involved, the data packets travel from the first station to the router. The router then examines the Layer Three address, consults its routing table, and places the packet onto the appropriate destination LAN or WAN link.

The big difference appears after a few packets have been forwarded through the MPS. The MPC doing the initial forwarding to the MPS notices that there is a string of packets with identical Layer Three subnet destination addresses. After a certain number of these packets have been sent, the MPC asks the MPS about the final ATM address of the packets. The MPS tells the MPC that destination ATM address, and the MPC can now send the packets directly to the final ATM address instead of routing them through the MPS. This is illustrated by arrow 2 in Figure 7.6. (Most situations are slightly more complex than this example, as more than one MPS may be involved in the data path.) MPOA therefore allows very efficient transfer of long datastreams among ATM-attached and LAN-attached devices on an ATM network.

MPOA has other advanced features. It can use the IETF's Multicast Address Resolution Server (MARS) [RFC 2022] to handle IP multicast addresses and multicast group membership. MPOA will also have the ability to use ATM QoS. It will be possible for MPOA edge devices to examine other types of QoS—such as IP's Diff-Serv—and map them into ATM QoS.

Classical IP over ATM (RFC 2225)

If ATM is being used to connect IP-based networks, Classical IP over ATM, as specified in RFC 2225 (previously specified in RFC 1577), can be used. Unlike LANE and MPOA, which involve mapping IP addresses to LAN addresses and then LAN addresses to ATM addresses, RFC 2225 allows IP addresses to be mapped directly to ATM addresses.

In RFC 2225, an ATMARP Server provides the address mapping function. When edge devices are initialized, they register their IP and ATM addresses with the ATMARP Server. Then the edge devices, upon receiving an incoming IP packet, either use existing ATM PVCs or ask the ATMARP server to map that packet's IP address to an ATM address. That mapping is cached in the edge device for later packets, and it's used to create an SVC, if needed, to the destination edge device on the other side of the ATM network. RFC 2225 edge devices use UBR and AAL5 to carry IP frames over the ATM network.

RFC 2225 mappings take place only within an IP subnet, called the Logical IP Subnet (LIS); RFC 2225 does not provide routing functions. Although there can be many different LISes within a single ATM network, they must use a real router to interconnect themselves.

Advantages of RFC 2225 include its relative simplicity and the large packet sizes that it can accommodate. However, classical IP over ATM, as specified in RFC 2225, cannot use ATM's QoS facilities; it is unaware of multicast or broadcast; it doesn't provide inter-subnet routing; and it's restricted to IP only.

Frame Relay Interworking

The Frame Relay Forum (www.frforum.com) standard, "Frame Relay/ATM PVC Network Interworking Implementation Agreement," [FRF.5] and the standard, "Frame Relay/ATM PVC Service Implementation Agreement," [FRF.8] specify the interconnection of Frame Relay and ATM's AAL-5 (ATM Adoption Layer 5) interface. These specify two types of interconnection: Frame Relay can be carried over ATM and restored to Frame Relay formats and behaviors at the other end of the connection, or Frame Relay can be connected to an ATM system and thereby talk directly to an ATM user. As part of the interconnection, Frame Relay's DE header bit can be mapped to and from the ATM Cell Loss Priority (CLP) header bit. The FECN and BECN bits in Frame Relay are carried through an ATM network for the case where Frame Relay is carried over ATM, but they are not normally mapped to ATM's Explicit Forward Congestion Indication (EFCI). If ATM congestion is experienced, that congestion can be mapped to Frame Relay FECN and BECN bits.

IP Type of Service (TOS) and Filtering

The basic IP QoS system that has been used for many years is based on the filtering capabilities of IP routers and, in some cases, on the IPv4 Type of Service (TOS) byte. Most IP routers can classify incoming packets according to their packet headers and then apply rudimentary QoS handling that depends on that classification. The system is usually configured for each router separately, and there can be a lot of manual record keeping and router maintenance involved. Most network administrations have used it to provide one or two special traffic classes; a typical example is a traffic class dedicated to SNA traffic. Unfortunately, providing more than a couple of classes is too complex an administrative job for most network managers; other IP-based solutions promise to be easier to manage for large networks.

Architecture

The basic Internet Protocol, IP, has a simple packet header that contains the source and destination IP address of each packet. The entire IP address is used by each router in the packet's path as it makes routing decisions; there aren't any abbreviated addresses or virtual circuit identifiers as there are with other systems such as ATM or Frame Relay. When a packet arrives at a router, that router looks at the entire IP address, compares it to a routing table, and picks the appropriate outgoing communication link depending on the entries in that table. Each router makes its own decisions, and it's possible that a particular packet may end up taking a path through the network that would surprise the first routers in the path if they knew. It's therefore not possible in normal IP networks to establish an end-to-end route and provision it for special QoS characteristics before the first packets begin to flow on the connection. Indeed, even if arrangements are made to configure all of the routers in a particular path, there's no assurance that the packets involved in the flow will flow along that path. Congestion or other problems can cause packet rerouting at any time, and some packets may even arrive in the wrong order at the destination because they took a different path than the other packets.

Because of the somewhat uncontrolled nature of IP routing, early QoS facilities in IP networks depended on the packet carrying all of its QoS information within its header. Therefore, the IP header contains a special byte, the Type of Service (TOS) byte, to carry simple QoS classification data. But router manufacturers also looked at other IP header fields to enable their routers to classify packets without requiring that the TOS byte be set properly. The set of IP header fields examined by routers for classification purposes often included the protocol type, which indicated the identity of the higher-layer protocol involved in the flow, and both source and destination addresses and IP port numbers, which usually indicated the identity of the applications at either end. (This set of five numbers is sometimes called the *five-tuple*.) Surprisingly, there are very few IP APIs that allow programmers to set the TOS byte; therefore, virtually all IP QoS classification is done implicitly, by administrators configuring their routers to examine IP header addresses and other characteristics.

Using the TOS byte and other IP header information, the routers can then classify individual packets and handle them differently, giving some priority over others in queues, for example. Routing decisions in IP networks are not usually affected by QoS, although some advanced IP routing protocols, such as OSPF, have included simple QoS-routing capabilities that can take QoS classes into account when selecting the next hop for a packet. However, the benefit of using QoS-routing capabilities in a normal IP-routed network are usually considered to be greatly outweighed by the cost and administrative complexity of implementing them.

QoS Facilities

The IPv4 packet header contains a Type of Service (TOS) byte, shown in Figure 7.7, that was originally intended to carry a 3-bit precedence level and a set of four type-of-service bits. That byte has recently been redefined as the DS-Byte, which is a part of IP Differentiated Services, described later. Nevertheless, the original IPv4 definition as the TOS byte is still in use in many networks. The IPv6 header does not contain a TOS byte; its comparable byte, the Traffic Class byte, is used only as an IP Differentiated Services DS-Byte.

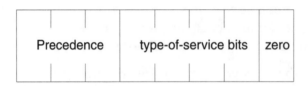

Figure 7.7 IP's Type of Service (TOS) byte.

As described in RFC 791, the TOS byte's 3-bit precedence level could take any of eight values. These corresponded to the military precedence levels of Routine (with a precedence value of zero) through CRITIC/ECP (with a precedence value of five). The highest two levels were reserved for network control: Internetwork Control was precedence value six, and Network Control was precedence value seven. Individual network administrators sometimes configured their networks to use the precedence levels, but there was never any Internet-wide usage of them. Indeed, the great majority of APIs do not give programmers any access to the precedence level.

The TOS byte also contains type-of-service bits, and their use was standardized by RFC 1349. These four bits can be turned on individually, but only one bit is to be turned on at a time. When on, the bits mean that the router should minimize delay, maximize throughput, maximize reliability, or minimize monetary cost. Some TCP/IP stacks set these bits automatically, depending on the application using the stack. For example, Telnet might be set to minimize delay, whereas FTP datastreams would be set to maximize throughput. As is true for the precedence level, most APIs do not allow programmers to change these bits.

The various router manufacturers implemented a much more flexible system than one that depends solely on the TOS byte. Instead of looking only at the value of the TOS byte, these router systems apply administrator-defined filters to all incoming packets. The filters look at a whole set of packet characteristics, typically including, along with the TOS byte, the source and destination IP addresses, the source and destination IP port, and the protocol type. Many routers can also include, as filter components, the physical port on which the packet arrived or the length of the packet.

After a filter has identified particular flows, the router can give those flows special treatment by assigning them to special queues or by giving them other forms of special handling or prioritization. For example, a set of flows identified by protocol type as being DECnet could be given a very high priority, or SNA packets encapsulated in TCP could be identified by IP port number and given special handling. In some cases, network administrators may find it easier to send high-priority packets over a special link, isolated from lower-priority packets. In that case, packets arriving on specific physical ports could be easily recognized as high priority, and part of their special handling could be ensuring that they leave the router only on certain special physical ports.

It's often possible to use a router or switch at the edge of a network to apply a filter and then set the TOS byte accordingly, so that routers in the core of the network need to look only at the TOS byte instead of having to examine all of the other header characteristics. In this case, the edge routers overwrite any existing value in the TOS byte, so the user has no control of the TOS byte's value. This is a predecessor to the modern Differentiated Services design, discussed later.

The major large-scale IP routing protocols, such as OSPF (Open Shortest Path First) and IS-IS (Intermediate System to Intermediate System), can use TOS type-of-service bits (such as the bit indicating that the router should

IP Type of Service (TOS) and Filtering QoS Characteristics

TOS and filtering are commonly used to provide coarse prioritization, such as that needed to keep SNA transaction traffic flowing over IP networks.

Bandwidth Control

Routers can be set to guarantee bandwidth to particular flows, identified by TOS or filtering, but those guarantees are only within the router queues themselves. There is no general way of providing an end-to-end guarantee because the end-to-end flow path cannot be predicted unless a network is very carefully designed with only a limited number of paths and with careful individual configuration of each router.

Discard Control

No discard control is provided by TOS and filtering, other than the indirect control that's the result of lower-priority packets being discarded before higher-priority packets. Within a particular datastream, there's no way to designate particular packets as more or less important than others.

Latency and Jitter Control

Latency and jitter guarantees are not normally provided by TOS or filtering, but they could be used to provide such guarantees in the same way that TOS or filtering could be used to provide bandwidth control. A relatively small network could be carefully designed to have only a few paths between two users that needed latency and jitter control. Then the routers in that path could be configured with the necessary filtering and minimize delay) in their routing decisions. In effect, they can maintain separate routing tables, using different tables for different settings of the TOS type-of-service bits. This allows the TOS to affect both the router's internal queuing operation and the routing decisions. But there's a lot of complexity and cost in maintaining the separate routing tables and in setting up the detailed configuration information that the routers will need to make their decisions. Therefore, IP QoS levels are not usually used to influence routing decisions within an enterprise's network, apart from the occasional use to select an outgoing physical port if there are a special set of ports used for only high-priority traffic. (BGP-4, the special routing protocol used for extremely large enterprises and for the Internet itself, has its own special methods for providing QoS for an IP network. It's beyond the scope of this book, which focuses on enterprise networks.)

queuing options to identify the user datastreams and provide the guarantees regardless of any possible route taken by the packets.

Prioritization Control

The TOS byte contains precedence indicators, although they can almost never be set by a user's API. Instead, the network administrator can usually configure routers to give various priority levels to flows identified by various IP header fields, such as IP address, port, and protocol identifier. The routers can then alter the precedence indicators, if desired.

Error Control

The only error control choice available is the maximize reliability type-of-service bit in the TOS byte, but this is almost never used by routers and only rarely appears in a user's API. An indirect way of influencing error rates is to use filtering and then select particular physical output links from the router that are known to have certain error characteristics. Selection of high-priority queues could also indirectly improve error characteristics.

QoS Signaling and Policy

As there are very few IP APIs that provide TOS signaling, virtually all the signaling for this method of QoS is implicit, done through filtering in the routers.

Some vendors can provide IP admission control, traffic policing, and policy based on IP TOS and filtering. Their routers can be configured with sophisticated policy control commands that use filtering and TOS to apply those policies to flows. COPS technology, described later, in the section "QoS Policy Management and Measurement," can also interoperate with TOS to provide policy control.

Indeed, most administrators use TOS bytes and filtering to provide only very coarse prioritization within the router queues. At most, one or two classes of traffic, such as SNA transactions, are given priority over other traffic in the queues; no strict QoS guarantees are made; and there is no attempt to influence routing decisions at all. Even for these simple QoS features, someone usually has to sit down and plan the QoS parameters for each router, design the filters and the corresponding queuing and special-handling facilities, then enter those characteristics into the router by typing into an operator interface. Automated systems to configure an entire network of routers are not in widespread use. And there's no end-to-end QoS guarantee after all the work is done—there's only a router-by-router guarantee. If there's congestion in the network—the time when QoS is most useful—the routers may suddenly decide to send some traffic through an unanticipated sequence of router hops, using routers that haven't been preconfigured appropriately to provide the right QoS levels.

Integration with Other QoS Technologies

The TOS byte, which can often be set as a result of filtering, can sometimes be used to map to other QoS facilities. For example, a router could filter on IP addresses and then set the TOS byte, and that TOS byte could later be used to influence an 802.1p LAN QoS priority setting. Most integration work by non-IP QoS facilities such as ATM will be done with the newer IP QoS facilities, however: RSVP, Integrated Services, and Differentiated Services. Those new IP QoS facilities are themselves designed to map to the older TOS byte at their boundaries or, in the case of Differentiated Services, to coexist with the TOS byte. (The Differentiated Services specification includes compatibility with the precedence portion of the TOS byte, although not with the four type-of-service bits. This is discussed in detail in the "Differentiated Services" section of this chapter.)

Integrated Services and RSVP

The Internet architecture was not designed to provide sophisticated QoS, and it was usually impossible for a program to affect its QoS level through API commands. As discussed in the previous section, the only QoS facility provided was the rudimentary TOS byte in the IP header, but the great majority of TCP/IP protocol stacks didn't allow users to set that byte through the API. Therefore, the only way for an application to obtain even the rudimentary enhanced services available on an IP-based network was for the application to use an identifiable Internet address, port number, or protocol, and for the network administrator to manually configure each individual router in the flow's path to recognize those addresses, port numbers, and protocols and then provide the appropriate service. Because there wasn't a QoS API, programmers couldn't change their QoS level once it had been assigned by the administrator. Worse, because each router had to be individually configured, adding a new path through the network (possibly because of a new user) might require reconfiguration of routers that had not previously had to deal with the datastream needing QoS.

Even if a network administrator was willing to do the work to configure all of the routers, he still faced a nightmare if he wanted to provide the strict QoS guarantees of latency, jitter, bandwidth, or error rate that some applications required. He would have to predict all of the possible paths through the network for each flow, somehow ensure that the flows wouldn't exceed a certain size, calculate the buffering options required at each router to ensure that the router wouldn't exceed its budget for the particular QoS characteristic, take link latency and router processing overhead into consideration, and only then begin the time-consuming work of manual router configuration. Each router had to have filters set up to identify the flows, and the queuing and routing decisions had to be carefully tuned. For all but the smallest networks, the task of designing and configuring all these options on all of the individual routers was unthinkable.

The Resource reSerVation Protocol (RSVP), a component of the IETF's Integrated Services architecture for IP QoS, was designed to overcome these problems. It provides a QoS API for IP users, and it automatically signals the QoS requirements of a datastream to all routers in the datastream's path. It then handles the necessary calculations to ensure that QoS guarantees can be met, and it reserves the necessary resources at each router in the path or rejects QoS requests if they can't be accommodated. The Integrated Services architecture also provides the definitions of the flow traffic characteristics and of the QoS services to be provided.

RSVP and Integrated Services are complex, and they may be too complex for use in very large-scale networks and by ISPs. They require that RSVP-aware routers be able to remember the characteristics of each individual QoS-controlled flow passing through them. Therefore, in some cases, parts of the RSVP specification are being used without the rest of the RSVP design or the Integrated Services architecture. This approach, discussed in detail in the "Differentiated Services" section, allows the end-user signaling portion of RSVP to be used without including the scaling difficulties of a full RSVP and Integrated Services implementation.

Architecture

The problem faced by RSVP's designers was that IP is a datagram protocol; that is, it doesn't first create a connection (a virtual circuit) and then send data over it using an abbreviated address. Instead, each individual packet contains the entire destination address and is routed independently of all the other packets. There isn't any guarantee that the particular route picked by any one packet will be the same as the route picked by subsequent packets. There isn't any connection setup phase during which QoS parameters can be negotiated and appropriate routes chosen. So there's no simple way to identify all of the routers that will be involved in a particular flow, and there's no simple way to preconfigure them during a connection setup phase.

RSVP therefore was created as a completely new protocol designed to live in the somewhat changeable world of IP routing. It's truly a new protocol, with its own protocol ID, separate from UDP, TCP, and the other IP-based protocols. The RSVP packets are carried by IP, and they therefore use the same routing tables and follow the same routes as UDP and TCP packets, but, unlike those packets, they interact with the routers along the path. If the routing tables change, as they do occasionally, both the flow packets and the RSVP packets will follow the new route.

The source of a flow uses the RSVP API to start the process of configuring QoS for that flow. For example, a server that has been contacted by a new user will issue RSVP commands to provide QoS for its new flow to that user, or a server that's starting a multicast will issue RSVP commands for that multicast's outgoing flow. The RSVP commands create an RSVP protocol message called a PATH message, which is addressed to the flow's ultimate destination but which actively interacts with all of the RSVP-aware routers as it travels downstream along the path to that destination, setting up control blocks as it goes. (See Figure 7.8.) The PATH message identifies the relevant flow by the usual method: the IP address, IP port, and protocol identifier. All of the routers in the path, upon receiving the PATH message, will now have the information they need to recognize the flow when it appears at one of their interfaces. The PATH

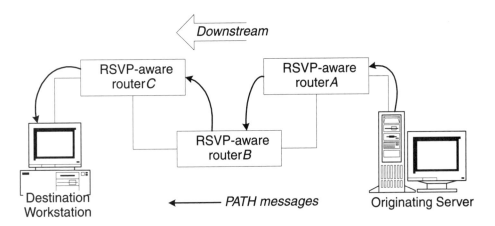

Figure 7.8 RSVP PATH message flow.

message also carries the traffic characteristics of the flow (average and peak data rates, etc.), so that the routers will know how much of their capacity that flow will require. Finally, the PATH message can contain fields used by all of the RSVP-aware routers in the path to indicate the QoS services that they can provide and how much of their resources they can afford to dedicate to this flow. This last group of fields, called the AdSpec, can count the number of RSVP-aware routers in the path, estimate the total available bandwidth, give the maximum packet size that can pass along the route without being fragmented, and estimate the minimum available latency, based on each router's updating the minimum_path_latency field as the PATH message passes through on the way to its final destination. Note that *no actual QoS reservations are being made by the PATH message*; it's simply setting up RSVP control blocks in the various RSVP-aware routers that it's passing through and accumulating interesting QoS information.

When the PATH message finally arrives at its destination, which is also the destination of the flow, it contains valuable information about the characteristics of that flow and about the characteristics of the path that the flow will take on its way from the source. The destination can then, if it wants, ask to make a QoS reservation for the flow. That reservation is made by the RESV message, which follows the path of the PATH message backward, upstream to the data source.

Following the PATH message's path backward isn't as simple as it first appears. IP networks are known for having asymmetric routing; that is, the flow in one direction often follows a different path from the flow in the opposite direction. The path from user A to user B is often completely different from the path from user B to user A! There are a variety of reasons for this, but the result is that RSVP cannot simply assume that it can backtrack over the PATH message's path by blindly following the standard routing tables back to the source as if it were an ordinary IP packet. Instead, the PATH message, as it travels from the flow source to the destination, takes care to place a special Previous Hop (PHOP) address in each control block that it sets up. For example, if the PATH message travels from Router A to Router B, it will place Router A's address into the control block that it builds for its flow in Router B. If it then travels on to Router C, it will place Router B's address into the control block that it builds for its flow in Router C, and so on until it reaches its final destination.

The result is that if that final destination decides to ask for an RSVP reservation by issuing a RESV message, the RESV message will be able to follow the PATH message's path backward by looking at the PHOP addresses stored in all the control blocks. In our example, it will look at Router C's PHOP to discover that the previous router was Router B. The RESV message will then go to Router B, make its necessary changes to the control block it finds there, and then travel on to Router A. The RESV message will continue upstream, making changes in all the router control blocks as needed to install the desired QoS reservation, until it finally reaches the flow source. At that time, it will know if it was able to make the reservation successfully in all of the involved routers, and it can send a confirmation message back to the requester at the flow's destination address. (If there is a problem at one of the intermediate router hops, that router will send an error message immediately to the destination, which can then decide if it wants to try asking for a different set of QoS characteristics.)

The RSVP system handles the changeable nature of IP routing paths by associating a timeout interval with each RSVP control block in each router. Instead of sending the PATH message and the RESV message once, they're sent repeatedly by the source and the destination stations. Each transmission of the PATH message and the RESV message refreshes the RSVP control blocks and resets the timeout timers. If the path changes, these retransmissions of the PATH message and RESV message will tell the new routers about the QoS reservation, and the abandoned routers will eventually discard their RSVP control blocks for the flow when the timeout timers expire. This technique is called *soft state*.

What types of QoS reservations can RSVP make? The IETF Integrated Services architecture includes two basic reservation classes and three different styles. The classes are Guaranteed Service, which provides a bandwidth guarantee and a maximum end-to-end latency, and Controlled Load, which provides a prioritized service that is supposed to approximate the service a user would receive on an uncongested network. The RSVP system allows a user who has received a QoS reservation to continue probing the network to try and get larger and larger QoS allocations without losing his or her previous reservation.

The RSVP system also knows how to handle reservations for multicasts. The three reservation styles are used to indicate the different ways in which a destination is willing to have its incoming flows share bandwidth. This capability can be useful if the routers leading to a destination are congested; it lets the destination decide how the limited bandwidth should be shared among incoming datastreams when the alternative, insisting on a separate set of QoS guarantees for each datastream, might lead to rejection of some reservation attempts by the overburdened routers. For example, a speech-only conference call only needs to allow one speaker at a time; it's wasteful to insist on full bandwidth reservations for all possible speakers simultaneously.

Although RSVP was originally designed as a piece of the IETF's Integrated Services architecture, pieces of it have recently appeared as components of other IP QoS architectures, such as Differentiated Services, discussed later in this chapter. The piece that's most often used is the RSVP API and the signaling mechanism at both sender and destination; sometimes most of the router-to-router signaling system and RSVP control block structure is left out and replaced by a different design. It's important to realize, therefore, that the term RSVP is not always inextricably linked to the Integrated Services architecture and to the complete RSVP designs.

QoS Facilities

RSVP provides the user with access to the IETF's Integrated Services reservation classes. There were originally supposed to be four classes, but only two have been defined: Guaranteed Service and Controlled Load. We'll look at them after we look at the traffic descriptors that Integrated Service uses to describe the characteristics of the flow. RSVP includes those traffic descriptors in the PATH message that the source of the datastream sends down the path to the destination before the actual reservations are made.

Traffic Descriptors

The Integrated Services traffic characteristics are given in a special format known as the Tspec, and they specify the flow characteristics in token bucket terms. The Tspec traffic specification includes five items:

Token Rate (r). The average data rate in bytes per second.

Token Bucket Size (b). The number of bytes that can be held in the token bucket before it overflows (a good estimate of the burstiness of the flow).

Peak Data Rate (p). The maximum data rate in bytes per second.

Minimum Policed Unit (m). The minimum packet size, in bytes, for purposes of computing the per-packet flow characteristics from the other Tspec parameters. (The real packets can be smaller than this value.) For example, the Peak Data Rate divided by the Minimum Policed Unit gives the maximum number of packets per second.

Maximum Packet Size (M). The largest allowed packet, in bytes. Larger packets are considered nonconforming and may not get QoS handling.

The Tspec is included in the PATH message sent by the flow's source, and it's repeated in the RESV message used to make the QoS reservation. It tells the routers the characteristics of the flow that needs QoS services. This helps the router decide if it can honor the RESV message asking for QoS.

QoS Parameters

These parameters are used in the Flow Specification part of the RESV message that is sent upstream by the destination of a flow. The QoS parameters of concern to us are those that describe the two possible Integrated Services Classes: Guaranteed Service, which makes quantitative guarantees of particular latency values, and Controlled Load, which is qualitative, promising only a level of performance that is relatively better than other levels of performance.

The Guaranteed Service class is specified by the Tspec parameters, which are repeated in the RESV message to specify the traffic characteristics of the flow, and by two additional parameters: the Rate and the Slack Term.

The Rate is the required average data rate in bytes per second, which must be equal to or greater than the Token Rate in the Tspec. The RSVP software at the destination of the flow, using the information that it received in the PATH message, can calculate the Rate that it should request if it wants a particular end-to-end maximum latency. The Slack Term, measured in units of time, tells the routers how much flexibility the destination has in its willingness to trade increased latency for decreased bandwidth requirements.

The important thing to notice here is that the Guaranteed Service class allows the recipient of a flow to specify the maximum allowable end-to-end latency. It does not allow specification of minimum latency, jitter, or error rate. It is also important to note that these guarantees may fail temporarily if the flow is rerouted; the new routers in the flow's path won't know about the QoS guarantees until the soft state is refreshed by the PATH and RESV messages that are automatically repeated at regular intervals.

The other Integrated Service class is Controlled Load, which was designed to approximate the end-to-end performance of an uncongested network. The RESV message asking for Controlled Load simply repeats the Tspec parameters; there aren't any additional parameters. Controlled load does not try to make any latency guarantees or any other type of guarantee, although it does imply that the requested bandwidth will be available at low error rates and reasonable latency. It just tries to ensure that performance will be that of an unloaded network. If a router doesn't think that it can provide such performance, it will reject the QoS request.

Integration with Other QoS Technologies

RSVP and the Integrated Services architecture are an important new IP QoS architecture, and as such, are being mapped into other modern QoS architectures. This is especially true of the ATM, LAN QoS, and Differentiated Services architectures.

RFCs 2379 through 2382 concern the interoperation of RSVP and ATM :

- Guaranteed Service class can be mapped into ATM's CBR or rt-VBR services, with the Guaranteed Service's Rate parameter corresponding to ATM's parameter SCR (sustainable cell rate), Tspec's parameter p (peak data rate) corresponding to ATM's parameter PCR (peak cell rate), and Tspec's parameter b (token bucket size) corresponding to ATM's parameter MBS (maximum burst size).

- Controlled Load service class can be mapped into nrt-VBR with the PCR set equal to Tspec's p, SCR set equal to Tspec's r (token rate), and MBS set equal to Tspec's b.

- Controlled Load service class can also be mapped into ABR, with PCR set equal to Tspec's p and MCR (Minimum Cell Rate) set equal to Tspec's r. The boundary devices at the interconnection of ATM and the IP routed network should have enough buffer capacity to absorb bursts of the size given by Tspec's b.

RSVP can also interoperate with ATM's LANE v2 and MPOA, which can use ABR and therefore can provide Controlled Load QoS characteristics.

Integrated Services and RSVP QoS Characteristics

Integrated Services and RSVP are used in some production environments, but they require that each RSVP-aware router maintain a control block for each individual flow that requires special QoS handling. This is practical in moderate-sized networks, but it is completely impractical for very large enterprises or the Internet. As RFC 2208 says, "The operators of [high bandwidth] backbones will probably not choose to naively implement RSVP for each separate stream. Rather, techniques are being developed that will, at the 'edge' of the backbone, aggregate together the streams that require special treatment. Within the backbone, various less costly approaches [such as Diff-Serv, discussed later] would then be used to set aside resources for the aggregate as a whole, as a way of meeting end-to-end requirements of individual flows."

Bandwidth Control

Guaranteed Service and Controlled Load both specify the bandwidth required in token bucket terms that allow for the specification of variable-rate flows. Both of these service classes can provide the effect of a bandwidth guarantee.

Discard Control

No discard control is provided by Integrated Services and RSVP, other than the indirect control that's the result of better performance for flows with Guaranteed Service or Controlled Load QoS. Within a particular datastream there's no way to designate particular packets as more or less important than others.

Latency and Jitter Control

Controlled Load provides no latency or jitter control, and Guaranteed Service provides only maximum latency control. It's possible that, with Guaranteed Service, the end-to-end latency will jitter between almost zero and the maximum latency that was guaranteed.

These technologies allow both IP destination addresses and QoS to be signaled into the underlying ATM network from the boundary devices, giving a seamless, routed IP connection to and over an ATM backbone.

Integrated Services and RSVP are also being designed to interoperate with LAN QoS through the use of the Subnetwork Bandwidth Manager (SBM). And SBM will be able to use the priority bits in the new 802.1 LAN header to create a few QoS classes that can then be coarsely mapped to groups of Integrated Services QoS characteristics. For example, one priority level could be reserved for the equivalent of the Controlled Load service class, and the SBM, acting as if it were an RSVP-aware router,

Prioritization Control

No prioritization control is provided, although the effect of Controlled Load is that of providing a high-priority path through the network. Guaranteed Service, of course, is a different type of QoS guarantee that is far stronger than that of simple prioritization.

Error Control

No error control beyond that normally provided by IP is explicitly provided by Integrated Services and RSVP.

QoS Signaling and Policy

QoS is signaled through the RSVP API, which is controlled by the application programmer. These APIs have been incorporated in many common TCP/IP protocol stack APIs, such as the Windows WinSock 2.0 API, the Sun Microsystems Solaris Bandwidth Manager API, and IETF's model RSVP API, RAPI, which is available on some UNIX platforms.

Because RSVP is controlled by the applications programmer, the issue of policy control and policing is important. "If first-class upgrades are free, everyone will fly first-class." Admission control, traffic policing, and policy are being incorporated into the Integrated Services model, and the RSVP system can carry a Policy Data specification in its PATH and RESV messages. These Policy Data specifications are used in conjunction with the policy and traffic management tools described later in this chapter. They help ensure that QoS reservation requests are validated against a database controlled by the network administration before they are granted.

In any case, the RSVP system incorporates a policing mechanism that examines flows to ensure that they do not exceed their Tspec. Data packets outside the Tspec given in the RESV message that created their QoS reservation can be discarded or handled as if they were normal IP traffic, without any special QoS reservation. Note that traffic shaping may be needed, either in the flow source or within the routers, to ensure that the flow remains within the Tspec's token bucket style of specification. If packets clump up at some point, they may exceed the Token Bucket Size or Peak Data Rate and be discarded.

would accept only as many RSVP reservations as could be accommodated in the LAN without congesting that particular priority level. A couple of other levels could be reserved in a similar manner for various maximum latencies, which would help provide the rough equivalent to Guaranteed Service.

Finally, Integrated Services are being connected to the latest IP QoS design, Differentiated Services, which is a way of grouping large numbers of flows requiring similar QoS levels into a few large classes. RSVP is still used at the edges to signal QoS requirements, but the core of the network, where keeping track of thousands of different flows might be overwhelming, can use the Differentiated Services architecture. The routers at the boundary between Integrated Services and Differentiated Services are responsible for processing the RSVP PATH and RESV messages appropriately. For example, a router on the boundary would accept an RESV message that's traveling upstream, examine it, and work within the Differentiated Services system to make the appropriate reservations within the appropriate Differentiated Services class to cross the core of the network. If the reservation can be made, it would then transparently forward the RESV message upstream to the router at the exit of the Differentiated Services section of the network, and that boundary router would then continue with the RSVP work as if there had been no interruption.

Differentiated Services

Integrated Services and RSVP provide a structure for very detailed control of the QoS of individual flows as they pass through a network of IP routers. Unfortunately, the scalability of that solution is still in doubt. Routers that are RSVP-aware must process and remember the state of every individual flow that's going through them, and rerouted flows don't get QoS handling until the next RSVP soft-state refresh. This could be tolerable in smaller systems, with limited numbers of routers and limited numbers of flows at any one time, but it's an overwhelming task in the Internet as a whole.

Differentiated Services (Diff-Serv) was developed as a way of providing something between the simplicity of IP TOS and the exceedingly fine granularity of Integrated Services and RSVP. As does Integrated Services, it can provide both guarantees (quantitative services) and relative performance levels (qualitative services.) It does that by using a byte in the IP header to indicate the QoS class. All the information that the router needs to handle the packet is contained in the packet header, so routers don't need to learn or store information about individual flows. There's no need for soft-state refresh messages; there's no worry about packets that temporarily don't get their proper QoS handling after they've been rerouted. There are no scalability worries associated with the need for routers to store information about flows. The disadvantage of Differentiated Services is that flows must be handled as part of larger groups; it's not possible to single out a particular flow for special handling, independent of other flows. Instead, it must be grouped with many other flows for its trip through all the routers, and it will receive the same handling as all of the other flows in its group.

For large-scale networks and the ISPs making up the Internet backbone, the granularity disadvantage of Differentiated Services is very small compared to the advantages. Differentiated Services will allow ISPs and large networks to offer different classes of QoS at different price points, something that Integrated Services/RSVP was too complex to do. The ISP executive or the network administrator of a large network doesn't want to offer hundreds of different service-level agreement (SLA) options and prices; they would be impossible to administer or to sell. Differentiated Services, which can easily provide a handful of distinct SLA options at different price levels, is ideal.

Differentiated Services appeals to small and midsized networks also. The flexibility offered by Integrated Services/RSVP may simply be an invitation to excessive complexity with no major advantages for most applications. A couple of Differentiated Services levels may be all that's needed to separate real-time, delay-intolerant traffic such as interactive voice from more tolerant traffic such as streaming video. Finer distinctions among different interactive voice flows may not be necessary.

Because of the broad appeal of Differentiated Services, there's a lot of work being done to provide interoperability between it and other QoS technologies, such as LAN QoS, ATM, IP TOS, and Integrated Services/RSVP. For example, Integrated Services/RSVP could be used at the edge of a large enterprise network, possibly in a lab needing finely tuned QoS, and a border router could convert the Integrated Services/RSVP signaling into Differentiated Services for those flows that needed to cross the core of the enterprise network—possibly to resurface in another small Integrated Services/RSVP network at the far side.

Architecture

Both Integrated Services/RSVP and the older IP Filtering technique required complex setup of each router in the flow's path. The routers had to be told about the individual flows requiring QoS. They had to store flow identification information, and they had to be told how to handle each of those individual flows. All this setup was done, either by network administration or by RSVP signaling, before the flows arrived. Flows that were rerouted because of network congestion, the very situation in which QoS could be most valuable, risked losing their QoS handling until the RSVP soft-state refresh signals caught up with them. In the case of IP Filtering, they might never get that QoS handling on the new route.

Instead of relying on stored QoS information in each router for each flow, Differentiated Services (Diff-Serv) relies on marking the individual packets for enhanced QoS services. All the signaling information that the router needs is embedded in the packet header in a standard place, called the DS-byte; no complex filtering is needed. That's a great advantage to router configuration and router processing overhead, but the problem facing the Diff-Serv designers was where to put that marking.

The problem of finding a home for the DS-Byte was solved by reusing the TOS byte that has always existed in the IPv4 header and by changing the IPv6 packet header to accommodate the new DS-Byte. The specification of the new DS-Byte in "Definition of the Differentiated Services Field (DS Field) in the IPv4 and IPv6 Headers" [RFC 2474], is the formal definition of how this new 8-bit field fits into both IPv4 and IPv6. Its use is uniform regardless of whether the IPv4 or IPv6 protocol is being used.

The great majority of the traffic on IP-based networks uses the IPv4 header, and that header has always had a TOS byte. Described in an earlier section, the TOS byte could be used to indicate both precedence and traffic classification (low latency, high throughput, etc.). The upper three bits gave the precedence, while the middle four bits gave the classification. The lowest bit was always zero. The TOS byte was rarely used, however. The DS-byte replaces it entirely, and the routers at the edge of new Diff-Serv networks are supposed to examine the incoming packets to ensure that any old-style TOS bytes are rewritten into the new DS-Bytes. Nevertheless, there is some compatibility between the two styles: the precedence field in the old TOS byte is given a reasonable interpretation when handled by DS-Byte rules.

In a DS-Byte (Figure 7.9), the upper three bits, which are the same three bits used by the TOS byte for its precedence field, are called the Class Selector. The values in the Class Selector must form a strict hierarchy, with 111 being the highest priority and 000 the lowest. Although the names are different, this is the same effect as for the TOS byte's precedence field. In particular, the highest two precedence values, 110 and 111, which were sometimes used in TOS-style networks to indicate network control packets, continue to be the highest priority in DS-style networks.

The other bits in the TOS byte didn't do as well in the transformation into the DS-Byte; they're completely incompatible. A TOS-style router looking at a DS-style header will be completely confused because the TOS byte was allowed to have only one of the middle four bits turned on at any time. In the DS-style header, there are often a whole set of these bits turned on at any time. A particular network administration may, however, decide to set up its DS-style routers to ignore the middle bits, thereby creating a network that's compatible with a TOS-style network.

Indeed, the real definition of the DS-Byte shows that it's not, strictly speaking, a concatenation of a priority field and a traffic classification field. Instead, the upper six bits of the DS-Byte are called Differentiated Services Code Points (DSCPs), and they're used to specify traffic classes. (The bottom two bits of the DS-Byte are unused and must be ignored.) These Code Points can be any value, and they can mean anything—subject to the requirement that the upper three bits be interpretable as a priority level. The lower three bits don't have any inherent meaning, and different Diff-Serv QoS services handle them in different ways, as we'll see. The specification makes a point of saying that a router isn't allowed to handle the six bits together as some sort of a priority field. Instead, it must use the entire six-bit field as an index into a table of router behaviors. This allows any combination of bits to be used to indicate any possible router behavior, without regard to what numerically adjacent Code Points mean. For example, some Code Points announce different sensitivities

Figure 7.9 Differentiated Service's DS-Byte.

to packet loss, while others provide QoS facilities that make the packet-switched system appear to be a constant bit rate leased line.

IPv6 was easier to adapt to Diff-Serv, as it was undergoing final specification while Diff-Serv was being designed. The first attempt at IPv6 specification contained a priority field with some similarities to that in IPv4. There was a 3-bit priority subfield, with network control traffic as the highest priority, and then there was an additional bit to distinguish between traffic that was sensitive to congestion and able to respond to feedback about bandwidth, and traffic that was insensitive and unable to respond. The original IPv6 also contained a 24-bit Flow Label field, which could be used to identify individual flows for special handling. The idea was that flows that needed unusual handling would set this field to a nonzero value, and all of the routers that handled the flow could use that value as an index into a hash table of prestored instructions for that flow.

The IPv6 priority field underwent some changes as the protocol was redesigned, and it eventually evolved into an 8-bit Traffic Class field in the RFC 2460 version of IPv6. (The IPv6 priority field grew by four bits, taking those bits from the Flow Label field in the original IPv6 specification. The Flow Label then became a 20-bit field.) The Traffic Class field was the placeholder for the DS-Byte, which now has the Traffic Class byte as its standardized home in IPv6's header.

The structure of a router designed to handle IP Diff-Serv is straightforward, and there are five different functions that most Diff-Serv routers need to perform. First, all Diff-Serv routers must start by performing the following:

Packet Classification. Very similar to IP Filtering, Diff-Serv devices need to classify packets for QoS handling. The simplest method, called Behavior Aggregate (BA) classification, is to look at the DS-byte only. BA classification is the best method for routers in the core of the network, where the workload is heavy. The other method, called Multi-Field (MF) classification, is similar to IP filtering and RSVP flow identification. An MF classifier looks at a range of fields, possibly including the DS-byte, IP address, IP ports, protocol type, and physical port on which the packet arrived. MF classification is best used in routers at the edge of a Diff-Serv network, where the router has a relatively light workload and can spare the CPU cycles to do the classification.

After the traffic is classified, there are four different traffic-conditioning functions that a Diff-Serv router may use. Depending on classification, some packets may use all of these; others may use only one or two. They are as follows:

Metering. This is a Diff-Serv router's traffic measurement and accounting function. It ensures that arriving traffic is within its traffic descriptor specifications (the Traffic Conditioning Agreement, TCA), and it accumulates accounting information for user billing. If there's a problem, it may send signals to the other traffic-conditioning functions inside the router. For example, depending on the packet's classification, it may decide to reshape (and delay) nonconformant traffic, or it may decide simply to re-mark or drop such traffic.

Marking. A packet that has been classified by MF classification almost certainly needs to have its DS-Byte set appropriately, and that's the job of the Marking function. But Marking is used in other cases, also. A traffic flow that is exceeding its allowable traffic specifications may have its DS-Byte changed to a lower category, and incoming packets with DS-Byte markings that aren't recognized by a differently configured DS-type network may need to have their DS-Bytes re-marked. Some routers may simply want to re-mark all incoming packets, to ensure that they have complete control over the possible Differentiated Services Code Points within their particular portion of the network.

Shaping. If incoming traffic is too bursty, the router may use a shaping function to delay some packets, reshaping them to fit inside of their allowed traffic specification. This is commonly done at the edge of a network, but it can also be needed inside the network's core. Note that some categories of traffic may not want to be shaped, as delayed traffic may be useless to them. For such categories, dropping or re-marking may be preferred.

Dropping. Traffic that's nonconformant to its traffic specification may simply be dropped. There may be different thresholds for dropping packets. The traffic classifier could classify incoming packets into three different categories, with different thresholds for packet dropping. Those packet dropping actions would then be implemented by the packet dropping function as signaled by the packet category.

The question of how to set up Diff-Serv categories and ensure that there will be sufficient resources to handle incoming packets at their required QoS level is complex. One alternative is to use a policy-based system to control all the routers and their willingness to admit new traffic flows; another is to use Integrated Services/RSVP to signal the needs for aggregated flows through the network, using RSVP to establish only a few, aggregated flows instead of individual flows.

A third method is to use the newly emerging MultiProtocol Label Switching (MPLS) architecture to create virtual circuits across IP-routed networks. MPLS is basically a traffic engineering architecture designed for handling the scalability problems in large networks, and it can be used to provide QoS facilities. It uses a new header field that's inserted into the packet between the Layer Two and Layer Three headers, although there are some cases where an existing field could be used—such as ATM's circuit identifiers. MPLS labels are used as if they were virtual circuit identifiers, providing a set of Label-Switched Paths (LSPs) from one side of the network to the other. Particular MPLS LSPs could be set aside for certain QoS levels, and groups of IP flows could be combined into one MPLS LSP for their trip through the network.

In any case, there's not yet much experience with the issue of setting up service-level agreements (SLAs) and their traffic descriptors (Traffic Conditioning Agreements, TCAs) that correspond to particular Diff-Serv classifications. Diff-Serv is very new, and the issues involved in standardizing SLAs and TCAs across administrative boundaries must be worked out. It's very possible that packets may need to be re-marked or shaped at these boundaries as they move from one network to another.

QoS Facilities

There are four QoS classes that are currently supported by Diff-Serv: Default, Class Selector, Assured Forwarding, and Expedited Forwarding.

Default Class is the same as today's best-effort forwarding. Its DS-Byte is all zeros, and it provides no QoS services.

Class Selector Class is the equivalent of the older TOS byte's precedence field. There are eight priority classes, or Code Points, and they are in strict priority order. These priority classes don't have to be handled separately by routers; that is, multiple adjacent priorities can be combined into one queue. However, a packet with one of the two highest Class Selector priorities must be given better handling than a packet with a Class Selector priority of zero. (This preserves the priority of network management packets that are marked with the old TOS classifications of 110 [six] or 111 [seven].)

Assured Forwarding Class (AF) combines prioritization with packet drop probabilities. There are four Assured Forwarding classes, and they are the priority equivalent of the lowest four non-zero Class Selector classes. (That is, AF Class One is the priority equivalent of a Class Selector packet in priority One, the lowest non-zero priority. AF Class Four is the priority equivalent of a Class Selector packet in priority Four.) There isn't any AF Class at priority zero, as the all-zero Code Point is reserved for Default Class traffic. The highest Class Selector priority classes, Five, Six, and Seven, don't have an AF Class equivalent. Packets marked with Class Selector priorities Six and Seven may be given higher priority than any AF Class packets.

Each AF Class contains three packet drop precedence levels. Within an AF Class, if there's a shortage of network resources, packets can be dropped by routers in order of packet drop precedence level. The router is expected to use an algorithm such as Random Early Detection (RED) and to do the dropping gradually. It isn't supposed to decide, abruptly, that it's in trouble and that all packets, from all packet drop precedence levels, must be dropped. It should start dropping packets smoothly, from the level that has the highest drop probability, and it should escalate to dropping packets from the other levels only if the congestion problems don't resolve themselves.

Expedited Forwarding Class (EF) is a single class that tries to emulate the assured bandwidth, low-latency, low-jitter, low-loss behavior of a leased line. There are no subclasses; either a packet is in Expedited Forwarding or it isn't. The Expedited Forwarding Code Point is at the precedence level of a Class Selector packet in priority Five. There aren't any specifications about the amount of latency, jitter, or packet loss to be provided by any particular network's EF Class; that's up to the network administration and the capabilities of the routers that are implementing EF.

Integration with Other QoS Technologies

Because Diff-Serv is very new, there are few existing specifications for the interoperation of Diff-Serv with other QoS Architectures. However, it's certain that they will appear.

■ Integrated Services/RSVP could be used at the edge of a large enterprise network, possibly in a lab needing finely tuned QoS, and a border router could convert the Integrated Services/RSVP signaling into Differentiated Services for those flows that needed to cross the core of the enterprise network—possibly to reappear in another small Integrated Services/RSVP network at the far side. The border router would verify that the Diff-Serv network could carry the Integrated Services/RSVP traffic, then it would appropriately mark the

Differentiated Services QoS Characteristics

Diff-Serv is a new technology that is being designed to provide QoS in a scalable manner over both small and very large IP-based networks. It's not as flexible as Integrated Services/RSVP, but it appears to be much more practical for large enterprises and ISPs. This is a very new architecture, however, and there isn't much experience with controlling access to particular QoS classes and to provisioning those classes automatically across a large network in such a way that QoS levels are maintained correctly.

Bandwidth Control

Expedited Forwarding Class allows a user to request bandwidth equivalent to that given by a leased line, although the exact methods for specifying that bandwidth and for assuring that it can be delivered are currently left up to the network administrator. This is a much coarser control than that offered by Integrated Services, as there is only one Code Point for Expedited Forwarding. In effect, the network's central policy control must somehow ensure that it isn't allowing too many users to make use of this facility. It must keep track of the bandwidth available in all routers and links, and it must be sure that there aren't aggregation points where that available bandwidth won't be sufficient to handle all the packets that appear at the router's input port with their DS-byte set to the Expedited Forwarding Class.

Discard Control

The Assured Forwarding Class provides three levels of discard control, and the Class Selector Class implies that higher priorities will suffer less packet loss than lower priorities. If an application wants to tag its packets with different packet discard preferences, Assured Forwarding Class is the best choice.

Latency and Jitter Control

The only class providing some latency and jitter control is the Explicit Forwarding Class, but the amount of that control and the exact parameters are left up to the particular network administration and the capabilities of its routers. As was true for Bandwidth Control, this is a much coarser control than that offered by Integrated Services; only one category is available. For example, a network administrator might provide an Explicit

DS-byte in the flow's packets and would transport the RSVP packets along with the flow packets through the Diff-Serv network.

- Diff-Serv's Class Selector class was designed to interoperate with the older IP TOS prioritization system. Border routers can re-mark packets as necessary.

Forwarding Class that guarantees a maximum end-to-end latency of 200 milliseconds and makes no other latency or jitter guarantees. The network's central policy control must somehow ensure that it isn't allowing too many users to make use of this facility. It must also be sure that there aren't aggregation points where there won't be sufficient capacity to handle all the packets that appear at the router's input port with their DS-Byte set to the Expedited Forwarding Class.

Prioritization Control

Prioritization Control is furnished by all of the Diff-Serv classes except Default Class, the lowest priority.

Error Control

Error Control beyond that normally provided by IP could be provided by any of the classes, depending on the particular network administrator and the capabilities of the routers. It is not explicitly required by the specifications, however.

QoS Signaling and Policy

The basic Diff-Serv model assumes that QoS categories will usually be signaled by filtering on an incoming flow, in the manner currently used by IP Filtering. The IP addresses, port numbers, protocol type, and other characteristics can be used by Diff-Serv's MF-classifier to determine QoS categories and set the DS-byte appropriately. However, RFC 2460 requires that "the service interface to the IPv6 service within a node must provide a means for an upper-layer protocol to supply the value of the Traffic Class bits . . . " The new programmer APIs, unlike the previous ones for IP, are being built to allow this. The result is that some flows will probably be directly controlled by applications.

Because Diff-Serv packet marking could be controlled by the applications programmer, the issue of policy control and policing is important to avoid overcommitting resources. As one way of doing this, the Diff-Serv boundary routers could examine and re-mark all incoming packets to enforce SLAs, validating QoS reservation requests against a database controlled by the network administration before they are granted. In any case, the Diff-Serv system's traffic conditioning functions can examine flows to ensure that they do not exceed their SLA's Traffic Conditioning Agreements. Data packets outside the agreements can be discarded or re-marked to lower QoS levels.

- Diff-Serv's classes could be mapped to LAN QoS through the use of the Subnetwork Bandwidth Manager (SBM).

- ATM and MPLS can be used to transport Diff-Serv traffic, providing appropriate guarantees for the various Diff-Serv classes.

In all of these cases, the method for specifying and controlling service-level agreements and their included traffic conditioning agreements will be the key to successful interoperability. The other technologies must somehow be able to interoperate with those agreements and control the traffic flowing across the boundaries, controlling admission and policing as necessary.

Traffic Shaping

Traffic shaping is a technique for delaying some network traffic in an attempt to spread out traffic peaks, making it less chunky and therefore less of a strain on network equipment. It is an intrinsic part of many networking technologies, most notably ATM and Diff-Serv, where there are explicit traffic-shaping components. The technology is described in Chapter 6, "Basic QoS Technologies," and this section is a very brief discussion of its use as a stand-alone network building block when it's not automatically included in the underlying network or QoS technology.

Stand-alone traffic shaping is most commonly used in IP networks, and it is implemented in routers as a separate function and in stand-alone boxes.

Router-based traffic shaping is usually a combination of queuing with a variant of Random Early Detection (RED) or Weighted RED, which can be configured on most modern routers. The queuing can be adjusted to provide the equivalent of leaky bucket or token bucket operation, and some routers can even adjust the rate depending on the congestion signals that they receive from transmission technologies such as Frame Relay.

Stand-alone boxes, such as those from Xedia and Packeteer, implement traffic shaping using the bucket technologies as well as by using class-based shaping or rate control (both discussed in Chapter 6). They can be inserted into a major communications link to shape all the traffic from a particular edge of the network, and many of these boxes also contain comprehensive traffic measurement and reporting tools. A typical advantage of the stand-alone boxes is that they have provided much finer configuration granularity than the router-based systems, allowing network managers to identify the particular flows needing QoS with great precision.

QoS Policy Management and Measurement

If billing is based on usage, managers will start asking to be given the controls they'll need to ensure that their telecommunications expenses are within budget. Such control requires real-time accounting across the network, to intercept unauthorized or excessive network usage as it occurs, possibly forcing that usage into a lower, less expensive QoS level. Policy management gives network managers the tools they need to measure and control network utilization.

Ideally, policy management systems should allow network managers to create sets of rules that control the use of network resources. These rules would specify the levels of QoS available to particular users, depending on the applications they're using, the servers involved, the time of day, the number of other users in the same group that are using network resources, and other factors. The network manager would set these rules after consultations with user groups, and they could be changed at any time to account for varying business needs, such as changed priorities at the end of the business quarter.

The policies would be administered from a central location but enforced throughout the network at all points where there is a need for QoS. Devices at the edge of the network would check with policy control before allowing a new datastream to start flowing at anything other than the lowest, best-effort QoS level, and they would make sure that any user-requested QoS levels were allowed to the user under current policy rules. They would also ensure that new datastreams could be safely allowed into the network without overloading any network components and without breaking any existing policy promises for existing flows. It wouldn't just be at the network edge that QoS policies would be implemented. Devices all throughout the network would be configured by the policy control devices to support QoS datastreams. IP filters would be set appropriately, queue characteristics would be configured, and many other configuration parameters would be managed automatically to ensure that each QoS datastream that was admitted to the network would be supported at the promised QoS.

Some proprietary policy management methods for networks have been built by individual vendors, and some technologies, notably ATM, usually have extensive policy management facilities. But, in general, policy management is a very new area for the standards bodies, and few standards-oriented policy management systems are available [Saunders]. Recently, there has been a new development in the standards area. The Common Open Policy Service (COPS) has been developed—first for Integrated Services/RSVP, and then for other IP-based QoS facilities, notably Differentiated Services. We'll discuss COPS first, then the various QoS measurement techniques that are also available to network administrators.

Common Open Policy Service (COPS)

The Common Open Policy Service was designed to provide a scalable, standard client/server model for providing policy services. It defines a protocol that runs over TCP and interconnects Policy Decision Points (PDPs) that make policy decisions with Policy Enforcement Points (PEPs) that are the devices, such as routers, that ask for and enforce those decisions. The PDP and PEP constantly check to be sure that their connection is working, and the PEP will automatically connect to a backup PDP if the link fails. Both PEP and PDP remember the current state of all policy decisions, so that the PEP can continue to function even if it's temporarily unable to communicate with the PDP. In addition, the fact that the PDP remembers what is happening in all the PEPs allows it to push new policy instructions out to those PEPs that need them, even if the PEP hasn't explicitly asked for an update. This allows network administrators to change network policy and be sure that it will be quickly implemented, even in already approved flow connections.

The PDP is the source of all decisions, and it uses a set of policy rules that have been stored in a directory by network mangers. It's responsible for validating incoming requests from PEPs, checking their validity against stored policy rules, deciding whether to grant the QoS request after taking into account the state of the network and all the existing QoS flows, and configuring the network components to ensure that the granted QoS will actually be delivered by network components without causing harm to existing QoS-labeled flows. Whenever a change is made to the rules by network administrators, the PDP must check through its memory of all the existing QoS flows to find those that are affected by the change. It then sends out messages to all the concerned PEPs to make that change immediately.

The PEP can be located in any network device that must decide how to handle QoS flows, including switches, routers, and even endpoints such as server hosts and QoS-aware Ethernet cards. It connects to the PDP when it is initialized, and then it is ready to send queries to the PDP about QoS services. For example, the PEP may ask the PDP for a decision whenever it learns that a user is requesting QoS, whether through intercepting RSVP's RESV and PATH messages, by inspecting the DS-byte in a new incoming flow, or through some other means. In some cases, the PEP may be able to refer to decision rules previously passed to it by the PDP, or it may have to make decisions locally if the PDP is temporarily unavailable. But the PDP is still the ultimate authority. When a decision is reached, that decision is stored in the PEP, and the PEP then takes the appropriate action—accepting or refusing admission to a new datastream, marking or re-marking packet headers appropriately, allowing the progress of RSVP's RESV and PATH messages (sometimes with an additional Policy Data object inserted in the messages), or changing the configuration of the network device itself. The PEP will tell the PDP when a datastream's status changes and the QoS reservations can be removed from the system, and it also allows the PDP to change the rules applying to an existing datastream. The COPS system has been designed to handle multicast as well as point-to-point transmission, and it understands that different rules may apply to the different flows that branch out from a flow replication point inside a multicasting router.

Most vendors of COPS systems provide methods for integrating non-COPS devices into the system. They have created policy proxies that will send policy decision-based configuration information to non-COPS devices by using the Simple Network Management Protocol (SNMP), by emulating an operator at a configuration terminal, or through other means.

In the original design of COPS, for the Integrated Services/RSVP system, COPS always learned of new QoS requests when the PEP intercepted RSVP's RESV and PATH messages. In the new, expanded definitions of COPS, it now must work with QoS technologies that don't have RSVP-style signaling. For example, Diff-Serv may communicate directly with the PDP to set QoS rules that apply to all datastreams entering the network from certain network addresses, such as those that handle real-time voice traffic. This modification for Diff-Serv is only the start of a number of modifications that will be made as COPS expands to include interoperation with many different types of QoS and networking technologies.

Finally, it's important to note that COPS does not need to be installed in every node in the policy-based network; it just needs to be installed in nodes that must make policy decisions. For example, it could be sufficient for a network to have PEPs only in the routers that form the boundary of a subsection of the network. Routers inside the boundary could simply obey DS-Bytes in the IP packet headers without being aware of COPS at all; they would be Policy-Ignorant Nodes (PINs). The PDP would use PEP admission control at the network boundary to ensure that the network's core routers would never be loaded to the point that they'd be unable to furnish the required QoS.

QoS Measurement

Once users are paying for QoS, they'll start asking for accurate measurement and accounting. The basis for deciding what to measure is the set of requirements developed in the first half of this book. Network latency, jitter, packet loss, bit error rates, and availability are certainly candidates, but it's important to focus on the particular applications and users involved.

In some applications, for example, delay is not a QoS requirement to be measured. File transfers, electronic mail, fax transmission, communications with voicemail mailboxes, streaming video and streaming audio—none of these has stringent delay requirements. Instead, they have throughput and elapsed time requirements. Their throughput performance may depend on delay, but it's the throughput, not the delay, that is important to the end user. Simple measurements of the delay may be misleading because there are many reasons for poor throughput in addition to long transmission delays.

Surprisingly, Web pages usually don't have a strict QoS delay requirement; their quality, as perceived by users, is based on the total download time of the files that make up the Web page. The latency of individual packets is only roughly associated with Web download times because it doesn't take the interpacket spacing into consideration. Low-latency transmission of individual packets doesn't guarantee excellent user-perceived Web download speed quality if those packets are widely spaced because of congestion in the network or if they require many retransmissions because of errors.

It's also important to determine if the users will accept statistical sampling or measurements by proxy workstations controlled by network management instead of precise accounting for every packet and connection. Statistical sampling of networks based on Ethernet or Internet technology can be difficult because of the self-similar nature of their traffic, but trying to measure each and every packet can be worse.

The Policy Decision Point in COPS and similar policy mechanisms in ATM and in various vendor's proprietary systems can furnish accounting and measurement information to network managers. There are also a number of separate tools dedicated to network measurement that can be used to evaluate QoS. The problem is in measuring the QoS accurately, and in a way that is meaningful to both network users and to network engineers.

The first distinction we must make is end-to-end versus point measurement. An end-to-end measurement is precisely that: a measurement that gives the performance of the network from one user all the way to another, through all the network devices, links, switches, and routers. It's the best measurement from the user's point of view, but it is often less useful for the network engineer who has to fix something—he or she may not know where the trouble lies in that long, convoluted path. Also remember, as discussed in Chapter 4, "Network QoS Design Specifications," that the round-trip measurement usually cannot be cut in half to give the one-way measurement. The packets may take different paths, and the buffer situations may be very different in the two directions. The IETF's IP Performance Metrics group is very active in this area. (See www.ietf.org/html.charters/ippm-charter.html.)

A point measurement, by contrast, is simply the measurement of traffic and network device characteristics at a single point: an individual router, or switch, or communications link (such as Frame Relay). Point measurements can be obtained from virtually all network devices, and some end stations, through the use of the standard Simple Network Measurement Protocol (SNMP) and its associated data records, the Management Information Base (MIB). This is very meaningful for a network engineer, as it can immediately show the status of the device: the traffic going through it, the CPU and memory utilization, the state of the various queues, and even, sometimes, the identity of the heaviest users and some information about the flows among them through the use of the Remote Network Monitoring MIB, RMON. Unfortunately, it can mean little to the users. They aren't concerned with a single device; they are concerned only with their end-to-end experience.

How, then, can a network manager provide both end-to-end and point measurements, satisfying the users and the network engineers who have to fix the system? The simple answer is that there isn't a simple answer. Many systems try to do this through time correlation. (If a particular node has severe queue and capacity problems at the same time that end-to-end performance falls apart, then we can guess the cause.) Others are more sophisticated, trying to correlate point measurements by tracking flows from one network device to the next, or using tools to trace the path of a packet through the network. After discovering the path that's in trouble, these tools then measure shorter and shorter segments of that path in an end-to-end manner and look at the point measurements of all the devices in the path.

In all these cases, a key is evaluating the performance of a particular QoS level or flow, usually as contrasted with the performance at a different QoS level. But most measurement tools are designed with the assumption that all traffic is handled in the same way. There's no way to track the end-to-end performance of a flow with a certain QoS; the tool usually can't distinguish among flows at the various QoS levels. The point measurement devices also may have difficulty evaluating the effectiveness of various network components in forwarding traffic at a particular level of QoS. Let's look at some examples of how these tools must be adapted for QoS situations.

There are two types of tools for measurement: active and passive. The active tools inject an actual flow into the network or the network component (such as a communications link) and evaluate what happens to it. The passive tools either watch an existing flow (tracking it by looking at some internal value, such as the header fields or an application-level transaction ID) or refer to statistics tables, such as the MIBs maintained by the network devices. This latter use of MIBs can be quite sophisticated; the RSVP MIB, for example, stores information about all of the QoS flows passing through the device. Using that information from adjacent RSVP-aware devices, a passive monitor could reconstruct the path of a particular flow.

That use of the RSVP MIB is a good example of how passive monitors could evaluate QoS performance. They could track flows through the RSVP MIBs, then use the other router and switch MIBs to learn about traffic levels on the links, the state of internal queues, and other state information. It should then be possible to derive the end-to-end performance of various flows by looking at the situation in each device and link that they must pass through. Passive watching of selected flows (by filtering on their network addresses or by watching for their appearance in the various MIB tables that track QoS and high-volume traffic flows) would add to the information available. An advantage of this technique is that any problems in the flow's path would be immediately isolated to the component causing the difficulty. Unfortunately, this type of passive monitoring to track end-to-end performance requires a lot of work from the central monitoring console.

Therefore, most end-to-end performance measurement is done with end-to-end tools—some passive, some active. An example of a passive tool is a Java applet embedded in a browser or a special software module inserted between an application and the communications protocol stack. These tools can identify transactions by watching packet identifiers or application-level transaction identifiers, then recording the round-trip time and other characteristics. They can build a histogram of the resulting information for datastreams at various QoS levels and report to a central console when polled.

Active tools are also used for end-to-end monitoring. The IP community has long used the ping, TReno (ftp://ftp.psc.edu/pub/networking/tools/), and traceroute tools to get a rough estimate of end-to-end network performance, and far more sophisticated tools are available from a number of vendors. These sophisticated tools, available for all network architectures, can run scripts to emulate user transactions or download Web pages and record the performance data. Network administrators may want to connect such a tool permanently to the network at key points to measure end-to-end performance at various QoS levels.

In some cases, end-to-end measurement is needed, but the administrator doesn't have access to the software or device at one end. The classic example is provided by the World Wide Web, in which an administrator can be keenly aware of the need for end-to-end performance measurement but may not be allowed to insert a Java applet into the user's browser if that user isn't an employee. Active tools can be used in these situations to substitute for the remote users. These tools can be installed at field offices to measure the Web performance from centrally located Internet servers, or a service provider such as Keynote Systems (www .keynote.com) can supply a service to measure Web page downloads and transactions. The Keynote Systems service can measure any Web page download or transaction from over 150 locations worldwide, and the measurement data is complete with details of Web and Internet performance such as DNS lookup time, TCP connect delay, and the time lag before the arrival of the first and last data packets. This real-time information is invaluable to any e-commerce Web site that's concerned about customer experience. Keynote and other suppliers are also expanding their service offerings to measure the performance aspects of many different types of applications on the Internet.

Examples

A few quick examples should show how these technologies can work. We'll look at four:

- A research lab using Gigabit Ethernet
- A manufacturing company using SNA and other legacy protocols along with IP
- A hospital campus based on ATM
- An IP-based industrial corporation using a core technology of Diff-Serv

The Research Lab (Overprovisioning/Isolation)

Overprovisioning, usually with Gigabit Ethernet, is the typical solution for a lab requiring high-speed connectivity that is located in a single geographic area—within the range of a LAN. An ideal lab for overprovisioning with Gigabit Ethernet has bursts of intense LAN use as huge files are transferred, but has relatively low use when averaged over long intervals and has little need for guaranteed QoS. For file transfers and most lab work, and even for real-time voice and video if occasional interference is acceptable, overprovisioning is all that's needed.

Gigabit Ethernet has a lot of virtues as a solution for overprovisioning a lab. Ethernet is a very familiar technology, usually a common feature of all lab equipment. The lab workers can therefore easily configure their equipment to use Gigabit Ethernet without any modification. Expanding a small Gigabit Ethernet network to keep far ahead of increased loads is also simple. If LAN use increases to the point that there are capacity problems, the LAN can be segmented by adding a couple of LAN switches.

Overprovisioning can even be used if the lab networks must carry some real-time traffic, such as low-volume data flows between sensors and monitoring equipment. One method is to segment the LAN by using LAN switches to create branches of the LAN that have very little traffic and are therefore massively overprovisioned. In extreme cases, if it can't be guaranteed that there will almost always be enough open capacity to handle the data flows in a timely manner, an additional LAN could be installed for use by real-time traffic only. That's probably simpler than building a LAN with QoS capabilities and adapting the various pieces of lab equipment to run over such a LAN.

The weak point of all overprovising designs is aggregation and scalability. Aggregation might be a problem if near real-time performance is needed and if there's a heavily used focus of the LAN traffic, such as a central server, or if there's a congested WAN link. Scalability becomes a problem if the LAN grows so large that there are times when the traffic through some of the LAN switches often invokes the flow control mechanisms. For such cases, a more complex solution, possibly involving LAN QoS and a WAN gateway, may be necessary. The Gigabit Ethernet LAN will still be usable as part of the new design, however.

The Manufacturing Company (Filtering and SNA)

Probably the most common use of QoS is for construction of a non-real-time, multiservice network that carries IP traffic along with SNA and other protocols. The real-time requirements aren't strict, but some SNA traffic may fail if it is overly delayed. Other protocols, such as NetWare's IPX and Apple protocols, may also need to be carried.

This situation is usually handled by multiprotocol routers, spoofing, encapsulation, and filtering. Multiprotocol routers can be configured to handle a couple of different protocol families concurrently. This is, for example, a simple way of handling IP and IPX in the same network. In other cases, one protocol may be spoofed and encapsulated inside of another; one example is the case where SNA data flows are encapsulated inside IP by using the DLSw (Data Link Switching) standard [RFC 1795].

The DLSw gateways use a lot of the mechanisms described in Chapter 3:

- They spoof the Layer 2 SNA acknowledgements to keep traffic flowing smoothly and rapidly without waiting for acknowledgements to travel across the entire IP network.

- They use directories and caching to remove repetitive address search broadcasts from the IP network.

- They encapsulate the SNA data structures inside TCP for transport.

The resulting DLSw encapsulated data flows are identified by IP filtering to be given precedence in router queues. (SNA can also be carried across IP networks by many other methods, some of which are much more sensitive to latency than DLSw. See [Nolle] and [Guruge] for more information and tables of acceptable latencies and error rates for encapsulated SNA.)

In all these cases, each router in the network must be configured to identify the protocols to be given precedence—whether by protocol identification or by filtering on IP protocol type, port, or address. As all of the data flows share the same communications links, the protocols that need a higher priority are then given precedence in the router queues for the links. Configuration of the routers in a large network can be a chore, but it's practical in cases where a few legacy applications are used or where those applications tend to be focussed on a relatively few major servers at fixed addresses.

Simple filtering and queue precedence as used in these situations isn't good enough to guarantee latency or jitter, but it's enough to enable legacy protocols to function well over IP-based and multiservice networks. If a few real-time applications need to be added to such a network, it's simplest to create a completely separate network for them. For example, adding a few teleconferencing facilities could be done with some ISDN lines, not a complete redesign of the backbone network's QoS facilities.

The Hospital Campus (ATM)

For campus-wide situations that require extensive, proven QoS capabilities, ATM is a frequent choice. Large hospital complexes are a good example of this situation. They require a lot of multimedia; they have equipment that transfers a large number of detailed image files frequently; there's a lot of transaction and database work that simply can't be interrupted by anything; researchers in the hospital need access to high-speed links to other research centers; and the hospital is constantly being reorganized. ATM may be tricky to configure, especially in multivendor environments, but it's here and it works. IP's modern QoS offerings—RSVP and Diff-Serv—are simply too new and unproven for a lot of hospitals to accept.

The hospital campus typically installs carrier-class ATM switches in its backbone, and it provides native ATM connections for major multimedia installations. Permanent (nailed up) ATM connections can be used to handle bridging among LAN switches and routers for user equipment that needs QoS but doesn't understand ATM or QoS signaling. Network administrators can assign special QoS levels to the nailed up ATM connections as needed, and the connections can be quickly reconfigured by network administrators to keep pace with hospital changes. These nailed up connections can also supply the equivalent of leased lines among devices that perform massive file transfers, and they can link any device in the hospital directly to the high-speed links that go to other research centers.

For general-purpose network use, LANE and MPOA provide IP networking capabilities over the ATM backbone as well as connectivity to the multimedia servers. Their QoS capabilities aren't currently as good as native ATM, but anything needing high-quality guarantees can easily get them through arrangements with the ATM administration. Meanwhile, normal Web browsing, e-mail, and transaction traffic can flow easily over the same backbone that is carrying all the other traffic in the hospital.

The IP-Based Corporation (Diff-Serv, LAN QoS, and RSVP)

This is an example of what the near future holds: an IP-based QoS system that extends over an entire corporation, from LAN to WAN. The core is based on IP Diff-Serv and MPLS, while the edge networks are based on LAN QoS. RSVP is used for signaling, and policy management is used for coordination.

In our example, the administration of the network has established a few basic QoS categories into which all traffic must fit: a couple for real-time speech (telephone) and for real-time multimedia or video, a couple for high-priority transactions, and a couple for lower-priority streaming video, Web browsing, e-mail, and bulk file transfer. Each major group in the corporation has agreed to pay for a certain amount of access to each of these categories when traversing QoS-controlled parts of the network (such as constricted WAN links), and the policy management system will hold them to those promises. The groups are responsible for keeping their QoS usage within the limits they have paid for. If a group has difficulties staying within its limits and finds that its members are being forced into lower QoS categories than they want because the group's allocation is being used up, then the group's managers can decide whether or not to purchase more QoS capacity from the network administration.

This system of group allocations within broad QoS categories is much easier to administer (and the resulting bills to the end-users are simpler and easier to understand) than a system that depends on detailed QoS design for each traffic flow before anything can be built. For example, a group can place a new application on the network by using their existing QoS category allocations. Any resulting performance problems will only affect other members of the group, and the group managers can then decide whether to tune the application for better performance or pay the network administration for more capacity at the needed QoS level.

We'll discuss the edge of the network and LAN QoS design of our example first. Then we'll talk about the boundary routers that connect those edge networks to the core network, and we'll mention the use of public networks inside the core.

The edge of the network in our example depends on high-speed Ethernet switches using LAN QoS to differentiate among a few QoS classes. It's quite possible that not all of the class distinctions made by the network administrators will be used in the LAN; instead, there might be only two or three categories. For example, giving interactive voice and video priority over other traffic might be the extent of classification on many LANs within the corporation. LAN QoS would be controlled by the policy manager and the Subnetwork Bandwidth Manager (SBM), coupled with RSVP signaling or some other type of classification marking (such as filtering or the IP TOS byte). It's probable that many LANs would have no QoS at all, but would have their frames classified and controlled only when they pass through an Ethernet switch into an important, somewhat-congested section of the corporate LAN.

Boundary routers are placed where the edge networks meet the network core. They prepare incoming packets for efficient routing, and they communicate with the policy manager as they enforce the administration's classification rules. Boundary routers may need to interface with any LAN QoS frame markings, and they also handle any RSVP signaling to the edges of the network. They convert these markings and signals to and from DS-byte traffic classes, and they provide the Diff-Serv packet functions of classification, metering, marking, shaping, and dropping, as needed to enforce policy rules.

The core of the network depends on Diff-Serv routers. These are highly scalable and efficient, because the class markings are easily found in the DS-byte. No other filtering needs to be done; the router just looks at the address and the DS-byte, then decides. The routers can use advanced queuing, such as WFQ, to provide latency guarantees, because the policy manager will work with routers at the boundary of the network's core to restrict entry to latency-controlled classes as needed. Multi-Protocol Label Switching (MPLS) gives the traffic engineers a very powerful tool to design a network that can provided needed end-to-end QoS levels at the same time that it makes core network routers more efficient. The MPLS Label-Switched Paths (LSPs) can be provisioned whenever a particular QoS level needs some guaranteed paths across the core of the network, from one boundary router to another.

Finally, if core traffic has to cross a public network, it may be difficult—even in the case of ATM—to integrate the corporation's QoS signaling with the public carrier's QoS signaling. An alternative may therefore be attractive: The corporation's network administrator may make special arrangements with the public carriers to provide separate, overlapping interconnection facilities that have different QoS characteristics and capacities. Each major QoS level will have its own, dedicated network and specific capacity limitations. The corporation's routers at the edge of the network can then examine the DS-byte and consult the policy management system before deciding which public link to use for each data flow that must cross the public network.

Summary

The final chapter of the book looks at all the technologies available to build a QoS network. First, it looks at overprovisioning—the absence of QoS—and makes the argument that it's the simplest solution, appropriate for some small networks, but it can lead to problems in larger, enterprise-wide networks. Bandwidth needs can grow abruptly, and a network without QoS capabilities can't handle the capacity shortage gracefully while waiting for an upgrade.

The next short topic discusses using isolation to provide QoS. This is most useful for protocols or applications that don't work well in a multiservice network or that would require very high expenditures for limited return. A typical example is limited videoconferencing; it's not worth rebuilding an entire nationwide network just to support a few videoconferencing stations. Placing ISDN calls is far less expensive.

LAN QoS is the first major topic in the chapter, and it introduces the standard chapter format. The technology's architecture is discussed, followed by QoS facilities and interoperation considerations. In the case of LAN QoS, the main point is that most existing LAN QoS facilities are rarely used—either proprietary, with small market share, or seldom-used portions of LAN specifications. Ethernet, the most popular LAN technology, had no QoS capabilities at all until very recently, when a new IEEE 802.1p standard was developed. That new standard, now incorporated into the basic LAN standards, allows the insertion of an 8-level priority field into all the basic LAN types. Coupled with the newly developed Subnetwork Bandwidth Manager, there's now a blueprint for future LAN QoS development.

Frame Relay, a popular technology, is next. Unfortunately, it has minimal QoS facilities. There are some proprietary extensions, but they're very limited.

Following Frame Relay is ATM, with the most extensive QoS capabilities by far. ATM has been in production use for a number of years and is well proven; it can supply virtually any type of QoS needed—at the cost of complexity. For enterprises that need true end-to-end QoS guarantees, however, ATM is the only proven technology today. It also has an extensive set of allied technologies to allow it to interoperate with the other QoS technologies.

The chapter then discusses three different methods for providing QoS to IP-based networks: the use of the Type of Service (TOS) byte and filtering in IPv4, the use of Integrated Services/RSVP, and the use of Differentiated Services. The TOS byte and filtering are the methods most commonly used today, and they work well if all you need to do is give priority to some legacy traffic (such as IBM SNA) over a limited portion of the network. Integrated Services/RSVP is the most flexible and extensive solution, providing both a guaranteed maximum-latency service and a prioritization service, but it's quite complex and may have problems scaling to a large network. Differentiated Services (Diff-Serv) is the latest IP QoS development; it will probably scale well, but it can handle only a few separate traffic classes. Unlike Integrated Services/RSVP, which must store state in each router for each flow, Diff-Serv stores nothing in the core routers. Instead, it marks the QoS level in the packet header, using the old TOS byte field.

The chapter then closes with a discussion of QoS policy management and measurement, as few people will be willing to pay for the glories of QoS if the network administrators can't prove that they're actually receiving better service!

QoS Characteristics of Major Network Technologies

	LAN QOS	FRAME RELAY	ATM
Bandwidth control	limited, for FDDI and some unusual LANs	none	extensive, precise CBR and VBR
Discard control	none	one level of discard precedence	two levels of discard precedence
Latency and jitter control	very limited, for FDDI and some unusual LANs	none	extensive, precise control
Prioritization control	limited, for FDDI and for some unusual LANs; will be more available in future	some limited proprietary solutions	through admission control
Error control	basic	basic	advanced
Signaling	implicit	none	implicit and explicit, including policy servers
Integration with other technologies	future, with IP and ATM	limited, with ATM and some IP routers	extensive with LANs and IP, IPX, multicast, Frame Relay

Note: This is a very general, oversimplified table. Be sure to read the appropriate sections of this chapter!

IP TOS AND FILTERING	IP INT-SERV / RSVP	IP DIFF-SERV
possible, but difficult to manage	limited CBR and VBR	limited CBR
indirect, through WRED	none	three levels of discard precedence
possible control of maximum latency only; very difficult to manage	possible control of maximum latency only	possible control of maximum latency only
limited; moderately difficult to manage	limited, a side effect	similar to IP TOS, easier to manage
basic	basic	basic
implicit, some explicit	explicit	implicit and explicit
with other IP and with LAN QoS	with other IP and with ATM, LAN QoS	with other IP and with ATM, LAN QoS

Cell. The 53-byte transmission block used by ATM. It has a five-byte header and a 48-byte payload.

CER (Cell Error Ratio). The ratio of good to damaged ATM cells.

Choke Packet. A notification sent to input sources by a network element that's being overrun with input traffic. It asks the sources to stop transmitting or to decrease their transmission rate.

CIF (Common Intermediate Format). A teleconferencing standard for a video image size that is 352×288 gray-scale pixels.

CIR (Committed Information Rate). The contractual data rate to which a Frame Relay carrier has agreed. If the input datastream to the network exceeds this rate, the network may discard it.

Class Selector Class. The Diff-Serv traffic class that uses the upper three bits of the DS-byte as a rough equivalent to IPv4's TOS byte precedence.

Client/Server. An architecture for designing software systems that relies on coordinated processing both at the central host computer (the server) and at the user's site (the client).

CLP (Cell Loss Priority). The discard eligible marking in an ATM cell.

CLR (Cell Loss Ratio). The ratio of lost cells to total transmitted cells on an ATM network.

CMR (Cell Misinsertion Rate). The rate at which ATM cells have bad headers, are in the wrong place in the datastream, or belong to another datastream altogether.

Codec (coder-decoder). A device that encodes and decodes analog signals, such as those from audio or video, into and out of digital signals.

Conformance Definitions. The ATM specification of the traffic policing rules that the ATM network will use.

Connection-Oriented. The requirement that signaling be used to establish a path through the network before data is transmitted.

Controlled Load. A prioritized service provided by Diff-Serv that is supposed to approximate the service a user would receive on an uncongested network.

COPS (Common Open Policy Service). A protocol that interconnects Policy Decision Points that make network policy decisions with Policy Enforcement Points that reside inside network devices and enforce those decisions.

COS (Class of Service). A QoS design that classifies packets into one of a few categories. All packets within a particular category are then handled in the same way.

CRC (Cyclic Redundancy Check). A number appended to a data block that is based on calculation at the transmitter and is used by the receiver to detect errors in the transmission.

Datagram. A packet-switched technology that doesn't require that the path through the network be established through signaling before data is transmitted. Instead, each packet contains all the information necessary to route it to its destination.

DE (Discard Eligible). A flag set in the header of a packet or frame to indicate that it should be discarded if there's congestion in the network.

Dejitter Buffer. A buffer used in the receiver of a data flow to smooth out any jitter.

Diff-Serv (Differentiated Services). A QoS architecture based on Class of Service categorization of data packets by a special byte (the DS-byte) in the packet header.

Digital. Signals that can take only specified, clearly distinct values.

DLCI (Data Link Connection Indicator). The abbreviated address used in a Frame Relay header.

Downstream. In the direction heading toward the destination of a data flow.

DS-byte. The Class of Service categorization byte in a IP packet that is used by the Diff-Serv QoS architecture. This byte occupies the place formerly used by the TOS byte in IPv4, and it occupies the Traffic Class field in IPv6.

DSCP (Differentiated Services Code Point). The upper six bits of the DS-byte, used to specify Diff-Serv traffic classes.

EF (Expedited Forwarding) Class. The Diff-Serv traffic class that's the rough equivalent of a Constant Bit Rate service.

Enabling. Using a technology not for immediate benefit to the enterprise but because it will form the base from which some future, still unspecified, jump into a new market can be made.

Encapsulation. The process of encasing one protocol inside another one for transmission across a network.

FCS (Frame Check Sequence). A number appended to a data block that is based on calculation at the transmitter and is used by the receiver to detect errors in the transmission.

FDDI (Fiber Distributed Data Interface). A 100-mbps LAN using fiber-optic cabling and token-passing technology.

FEC (Forward Error Correcting). A way of encoding data for transmission to allow the receiver to detect and correct most errors without needing to ask for a retransmission.

FECN (Forward Explicit Congestion Notification). The notification that a Frame Relay network sends to a receiver to request that the transmission rate to that receiver be lowered.

FIFO (First-In, First-Out). A queuing technology that stores incoming packets in order of arrival. No attention is paid to packet size, priority, or any other criteria. The longest-waiting packet is always transmitted first.

Filtering. The process of examining a packet header for flow classification information.

Five-tuple. The combination of the source and destination addresses, IP port numbers, and protocol type used to identify an individual flow.

Flag. A unique identifier that marks the beginning and end of a data frame or packet. Sometimes also refers to a control bit inside a frame or packet header.

Flow. A sequence of data packets sharing the same combination of source and destination address, along with any other distinguishing characteristics that may be necessary to differentiate it from other flows sharing the same address pair. A flow in a packet-switched network is very similar to the concept of a circuit in a circuit-switched network or a virtual circuit in a frame relay, X.25, or ATM network.

FPS (Frames Per Second). The number of complete video frames shown every second.

FQ (Fair Queuing). A queuing technology in which only one packet at a time is taken from each flow for transmission, in round-robin fashion, thereby ensuring that no one flow can monopolize the output link.

FRAD (Frame Relay Access Device). The device that connects a user to a Frame Relay network.

Frame. A block of data transmitted across a link with a header that contains addressing and control information. A frame is usually a link-level data block.

Frame Relay. A packet-switched network service available from public carriers that has a requirement that the path through the network be established through signaling before data is transmitted. It can be thought of as a streamlined version of X.25.

FTP (File Transfer Protocol). A protocol that uses TCP for transmitting files between two network users.

Full Duplex. A data transmission path that allows transmission in both directions simultaneously.

Geosynchronous Satellite. A satellite that appears to remain above the same spot on the Earth's surface.

GFR (Guaranteed Frame Rate). A non-real-time ATM service designed for IP traffic that doesn't need a constant timing synchronization clock or guarantees of latency or jitter.

GOP (Group of Pictures). The sequence of MPEG video compression frames beginning with an I frame and ending with the frame before the next I frame.

Guaranteed Service. An Integrated Services QoS service that provides a bandwidth guarantee and a maximum end-to-end latency.

GUI (Graphical User Interface). A user interface that's based on graphics or images, instead of on pure text.

Half Duplex. A data transmission path that allows transmission in only one direction at a time.

HDLC (High-level Data Link Control). A protocol used to guarantee that data is transmitted without errors across a physical link.

Header. The portion of a data frame or packet that contains addressing and control information used by the network.

Heartbeat. A packet transmitted at regular intervals to signal that that communications link and the attached stations are still functioning.

Hop. One step across a network; typically a single jump from one switch or router to the next one in the path.

ICMP (Internet Control Message Protocol). A protocol in the Internet IP family that provides feedback about network operation and packet-handling errors.

IEEE (Institute of Electrical and Electronics Engineers). The professional organization for electrical and electronics engineers. In the context of this book, the group that develops some LAN standards.

IETF (Internet Engineering Task Force). A standards-making body focused on Internet technologies. (See www.ietf.org.)

I-Frame. A fully intra-coded compressed video frame. A Key Frame.

Inter-coding. The process of encoding a compressed video frame by reference to frames that precede or follow it in time.

Internet. The global, interconnected set of packet-switched networks based on IP technology.

Intra-coding. The process of encoding a single video frame or portion of a frame without any information from frames that precede or follow it in time.

Intranet. Networks that use the same technology as the public Internet but are operated for private use.

Int-Serv (Integrated Services). A QoS technology for Internet use that provides very precise control of QoS for each separate data flow, at the expense of considerable complexity and network overhead.

IP (Internet Protocol). The basic internetworking protocol that carries datagrams on the Internet.

IPv4 (Internet Protocol version 4). The most widely-used version of IP.

IPv6 (Internet Protocol version 6). The generation of IP that follows IPv4; not yet in widespread use.

IPX (Internet Packet Exchange). A proprietary network-layer protocol used by Novell NetWare systems.

ISDN (Integrated Services Digital Network). A public switched digital network.

IS-IS (Intermediate System to Intermediate System). A routing protocol used by OSI networks, similar to OSPF.

ISP (Internet Service Provider). An enterprise that sells Internet connectivity and services.

Jitter. The variation in latency.

JND (Just Noticeable Difference). A measure of video quality developed by the Sarnoff Corporation.

Key Frame A fully intra-coded compressed video frame, used as a synchronization point.

LAN (Local Area Network). A communications network that interconnects stations in a limited geographical area, usually at high speeds.

LANE (LAN Emulation). An ATM technology that allows ATM networks to interoperate with LANs.

Latency. The time delay from one point in a network to another.

Leaky Bucket. A queuing technique that can be used to create a constant rate traffic flow out of a varying rate flow. The input rate to the leaky bucket can vary, but the output rate of the leaky bucket is a constant.

Leased Line. An unswitched communications link leased from a telephone company and normally operated at a fixed data rate.

LEC (LANE Client). The ATM LANE process that transmits LAN frames over the ATM network.

LECS (LAN Emulation Configuration Server). The ATM LANE process that provides basic configuration information to new ATM LANE users.

Legacy. Older communications technologies that use proprietary protocols.

LEO (Low Earth Orbit). A satellite placed close to the earth's surface.

LES (LAN Emulation Server). The ATM LANE process that handles address mapping.

Macroblock. A group of pixels that is handled as a group during video compression.

MAN (Metropolitan Area Network). A communications network that interconnects stations in a limited geographical area, usually limited to a campus or city.

maxCTD (Maximum Cell Transfer Delay). The sum of the latency and the maximum acceptable jitter across an entire ATM network.

MBS (Maximum Burst Size). The maximum number of ATM cells that will be transmitted by the user in a single burst at the Peak Cell Rate.

MCR (Minimum Cell Rate). The minimum ATM cell transmit rate needed by the user.

Medium. The physical material used to make a telecommunications link, typically copper, fiber optic, or free space.

MF (Multi-Field) Classification. The Diff-Serv mechanism for classifying flows by looking at multiple packet characteristics, such as DS-byte, addresses, and protocol type.

MIB (Management Information Base). A table of network statistics and control information maintained in a network component.

MOS (Mean Opinion Score). A method for ranking the user-perceived quality of speech encoding and compression technologies.

MP-3. One of the MPEG standards for audio compression.

MPC (MPOA Client). The ATM process that is designed to transmit packets over the ATM network as part of the MPOA system.

MPEG (Moving Picture Experts' Group). In the context of this book, used to refer to the MPEG standards for video compression.

MPLS (Multi Protocol Label Switching). A method for labeling packets to streamline their passage through a packet-switched network's core.

MPOA (Multi Protocol Over ATM). A system that was developed to allow inter-subnet connections over an ATM network without the use of a router.

MPS (MPOA Server). The process that handles the inter-subnet routing function in an ATM MPOA system.

MTBF (Mean Time Between Failures). The average time between failures of a component.

MTTR (Mean Time To Repair). The average time needed to repair a failed component.

Multicast. The process of transmitting a packet to more than one recipient simultaneously. The address in the packet is a special address that indicates multiple recipients.

Multidrop. A communications line with more than two attached stations.

Multiservice Network. A network designed to carry more than one protocol family.

Nailed-Up Connections. A method for interconnecting network bridges by using PVCs over an ATM network.

NIC (Network Interface Card). The hardware device that connects a network link to a computer's internal data paths.

nrt-VBR (Non-Real-Time Variable Bit Rate). An ATM service category that allows variations in the data flow rate and does not provides a constant, unvarying timing synchronization clock.

OSPF (Open Shortest Path First). A routing protocol designed for moderate to large networks.

Overprovisioning. Designing a network to have so much capacity that there is almost never any congestion or need for QoS.

Packet. A block of data transmitted across a network with a header that contains addressing and control information. A packet is usually a network-level data block.

Packet Switching. Technology to transmit digital data by breaking the data stream into separate packets and placing destination addresses in each packet's header. These addresses are read by switching equipment (routers).

Packet Voice. Technology used to transmit telephone or teleconferencing over a packet-switched network.

PATH Message. The message used by a data transmitter in the RSVP system to initiate QoS handling for its data.

PCM (Pulse Code Modulation). A method for encoding an analog signal by repeatedly measuring the signal's amplitude and encoding that measurement as a binary number.

PCR (Peak Cell Rate). The maximum rate that the user will transmit ATM cells.

PDP (Policy Decision Point). The function in a COPS system that makes policy decisions.

PEP (Policy Enforcement Point). The function in a COPS system that implements policy decisions.

Per-Flow Classification. Technology that allows special handling to be associated with each individual flow through a network component.

PIN (Policy-Ignorant Node). Network components in a COPS network that aren't aware of COPS.

Pixel (Picture Element). The smallest element of a digital image.

Point-to-Point. Transmission from one source to one destination; different from multipoint or broadcast.

Policies. Rules for network access and for management of network resources.

Policing. Monitoring a network user's flow to ensure that it isn't exceeding the traffic specifications that were submitted as a part of the user's original network service request.

Policy-Based Networking. Technology that provides facilities for end-to-end network usage control.

Policy Server. The process in a network that stores and manages network policies.

Polling. The transmission of a status query by a master station on a communications link to all of the secondary stations in sequence.

Port. A subaddress that's appended to the end of the network address—similar to an extension number used when telephoning into a large company. Also the physical connection to a network component.

PPP (Point-to-Point Protocol). A protocol used on a point-to-point link to handle limited data flow initialization and multiplexing; often used on dial-up lines.

PQ (Priority Queuing). A queuing technology in which there are a number of FIFO-type queues, one for each priority level. Packets are always picked for transmission from the highest priority level; lower levels transmit only when all of the higher-level queues are completely empty.

PQR (Picture Quality Rating). An objective measurement of video picture quality.

Protocol. A set of data formats and procedures for transmitting data.

PSQM (Perceptual Speech Quality Measure). An objective measure of speech quality, defined in [ITU P.861].

PSTN (Public Switched Telephone Network). The dial-up telephone network.

PVC (Permanent Virtual Connection). An abbreviated network addresses that is permanently associated with a particular destination.

QCIF (Quarter CIF). Teleconferencing standard for a video image size that is 176×144 gray-scale pixels.

QoS (Quality of Service). The technologies that classify network traffic and then ensure that some of that traffic receives special handling.

Quantization. The process of discarding picture detail during video compression.

Random Arrival. A situation in which there is no correlation among the times that individual items arrive to join a queue.

Rate Control. A technology for smoothing the flow of data packets by controlling transmission rate.

Real-time. A process that is very sensitive to transmission delay because the sender and receiver need to communicate without any user-noticeable time lag.

RED (Random Early Detection or Random Early Discard). A technique was designed to avoid massive buffer overflows in network switching devices. It notices when a buffer is becoming dangerously full and then selects individual data flows for selective packet discard before the buffers overflow and all packets, from all data flows, are lost. It relies on TCP's automatically reducing its transmission rate when it notices that it has lost a packet.

RESV Message. The message used by a data receiver in the RSVP system to request QoS handling for the data that it is receiving from a particular source.

RFP (Request For Proposals). A formal request to vendors for proposals to build a system.

RM (Resource Management). A signal sent by an ATM network's ABR service to inform the senders of the available bandwidth.

ROI (Return On Investment). The average annual profit on an investment, expressed as a percentage of the amount invested.

Routing. The process of forwarding data blocks across a network based on the addresses in the network packet layer.

RSVP (Resource reSerVation Protocol). A component of the IETF's Integrated Services architecture for IP QoS. It provides a QoS API for IP users, and it automatically reserves capacity in the network, if possible, for a data flow.

RTCP (Real Time Control Protocol). A control protocol used in conjunction with RTP.

RTP (Real-Time Protocol). A protocol that provides synchronization, timing, and control information for real-time data traffic.

rt-VBR (Real-Time Variable Bit Rate). An ATM service category that allows variations in the data flow rate and also provides a constant, unvarying timing synchronization clock.

SBM (Subnetwork Bandwidth Manager). A process that acts as a resource broker for a LAN.

SCR (Sustainable Cell Rate). The average ATM cell rate over a long period.

SECBR (Severely Errored Cell Block Ratio). The ratio of damaged ATM cell groups to undamaged cell groups.

Self-similar. A pattern that appears to be the same regardless of changes in scale.

Skew. Synchronization offset between the audio and video portions of a transmission.

SLA (Service Level Agreement). A contract between a network administration and a network user that guarantees a level of service, such as network availability, error rate, and maximum latency.

Slow Start. The slow increase in the number of packets a modern TCP stack is willing to transmit as it begins transmission of a data flow or begins the recovery from congestion-induced packet loss.

SNA (Systems Network Architecture). IBM's proprietary networking architecture and protocols.

Soft State. A term used in the RSVP system to refer to the fact that each network node remembers its QoS information for only a limited period. It must be constantly refreshed by new QoS information sent by the data flow transmitters and receivers.

Spoofing. A device that handles polling or other behavior as if it were the intended recipient, thereby fooling the remote station.

Stack. The software that handles a network protocol.

Station. A user of a communications link.

Streaming. Transmission of video or audio data over network for slightly delayed playback while the data is still arriving. This permits buffering for a limited period (typically a few seconds) to allow recovery from lost or delayed data packets. It is not used for real-time data.

SVC (Switched Virtual Connections). An abbreviated network address that is temporarily associated with a particular destination by signaling through the user's API.

TCO (Total Cost of Ownership). A business analysis technique that attempts to compute the total cost of a system, including acquisition, maintenance, and support costs as well as less tangible costs and benefits.

TCP (Transmission Control Protocol). The primary error-correcting protocol used on the Internet.

TDM (Time-Division Multiplexing). A technology for intermixing data flows for transmission over a shared facility. The intermixing is done by allocating time slots, which are wasted if not used.

Telnet. An Internet protocol used to emulate the operation of a simple character-oriented terminal.

Token Bucket. A queuing technique that can be used by a network to regulate the traffic flow, adjusting it depending on the amount of capacity available at any given time.

TOS (Type of Service) Byte. The packet precedence and traffic classification byte in the IPv4 header. This byte has been redefined as the DS-byte.

Traffic Class Field. The DS-byte in IPv6.

Traffic Shaping. A technology used to force incoming traffic to conform to an agreed-on traffic flow specification and to smooth traffic flow, reducing the chunkiness of data and the need for large queues.

Transcoder. A device that can convert between two different video or audio compression technologies or compression levels.

Tspec. The traffic specification in an RSVP system, giving the characteristics of a particular data flow.

Tunneling. The process of encapsulating one or more data flows for passage through a network that may use a different protocol family or that may not be secure.

UBR (Unspecified Bit Rate). A best-effort, non-real-time service, providing no constant timing synchronization clock and no guarantees of QoS or even of minimum available throughput.

UDP (User Datagram Protocol). The basic datagram protocol used by the Internet; it does not guarantee packet delivery.

UNI (User-Network Interface). The interface between the ATM network and the user.

UPC (Usage Parameter Control). The ATM's network's policing function.

Upstream. In the direction heading toward the source of a data flow.

VLAN (Virtual LAN). VLAN technology allows user stations on separate segments of a large, enterprise-wide switched LAN to function as if they were physically on the same shared-media segment.

Vocoder. A specialized type of codec designed for encoding the human voice for transmission.

VPN (Virtual Private Network). A technology, typically using encryption, that allows an enterprise to construct the equivalent of a private network over facilities provided by a public carrier.

VSAT (Very Small Aperture Terminal). A satellite broadcast system using small antenna dishes at one Earth station and, typically, a larger dish at the other Earth station.

WAN (Wide Area Network). A communications network that interconnects stations without regard to geographic location.

WFQ (Weighted Fair Queuing). An advanced queuing technology that can guarantee latency when coupled with admission control.

Window. The number of bytes or packets that can be transmitted before an acknowledgment is received.

X.25. An older packet-switched network technology that used variable-length packets and required that the path through the network be established through signaling before data is transmitted.

Cited References

[Cox] "On the Applications of Multimedia Processing to Communications," Richard V. Cox, Barry G. Haskell, Yann Lecun, Behzad Shahraray, Lawrence Rabiner, *Proceedings of the IEEE*, May 1998.

[Cuevas] "The Development of Performance and Availability Standards for Satellite ATM Networks," Enrique G. Cuevas, *IEEE Communications*, July 1999.

[Durham] *Inside the Internet's Resource reSerVation Protocol: Foundations for Quality of Service*, David Durham, Raj Yavatkar, New York: John Wiley & Sons, 1999.

[Ferguson] *Quality of Service: Delivering QoS on the Internet and in Corporate Networks*, Paul Ferguson, Geoff Huston, New York: John Wiley & Sons, 1998.

[Ghani] "TCP/IP Enhancements for Satellite Networks," Nasir Ghani, Sudhir Dixit, *IEEE Communications*, July 1999.

[Goodman] "Internet Telephony and Modem Delay," Bill Goodman, *IEEE Network*, May/June 1999.

[Gringeri] "Traffic Shaping, Bandwidth Allocation, and Quality Assessment for MPEG Video Distribution Over Broadband Networks," Steven Gringeri, Khaled Shuaib, Roman Egorov, Arianne Lewis, Bhumip Khasnabish, Bert Basch, *IEEE Network*, November/December 1998.

[Guruge] *Reengineering IBM Networks*, Anura Gurugé, New York: John Wiley & Sons, 1996.

[Ivancic] "NASA's Broadband Satellite Networking Research," William D. Ivancic, David Brooks, Brian Frantz, Doug Hoder, Dan Shell, David Beering, *IEEE Communications*, July 1999.

[Kleijn] *Speech Coding and Synthesis*, W. B. Kleijn, K. K. Paliwal (eds.), Amsterdam: Elsevier Science B. V., 1995.

[Kostas] "Real-Time Voice Over Packet-Switched Networks," Thomas J. Kostas, Michael S. Borella, Ikhlaq Sidhu, Guido M. Schuster, Jacek Grabiec, Jerry Mahler, *IEEE Network*, Jan/Feb 1998.

[Minoli-1998a] *Delivering Voice over Frame Relay and ATM*, Daniel Minoli, Emma Minoli, New York: John Wiley & Sons, 1998.

[Newman] "FRADs: Halfway There," David Newman, Tadesse Giorgis, Farhad Yavari-Issalou, *Data Communications*, September 21, 1998.

[Nolle] "SLAs for SNA: What's Wrong With This Picture?" Thomas Nolle, *Data Communications*, August 1998.

[Onvural] *Asynchronous Transfer Mode Networks: Performance Issues*, Raif O. Onvural, Boston: Artech House, 1994.

[Packeteer] *Controlling TCP/IP Bandwidth White Paper*, Packeteer Inc., Cupertino, California, 1998.

[Sahinoglu] "On Multimedia Networks: Self-Similar Traffic and Network Performance," Zafer Sahinoglu, Sirin Tekinay, *IEEE Communications*, January 1999.

[Saunders] "The Policy Makers," Stephen Saunders, *Data Communications*, May 1999.

[Stallings] *High-Speed Networks: TCP/IP and ATM Design Principles*, William Stallings, Upper Saddle River, NJ: Prentice Hall, 1998.

[Stevens] *TCP/IP Illustrated, Volume 1: The Protocols*, W. Richard Stevens, Reading, MA: Addison-Wesley, 1994.

[Tektronix-1997a] *A Guide to MPEG Fundamentals and Protocol Analysis (Including DVB and ATSC)*, Beaverton, Oregon: Tektronix Inc., 1997.

[Tektronix-1997b] *A Guide to Picture Quality Measurements for Modern Television Systems*, Beaverton, Oregon: Tektronix Inc., 1997.

[Wolf] "Measuring the End-to-End Performance of Digital Video Systems," Stephen Wolf, *IEEE Trans. Broadcast.*, September, 1997, http://ntia.its.bldrdoc.gov/n3/video/pdf/ieee97.pdf.

Recommended Reading

[Baldi] "End-to-End Delay of Videoconferencing Over Packet-Switched Networks," Mario Baldi, *IEEE Infocom 1998 vol. 3*.

[Chappell-1997] "Preserving WAN Bandwidth," Laura Chappell, *NetWare Connection*, August 1997.

[Chappell-1998] "Service Location Protocol: Discovering Services in a Pure IP Environment," Laura Chappell, *NetWare Connection*, July 1998.

[Cisco] *Cisco IOS Software Quality of Service Solutions White Paper*, Cisco Systems Inc, San Jose, California, 1998.

[Floyd] "Link-sharing and Resource Management Models for Packet Networks," Sally Floyd and Van Jacobson, *IEEE/ACM Transactions on Networking*, August 1995.

[Ginsburg] *ATM: Solutions for Enterprise Internetworking, 2nd ed.*, David Ginsburg, Harlow, England: Addison-Wesley, 1999.

[Goyal] "Traffic Management for TCP/IP over Satellite ATM Networks," Rohit Goyal, Raj Jain, Mukul Goyal, Sonia Fahmy, Bobby Vandalore, Sastri Kota, *IEEE Communications*, March 1999.

[Huitema] *Routing in the Internet*, Christian Huitema, Englewood Cliffs, NJ: Prentice-Hall PTR, 1995.

[Huston] *ISP Survival Guide: Strategies for Running a Competitive ISP*, Geoff Huston, New York: John Wiley & Sons, 1999.

[Kalyanaraman] "Performance and Buffering Requirements of Internet Protocols over ATM ABR and UBR Services," Shivkumar Kalyanaraman, Raj Jain, Sonia Fahmy, Rohit Goyal, *IEEE Communications*, June 1998.

[Koenen] "MPEG-4: Multimedia for Our Time," Rob Koenen, *IEEE Spectrum*, February 1999.

[Kosiur] *IP Multicasting: The Complete Guide to Interactive Corporate Networks*, Dave Kosiur, New York: John Wiley & Sons, 1998.

[Lakshman] "VBR Video: Tradeoffs and Potentials," T. V. Lakshman, Antonio Ortega, Amy R. Reibman, *Proceedings of the IEEE*, May 1998.

[Li] "Video Multicast over the Internet," Xue Li, Mostafa H. Ammar, Sanjoy Paul, *IEEE Network*, March/April 1999.

[Meijer] *Systems Network Architecture: A Tutorial*, Anton Meijer, London: Pitman, 1987.

[Minoli-1998b] *Network Layer Switched Services*, Daniel Minoli, Andrew Schmidt, New York: John Wiley & Sons, 1998.

[Park] *Electronics for Dogs*, Nick Park, Aardman Animations, London: BBC, 1995.

[Partridge] "TCP/IP Performance over Satellite Links," Craig Partridge, Timothy J. Shepard, *IEEE Network*, September/October 1997.

[Seifert] *Gigabit Ethernet: Technology and Applications for High-Speed LANs*, Rich Seifert, Reading, MA: Addison-Wesley, 1998.

[Spohn] *Data Network Design, 2nd ed*, Darren L. Spohn, New York: McGraw-Hill, 1997.

[Talluri] "Error-Resilient Video Coding in the ISO MPEG-4 Standard," Raj Talluri, *IEEE Communications*, June 1998.

[Xiao] "Internet QoS: A Big Picture," Xipeng Xiao, Lionel M. Ni, *IEEE Network*, March/April 1999.

[Zheng] "Traffic Management of Multimedia over ATM Networks," Bing Zheng, Mohammed Atiquzzaman, *IEEE Communications*, January 1999.

Standards

ANSI

ANSI standards are available from http://www.ansi.org/

[ANSI S.3.2] *ANSI S3.2-1989 (R 1995), American ational Standard for Measuring the Intelligibility of Speech Over Communication Systems*, ANSI, 1995.

[ANSI T1.801.03] *ANSI T1.801.03 (1996), American National Standard for Telecommunications—Digital Transport of One-Way Video Telephony Signals—Parameters for Objective Performance Assessment*, ANSI, 1996.

ATM Forum

ATM Forum standards are available from http://www.atmforum.org/

[ATM-1996] *ATM User-Network Interface (UNI) Signalling Specification Version 4.0*, ATM Forum, AF-SIG-0061.000, July 1996.

[ATM-1997a] *LAN Emulation Over ATM Version 2—LUNI Specification*, ATM Forum, AF-LANE-0084.000, July 1997.

[ATM-1997b] *Multi-Protocol Over ATM Version 1.0*, ATM Forum, AF-MPOA-0087.000, July 1997.

[ATM-1999a] *LAN Emulation over ATM Version 2—LNNI Specification*, ATM Forum, AF-LANE-0112.000, February 1999.

[ATM-1999b] *Voice and Telephony Over ATM to the Desktop Specification*, ATM Forum, AF-VTOA-0083.001, February 1999.

Frame Relay Forum

Frame Relay Forum standards are available from http://www.frforum.com/

[FRF.5] *Frame Relay / ATM PVC Network Interworking Implementation Agreement*, Frame Relay Forum, FRF.5, December 1994.

[FRF.8] *Frame Relay / ATM PVC Service Interworking Implementation Agreement*, Frame Relay Forum, FRF.8, April 1995.

[FRF.13] *Service Levels Definitions Implementation Agreement*, Frame Relay Forum, FRF.13, August 1998.

IEEE

IEEE standards are available from http://standards.ieee.org/

[IEEE 802.1D] *IEEE Standards for Local and Metropolitan Area Networks—Common specifications—Part 3: Media Access Control (MAC) bridges*, IEEE Std 802.1D-1998, 1998.

[IEEE 802.1p] *Supplement to MAC Bridges: Traffic Class Expediting and Dynamic Multicast Filtering*, IEEE Std. P802.1p, May 1997.

[IEEE 802.1Q] *IEEE Standards for Local and Metropolitan Area Networks: Virtual Bridged Local Area Networks*, IEEE Std. 802.1Q-1998, 1998.

[IEEE 802.3x] *IEEE Specification for 802.3 Full Duplex Operation*, 1997.

ITU

ITU standards are available from http://www.itu.int/

[ITU] *ITU-T Handbook on Telephonometry*, Geneva: ITU, 1993.

[ITU G.114] *ITU-T Recommendation G.114, General Recommendations on the Transmission Quality for an Entire International Telephone Connection: One Way Transmission Time*, ITU, 1996.

[ITU G.7xx] All these codec standards are ITU-T standards.

[ITU G.821] *ITU-T Recommendation G.821, Error Performance of an International Digital Connection Operating at a Bit Rate Below the Primary Rate and Forming Part of an Integrated Services Digital Network*, ITU, 1996.

[ITU H.xxx] All these are ITU-T standards.

[ITU P.800] *ITU-T Recommendation P.800, Telephone Transmission Quality Methods for Objective and Subjective Assessment of Quality—Methods for Subjective Determination of Transmission Quality*, ITU, 1996.

[ITU P.861] *ITU-T Recommendation P.861, Objective Quality Measurement of Telephone-band (300–3400 Hz) Speech Codecs*, ITU, 1998.

IETF

IETF standards are available from http://www.ietf.org/

[RFC 791] *Internet Protocol*, Information Sciences Institute, September 1981.

[RFC 1122] *Requirements for Internet Hosts—Communication Layer*, R. Braden, October 1989.

[RFC 1323] *TCP Extensions for High Performance*, D. Borman, R. Braden, V. Jacobson, May 1992.

[RFC 1349] *Type of Service in the Internet Protocol Suite*, P. Almquist, July 1992.

[RFC 1483] *Multiprotocol Encapsulation over ATM Adaptation Layer 5*, J. Heinanen, July 1993.

[RFC 1577] *Classical IP and ARP over ATM*, M. Laubach, January 1994.

[RFC 1661] *The Point-to-Point Protocol (PPP)*, W. Simpson, ed., July 1994.

[RFC 1795] *Data Link Switching: Switch-to-Switch Protocol*, L. Wells, A. Bartky, April 1995.

[RFC 1812] *Requirements for IP Version 4 Routers*, F. Baker, ed., June 1995.

[RFC 1821] *Integration of Real-time Services in an IP-ATM Network Architecture*, M. Borden, E. Crawley, B. Davie, S. Batsell, August 1995.

[RFC 1883] *Internet Protocol, Version 6 (IPv6) Specification*, S. Deering, R. Hinden, December 1995.

[RFC 1889] *RTP: A Transport Protocol for Real-Time Applications*, H. Schulzrinne, S. Casner, R. Frederick, V. Jacobson, January 1996.

[RFC 2001] *TCP Slow Start, Congestion Avoidance, Fast Retransmit, and Fast Recovery Algorithms*, W. Stevens, January 1997.

[RFC 2018] *TCP Selective Acknowledgement Options*, M. Mathis, J. Mahdavi, S. Floyd, A. Romanow, October 1996.

[RFC 2022] *Support for Multicast over UNI 3.0/3.1 Based ATM Networks*, G. Armitage, November 1996.

[RFC 2205] *Resource ReSerVation Protocol (RSVP) Version 1Functional Specification*, R. Braden, ed., L. Zhang, S. Berson, S. Herzog, S. Jamin, September 1997.

[RFC 2208] *Resource ReSerVation Protocol (RSVP) Version 1 Applicability Statement Some Guidelines on Deployment*, A. Mankin, ed., et al., September 1997.

[RFC 2210] *The Use of RSVP with IETF Integrated Services*, J. Wroclawski, September 1997.

[RFC 2211] *Specification of the Controlled-Load Network Element Service*, J. Wroclawski, September 1997.

[RFC 2212] *Specification of Guaranteed Quality of Service*, S. Shenker, C. Partridge, R. Guerin, September 1997.

[RFC 2225] *Classical IP and ARP over ATM*, M. Laubach, J. Halpern, April 1998.

[RFC 2330] *Framework for IP Performance Metrics*, V. Paxson, G. Almes, J. Mahdavi, M. Mathis, May 1998.

[RFC 3279] *RSVP over ATM Implementation Guidelines*, L. Berger, August 1998.

[RFC 2380] *RSVP over ATM Implementation Requirements*, L. Berger, August 1998.

[RFC 2381] *Interoperation of Controlled-Load Service and Guaranteed Service with ATM*, M. Garrett, M. Borden, August 1998.

[RFC 2382] *A Framework for Integrated Services and RSVP over ATM*, E. Crawley, L. Berger, S. Berson, F. Baker, M. Borden, J. Krawczyk, August 1998.

[RFC 2460] *Internet Protocol, Version 6 (IPv6)*, S. Deering, R. Hinden, December 1998.

[RFC 2474] *Definition of the Differentiated Services Field (DS Field) in the IPv4 and IPv6 Headers*, K. Nichols, S. Blake, F. Baker, D. Black, December 1998.

[RFC 2475] *An Architecture for Differentiated Services*, S. Blake, D. Black, M. Carlson, E. Davies, Z. Wang, W. Weiss, December 1998.

[RFC 2508] *Compressing IP/UDP/RTP Headers for Low-Speed Serial Links*, S. Casner, V. Jacobson, February 1999.

[RFC 2597] *Assured Forwarding PHB Group*, J. Heinanen, F. Baker, W. Weiss, J. Wroclawski, June 1999.

[RFC 2598] *An Expedited Forwarding PHB*, V. Jacobson, K. Nichols, K. Poduri, June 1999.

MPEG

MPEG standards are available from http://drogo.cselt.stet.it/mpeg/

MPEG-4 Requirements, version 9 (Atlantic City revision), ISO/IEC JTC1/SC29/WG11/N2456, October 1998.